THE LIEUTENANT DON'T KNOW

THE LIEUTENANT DON'T KNOW

One Marine's Story of Warfare and Combat Logistics in Afghanistan

BY JEFF CLEMENT

CASEMATE
Philadelphia & Oxford

Published in the United States of America and Great Britain in 2014 by
CASEMATE PUBLISHERS
908 Darby Road, Havertown, PA 19083
and
10 Hythe Bridge Street, Oxford, OX1 2EW

ISBN 978-1-61200-248-4
Digital Edition: ISBN 978-1-61200-249-1

Cataloging-in-publication data is available from the Library of Congress and
the British Library.

10 9 8 7 6 5 4 3 2 1

Printed and bound in the United States of America.

For a complete list of Casemate titles please contact:

CASEMATE PUBLISHERS (US)
Telephone (610) 853-9131, Fax (610) 853-9146
E-mail: casemate@casematepublishing.com

CASEMATE PUBLISHERS (UK)
Telephone (01865) 241249, Fax (01865) 794449
E-mail: casemate-uk@casematepublishing.co.uk

CONTENTS

WITH TREMENDOUS GRATITUDE TO MY WIFE, ALISON

DEDICATION

This book is dedicated to the five most influential Marines I have had the pleasure of serving with. In chronological order:

Lieutenant Colonel Ronald Peterson, USMC(Ret) was Marine Officer Instructor at Georgia Tech NROTC from August 2006 to May 2009. I learned what it means to be a Marine from him.

Major John Gallagher, USMC was Commanding Officer, Company A, Combat Logistics Battalion 6 from September 2009 to September 2010. I learned what it means to be calm under fire from him.

Gunnery Sergeant Joseph Caravalho, USMC was Platoon Sergeant, Second Platoon, Company A, Combat Logistics Battalion 6 from September 2009 to September 2010 and Career Planner, Combat Logistics Battalion 6 from September 2010 to May 2012. I learned how to be a Marine Officer from him.

Master Sergeant Mario Locklear, USMC was Operations Chief, Company A, Combat Logistics Battalion 6 from September 2009 to September 2010, and Unit Movement Coordination Chief, Combat Logistics Battalion 6 from September 2010 to May 2012. I learned that logistics is not personal from him.

Finally, Major Chris Charles, USMC was Coyote 44, Tactical Training Exercise Control Group, MCCAGC Twenty-Nine Palms from September 2007 to September 2010, and Operations Officer, Combat Logistics Battalion 6 from September 2010 to May 2012. I learned everything else from him.

FOREWORD

*By Gunnery Sergeant Joseph Caravalho; OEF 10-1 Platoon
Sergeant and SNCOIC, 2nd Platoon, Alpha Company, CLB-6*

NOVEMBER 2013: WOUNDED WARRIOR BATTALION
WEST, BALBOA DETACHMENT, SAN DIEGO, CA

Camp Lejeune, NC was my fourth duty station. Upon checking in, I was informed that Combat Logistics Battalion 6 was on the next rotation for deployment to Afghanistan. I was assigned as the platoon sergeant for 2nd Platoon, Alpha Company, a motor vehicle transportation or truck platoon.

In January 2010, we deployed to Afghanistan in support of Operation Enduring Freedom 10.1. We arrived at Camp Leatherneck and started operations with 1st Marine Logistics Group (Forward).

The platoon commander of 2nd Platoon was Lt. Clement AKA "Buzz." Buzz was his internal call sign as the convoy commander. Some were given and some were earned. My call sign as assistant convoy commander was "Smokecheck." A few of the others in the platoon were "Godfather," "Pee-Wee," "Gator," "Lollipop," and "Sweettooth." We took pride in our call signs, and they boosted morale and camaraderie. By the end of this deployment we had become stellar professionals in our billets and these call signs would go down in history among the Marines in CLB-6.

Seven months . . . some days seemed liked forever and the days blurred into weeks. Work was tough, demanding and never ending. Our mission was pushing through the Helmand Province. There were constant convoys, recovery missions and recon patrols. We mapped out routes and created roads that weren't there. Our convoys were huge, ranging from 60 to 100-plus vehicles at a time. These routes took us through unknown hostile terrain as well as

11

the heavily compounded area near the Salaam Bazaar, consisting of poppy fields, wadis and gullies. We were in an endless routine of discovering and striking IEDs, encountering enemy automatic fire, and indirect fire, as well as rocket propelled grenades and ambushes. Often times upon returning from a week-long convoy, we would have to do a Quick Reaction Force on short notice, building a recovery team and heading back out to recover damaged vehicles for the infantrymen we supported.

Lieutenant Clement stepped up and did amazing things. I have the utmost respect for him as an officer among all the officers I have worked with in my career. I have confidence in his leadership and decision-making and if he asked me to do something, I would do it with no questions asked even to this day.

Many of our Marines were young. They were fresh out of school, inexperienced and for many, it was their first deployment. However, by the time we left Afghanistan they had gained knowledge and expertise that can only be learned through living it. Anything that could have happened in a convoy, we encountered it. Any scenario taught in training, we did it and succeeded. Everything that could go wrong did go wrong, but we overcame it.

We were successful because of the leadership of the non-commissioned officers. We were successful because of the determination and commitment of the junior Marines and because of this every Marine made it home.

Everyone gave everything during this deployment and though many of the Marines were never formally recognized for it, our platoon built a bond of trust with each other. This was how we survived. We leaned on each other for support and somehow we got through it. This deployment was the toughest one to endure, but it was also the best. It was the definition of our Military Occupational Specialty: Motor T.

By Master Sergeant Mario Locklear, OEF 10-1
Operations Chief, Alpha Company, CLB-6

NOVEMBER 2013: MARINE WING SUPPORT SQUADRON 272, MARINE CORPS AIR STATION NEW RIVER, NC

It was September 2009 when three new second lieutenants checked into CLB 6. I had just graduated the Advanced Course, a professional military education course for gunnery sergeants, and walked into our company office. I was shocked at how young and new they all looked. Maybe one week after meeting the new second lieutenants our battalion did our first pre-Afghanistan field training operation. "What a goat rope!" was my first impression of our battalion, company and Marine leadership within it. Let's just say that first field operation was a learning experience for all of us—no one had a clue what was to be expected or what our commanding officer's intent was.

All of the staff NCOs had just returned from special duty assignments as recruiters or drill instructors, including myself, just four months earlier so it was, as you would say, a rebuilding phase for our unit. Especially with brand new lieutenants, (though that was no fault of theirs) the leadership was green. Unfortunately, we didn't have the luxury of time to rebuild—we were deploying in just a few months.

Moving on to the next phase of our pre-deployment training, our battalion went to Enhanced Mojave Viper at Twentynine Palms, CA. The company had already fired one of the staff sergeants who was a platoon sergeant, and put another sergeant in the billet. We were still a company of misfits shooting from the hip in everything we did. I kept asking myself, "When will it get better? When will people start clicking and working together better as a team?" Our battalion had everything from hazing incidents to vehicle rollovers. The arguments were continuous. Though the company seemed to be coming together a little, it was not nearly fast enough. By the end of EMV, the overall best platoon from Alpha Company was 2nd Platoon—the team of Second Lieutenant Clement with his platoon staff sergeant Caravalho. And even they weren't ready.

We arrived in Afghanistan in January 2010. Still not knowing what our mission was, we were sort of in a limbo status for the first few weeks. Again, I asked myself "What is going on?" Our unit had no equipment, we were living in temporary transient tents and we even seemed to be sharing our company workspace. It was horrible! Captain Gallagher, our company commander, was very eager to get us started so he took the initiative to get a group of us out on a convoy with one of the other logistics support units that was at Camp Leatherneck. What a nightmare! As we were preparing to go on this mission, Lieutenant Clement, Captain Gallagher and myself attended the mission planning briefs, but I felt that this other unit could have cared less if we were going with them or not. Our small group of Marines did the mission with the unit, but returned still feeling that our company was all on its own.

After being in Afghanistan for at least two months we got a better feeling of our mission and where we belonged. Our company finally started receiving equipment and we were able to move to permanent living quarters; we were also preparing to execute convoys.

But we were still undertrained, with untested leaders, and it felt like our command lacked confidence in our ability—it seemed they were hesitant to send us out on our first mission. Operations Lava 29 through 31, joint operations with three U.S. military branches and the British Army, were our first major convoys. Each had over 200 vehicles, 1000 personnel and took over 60 hours to complete, and established us as the company to beat. That series of operations set the tone for what the company would be doing for the rest of our seven-month tour.

I still scratch my head and wonder how we did all we did with so little . . . and why, even at the end, we still felt as if we didn't belong in the unit. Why did everyone have the mentality of us against them? We were the crash test dummies for so many different tactics and missions, but we made it happen and developed standard operating procedures for every unit after us about the best way to load vehicles with cargo, to do route recons, and to plan for convoys.

Alpha Company, callsign Arawak, was successful. We were the heavy movers, the logistics trains hauling everything from water and food, to ammo and fuel. We provided support to the grunts and were recognized when, along with the rest of the battalion, we received the Marine Corps' coveted Motor Transport Unit of the Year Award for 2011.

CLB-6 ALPHA COMPANY TABLE OF ORGANIZATION

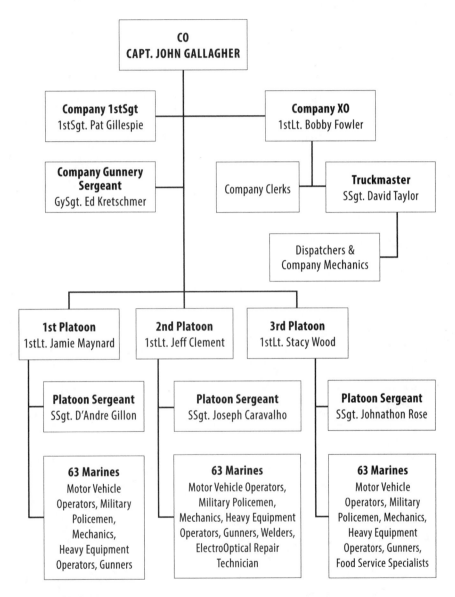

Alpha Company deployed with just over 200 Marines. Due to manning shortfalls, many Marines were filling billets outside their MOS, and were told to go "be Marines." Every platoon had trucks driven by cooks, guns manned by welders and electro-optical repair technicians, and radios calibrated by heavy equipment operators. The Marines learned quickly.

MAP OF HELMAND PROVINCE AND THE CLB-6 CONVOY ROUTES

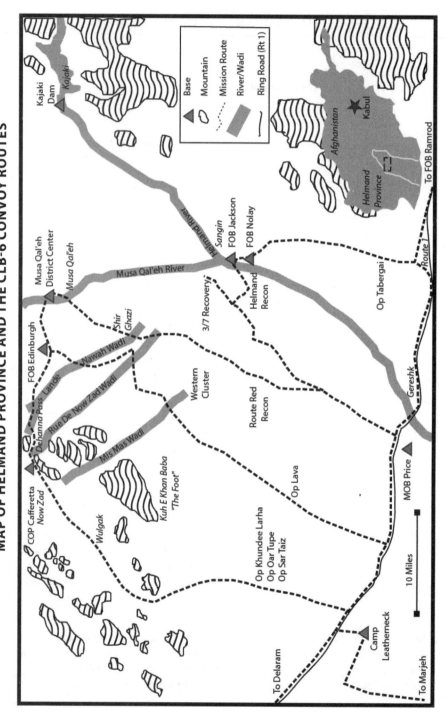

PREFACE

A lot of books have been written about Marines. Some of them by Marines, some by people who spent time around Marines, some by people who don't know anything about Marines, but all by people who think they know all there is to know about Marines. I suppose I am in the same boat as these individuals, because I too claim to know quite a bit about being a Marine.

I worked on this book off and on for a few years. The thing that kept me from really going ahead with it each time I picked it up was always the same—it ended up just being a litany of complaints—misery is the human condition and mine is worse than everybody else's, that sort of stuff.

In the TV sitcom *Seinfeld*, George Costanza once said, "If you take everything I've accomplished in my life and condense it down to one day, it looks decent." A lot of Marine Corps memoirs seem to do the same sort of thing, either with all the heroic accomplishments of their career or, just as common, all of their grievances. Neither tells the whole story, and neither is all that enjoyable to read.

So I waited to tell the story. I waited until I was a little less passionate about the events, until the edges were a little less raw. I think I've hit a sweet spot, where I can tell the story somewhat dispassionately but while the details haven't been completely forgotten.

Marines are allowed to lie when they tell war stories. Or rather, whether or not we're allowed to, we do lie when telling war stories. I could claim I won't lie, but that would (naturally) be a lie. With that being said, disregard everything I have to say (close the book now) or regard everything you disagree with as a lie. I am solely responsible for any inaccuracies.

I have written this based on what I remember. Where and when possible, I have tried to verify the sequence of events with other Marines who were there, from old notebooks, and from news and blog posts that are available online. At the end of the day though, this depicts the way I remember things happening. The tone that I take is based on my impression of the events, and those impressions shape memories. I don't guarantee 100% historical accuracy of the details and timelines, but the overall sequence of events and "moral of the story" is accurate.

Parts of the book will be most interesting to people who were in Afghanistan at the same time that I was, other parts to those who were Marines in years past and finally, some parts will be most relevant to people in the future, like young men and women who aspire to join the Corps. Some passages are written simply as a record of the things that the Marines of Combat Logistics Battalion 6 (CLB-6) did, so that maybe someday people will remember.

My experience was not supremely unique or extraordinary and to some degree that's what makes my experience important. The stuff in this book is the experience of the average Marine in Afghanistan. Thousands of Marines did these types of things, and more. We did what our country asked of us and what our country's elected representatives asked of us. We did this despite what often seemed like public indifference to our war.

My sense of what is possible and impossible will be forever shaped by what the Marines of CLB-6 did in Afghanistan. The basic premise of this book is that the Marines of CLB-6 were average Marines called to do what amounted to average combat tasks, and in the course of doing so, accomplished something extraordinary . . . something that most Americans cannot even fathom. Called to do these tasks, the average individual would decry them as terrifying and impossible. Despite the limitations of the equipment we were provided with, and the best efforts of an enemy who viewed us as an easy target, the Marines of CLB-6 lived up to the best of what it means to be an American. More importantly, they lived up to the pinnacle of what it means to be a Marine—refusing to be stopped.

In writing this book I often asked myself, "Do you deserve to write a book? Who do you think you are? Your experience wasn't that big a deal." My experience does not rise far above the baseline of any of the Marines in combat. There were firefights, where my Marines and I were shot at, and shot back. An IED exploded under my truck, causing permanent spinal and nerve damage and making it hard to concentrate at times. We MEDEVAC'd Marines on helicopters, not sure that we'd ever see them alive again. But no, my experience does not really rise above the baseline for combat.

So, for the Marines out there: This book was not written primarily with you in mind. There will be (long) passages where your reaction will be "I know all this already" or "every Marine does that . . . does he think he's special?" I am continually reminded that the civilian world at large doesn't know what we do. We need to tell them objectively and without agenda at every opportunity.

Every day that we were at war in Afghanistan, Marines had experiences like mine, but the general population of America was not aware of them. A few might watch *Generation Kill* or *Zero Dark Thirty* and say, "that's what the war is. The rest of the people over there are just killing time, playing XBOX and waiting to come home in seven months. No big deal."

And so here is my story. An average guy in combat. This is what war is. War is gritty. It is stressful. It is about compromises. It permanently impacts everyone it touches. I signed up for it, but nobody knows what they really signed up for until afterwards, and that's an important thing to realize.

CHAPTER ONE

NO REGRETS

If I die in a combat zone
Box me up and ship me home

Pin my medals upon my chest
Tell my Momma I did my best

Now Momma, Momma, don't you cry
The Marine Corps motto is "Do or Die."

—Traditional Marine Corps Running Cadence

APRIL 2010
SOMEWHERE SOUTH OF MUSA QAL'EH
HELMAND PROVINCE, AFGHANISTAN

The Afghan insurgents were aiming at me specifically, I was certain. The closer the bullets were to hitting my head, the slower time seemed to go, and the slower I seemed to be moving.

"Goddammit, where is that wrecker?" I yelled to my platoon sergeant.

"I don't know, sir, but it's gotta be coming up soon. Godfather went to go get it like ten minutes ago," Staff Sergeant Joseph Caravalho, my Hawaiian-borne platoon sergeant yelled back. Godfather was the callsign of one of our sergeants.

A hundred-plus pound IED had nailed one of our trucks. It was one of the biggest IEDs we had seen. The engine compartment was shredded, and tires had been thrown over a hundred feet in the air with a mushroom-shaped dust-filled shockwave. We couldn't recover this truck without our giant armored tow truck that we called a "wrecker." As soon as we were stopped by the IED, Afghan insurgents began firing at us from several directions and dropping mortar rounds on our position. Bullets ricocheted off the truck I was working on, inches from my head.

"What the hell am I doing here?" I asked quietly. I chuckled to myself and answered with a canned refrain, often heard among the Marine Corps' junior officers to describe their own obliviousness. "The lieutenant don't know."

DECEMBER 2012: CHRISTMAS COCKTAIL PARTY, SYRACUSE, NY

Every year, my in-laws throw an old-fashioned cocktail party, with drinks and hors d'oeuvres. I was talking with one of the guests at the party, I suppose one of the neighbors, when I was asked a question that I hadn't ever gotten.

"Do you regret becoming a Marine?" he asked.

I was taken aback, insulted even—but it was an honest question. I'm pretty sure that he could tell I was surprised (or maybe not—the libations flowed freely and he had drunk quite a bit), but I tried not to let it show on my face.

"No, you know, not at all," I responded. "I joined the Marine Corps to serve my country as cliché as that sounds and to learn, and to do stuff that I could never do anywhere else. I've gotten to do things that none of my college peers have gotten to do. So no, I don't regret joining the Marines."

I meant it, too. Even though I certainly had some difficult experiences, which, to be fair I expected—I also wanted them. I don't regret it. There are different variations to the question "Are you glad that you joined the Marines?" I think the best way that I have found to answer the question is that it was the right decision for me, at that time, with what I knew then.

People would almost always follow that up with a question about Afghanistan. It might be "What do you think about Afghanistan?" or "What's it like over there?" or the most irritating of all "Did you kill anyone?" As for Afghanistan, I'm proud of what I accomplished over there, and more so of what my Marines did, day in and day out. We answered the call of our country after 9/11, and did what we were asked to do.

SEPTEMBER 11, 2001: MR. JOHNSON'S HISTORY CLASS, GREEN HOPE HIGH SCHOOL, CARY, NC

I don't think any American will forget where they were when they first heard about the September 11th attacks on the World Trade Center and the Pentagon. I was a sophomore in high school. One of the students had gotten word of the first plane hitting the tower, but nobody believed him. In 2001, most kids didn't yet have cell phones, and smartphones were a thing of the future, so we had to ask permission from the teacher to use one of the computers in the classroom to check the news. Though he hadn't heard anything, Mr. Johnson consented, hoping that the report wouldn't be confirmed.

We couldn't quite believe it or understand the magnitude of the attack, but Mr. Johnson turned on the TV and we learned of the plane hitting the Pentagon and the second World Trade Center tower.

All students at the school, as most students did nationwide, spent the rest of the school day watching the news. The bells would ring, and we would all race to the next classroom, trying not to be away from a TV for too long. My English teacher got a phone call and through her tears she laughed sarcastically as she told us what was said. The administration had directed all teachers to turn off the TVs, to resume teaching according to their lesson plans, and that "today was a normal day."

"Today is a pivotal day in world history. You watch," she said to the class. "Today is not a normal day, and to pretend otherwise is ridiculous. You all have a right to be informed. You're not legal adults yet, but this will affect most of your adulthood."

Pretty much every news station played the same few clips of the planes striking the towers and of the smoking buildings. I don't think anybody really believed the World Trade Center Towers would hold, but it was still shocking watching them crumble an hour after the planes hit. Certainly after the first tower collapsed, everyone held their breath, hoping against hope that the second tower wouldn't follow suit.

The final list of casualties totaled 2,996, but during the day the estimates from the various "experts" ran as high as 30,000. The commentators speculated wildly, and nobody yet knew what had happened with United Airlines Flight 93 (which was deliberately crashed near Stoneycreek, PA by the hijackers as the passengers were about to regain control of the plane).

SEPTEMBER 11, 2001: PRAYER SERVICE, ST. MICHAEL'S CATHOLIC CHURCH, CARY, NC

I don't think I'm alone in saying that by about noon on September 11th, I was in a state of "emotional overload;" my capacity for further shock or devastation was exhausted. Like many others, my family went to church that night, where a special prayer service was held for the victims of the attack. Again, we didn't really know anything yet, but I agreed with Senator John McCain who said that this was an "act of war."

I had long planned on joining the Navy. Both of my parents and both grandfathers had been in the Navy. The September 11th attacks strengthened my resolve. As much as the prayers for the victims might be worthwhile, if I could help prevent another attack, I felt that I must. It's one thing to attack combatants—another entirely to attack people who are just going about their daily routine.

Sitting in that church in 2001, there were still seven years before I would commission in the military. I was sure that any counterattacks or wars would be resolved long before I would be old enough to play a part. After all, any military interventions would have to be twice as long as World War II for me to get a piece of the action, right? Still, I wanted to go to the Naval Academy, join the Navy, and help prevent another attack like 9/11.

FEBRUARY 2004: CARY, NC

I had been waiting for months for the admission decision letter from the Naval Academy to arrive. I knew the chances of being admitted to the Naval Academy were slim, but it is what I had always wanted to do. When I was at St. Bernadette's Catholic Elementary School growing up, I used to pretend that our blue and white uniforms were the uniforms of midshipmen, and when we walked in two neat lines as a class, I would pretend that we were marching. I was the only one in the class who would square the corners in the hallway. I thought I was pretty cool. Everyone else just thought I was weird. I was wrong; they were right.

But it had finally arrived. I still have that letter, actually. I pulled it out to make sure I got the words that I read that day just right:

> *Dear Jeffrey:*
> *Congratulations! We are pleased to announce that the Admissions Board has found you scholastically qualified for admission to the U.S. Naval Academy with the Class of 2008. You are guaranteed an offer of appointment . . . and so on . . . look forward to welcoming you as a member of the Brigade of Midshipmen.*
> *Sincerely,*
> *S.B. LATTA*
> *Captain, U.S. Navy*
> *Director of Admissions*

I was ready to sign the paperwork and send it back that day, but my mom was insistent that I wait.

"You don't have to send it in yet, so don't. You have a little more time to make the decision. Take the time. You might change your mind."

I was sure that she was wrong. But as usual, she was right. My parents had insisted that I look at a few other schools, just in case. I had gone to the prospective student orientation weekends at Georgia Tech, Virginia Tech, and NC State. I don't think I seriously looked at any other schools. I was so dead set on engineering, I didn't even look at any other majors.

The NROTC recruiter called me every week, asking me why I hadn't sent in my application yet. He didn't listen when I told him that it was because I didn't want to do NROTC. "Well, you'll submit your application eventually." He was right.

I don't remember when it hit me, but at some point I realized that it wasn't so much a conscious decision as a realization, that I didn't want to go to the Naval Academy. I think the academic challenge and the engineering student life at Georgia Tech was attractive, as was the idea of living in Atlanta.

I was still 100% committed to joining the Navy and I still wanted to be a surface warfare officer, but I was presented another road to get there. So I signed the NROTC papers and accepted admission to Georgia Tech. I was going to be a Ramblin' Wreck from Georgia Tech and a helluva engineer.

AUGUST 2004: GEORGIA TECH NAVAL RESERVE OFFICER TRAINING CORPS INDOCTRINATION, NAVAL SUBMARINE BASE KINGS BAY, GA

Freshman year at Georgia Tech began with INFORM, the Navy ROTC Indoctrination for Midshipmen. It was a weeklong orientation session run by a staff composed of senior midshipmen, the staff officers, and most memorably, the Marines assigned to the unit. Several Marines are assigned to each NROTC unit to assist in the training of young midshipmen. Instead of separate Marine ROTC units, midshipmen are all lumped together in the same unit and are designated as either "Navy Option" or "Marine Option" with slightly different program requirements for each group.

Although I was a Navy Option midshipman, I received "instruction" from the Marines at INFORM. One of the most fear-inspiring among them was Sergeant Joshua Roberts, who had just graduated from Marine Officer Candidate School. A Marine Enlisted Commissioning Education Program (MECEP) candidate, he was a sophomore at Georgia State University and a fearsome sight to behold for new midshipmen. INFORM left us with an introduction to the Navy and Marine Corps, and a definite impression that only a few were qualified to be Marines.

"Most of you Navy pukes couldn't hack it," Sergeant Roberts said, "but you're welcome to come out to Marine PT to see how much you suck."

Throughout my freshman year, I continued attending Marine PT, but I thought I still wanted to be in the Navy. I didn't begin to realize that I might want to be a Marine until the summer after my freshman year at CORTRAMID, a summer training program for midshipmen.

MAY 2005: CAREER ORIENTATION TRAINING FOR
MIDSHIPMEN, NAVAL STATION NORFOLK, VA

CORTRAMID stands for "Career Orientation Training For Midshipmen." The program is organized into four, one-week segments, each designed to expose young midshipmen to one of the major career paths that they might choose, both to help them make their career decisions and to give them some perspective on other types of naval operations. We would spend one week each with the Surface Navy, the Submarine Navy, Naval Aviation, and the Marines.

Getting to CORTRAMID was not as simple as I expected it to be. I had a set of paper military orders, as well as a paper itinerary and printout of my plane ticket from Raleigh to Norfolk. I tried to check in online, but got an error message. I chalked it up to the fact that the plane ticket had been booked through the military, and headed to the airport with my seabag. I got to the counter where the agent informed me that though my ticket had been reserved, it had never been paid for.

It looked like I would be late. Here I was, ten minutes into my career, literally on my first day of active duty, tasked with a simple assignment— move myself from Raleigh to Norfolk with a prepaid plane ticket—and I couldn't even get that done. After a while on hold with a few different customer service reps at the Defense Travel Service (DTS), the agent called me over to the counter.

"Alright, honey, there's good news and there's bad news. Your ticket has now been paid for. The bad news is that we just cancelled your flight."

"That's not good."

"But it looks like we can get you there just a few hours late. You'll have to go through Charlotte, but I think we can get you on a first class seat." I was rebooked on the later flight and managed to get to Norfolk. This was to be the first of many experiences with the military bureaucracy and administration that was less than stellar—although the pinnacle of administrative failures was not to come until a few years later, which resulted in every official document for the duration of my Marine Corps career having my first name spelled incorrectly.

The CORTRAMID staff met us at the airport and brought us to our home for the next few weeks at the Bachelor Enlisted Quarters at Naval Base Norfolk. After a few days of getting settled in, taking the Navy's Physical Readiness Test and other administrative tasks, we began our rotation.

Aviation Week was spent at Naval Air Station Oceana, near Virginia Beach. After completing swim quals to make sure we could float if the plane crashed, and the parachute simulator to learn how to bail out, every midshipman went up in a T-34. A two-seater, single engine propeller plane, the T-34 was the Navy and Marine Corps' version of an airplane with training wheels.

Definitely an unforgettable experience, a few minutes after taking off the pilot said, "You have the controls."

"I have the controls."

"You have the controls," he repeated, completing the last part of the three-step handover, a safety measure to ensure that someone is always in control of the aircraft. Under instruction from the pilot, I flew the plane out over the Atlantic Ocean. I figured we would turn around after a fairly sedate flight. Not so much. And it was awesome.

"Alright, you're going to do something called an Immelman turn now. Piece of cake. Pull back on the stick ... good ... now rudder and bank over now ... sweet. Level off." The Immelman is basically a U-turn in midair. I never really had an intense desire to be a pilot, but getting to do that at COR-TRAMID is definitely one of the coolest things I've ever done.

Surface Week was spent aboard the USS *Laboon*, a destroyer, and it was interesting, but not much more than that. I didn't have an unpleasant experience, but I didn't walk away with a burning desire to be a Surface Warfare Officer.

For Submarine Week, we flew down to Kings Bay, GA. The platoon of midshipmen spent a few days running simulators in the Trident Training Facility, where the expert crews of the Ohio Class ballistic missile nuclear submarines are trained. The life-size mockups of submarine control rooms and engine compartments move and tilt, flood, and fill with smoke. The following few days were spent underway aboard the USS *Albuquerque*. Jumping off the bow of a submarine into the pristine blue waters in the middle of the Atlantic was a good time, but I didn't think I had found my life's calling in the submarine force.

I still wanted to be a naval officer, but after experiencing the Navy-centric part of CORTRAMID, I was most looking forward to Marine week. My eighth grade math teacher, Harry Dudley, a 1969 graduate of the Naval Academy, had told our class about Marine Week. That had been in 1999, six years prior, and I had been looking forward to it ever since.

The platoon traveled from Norfolk to Camp Geiger, NC. Located near Camp Lejeune, Camp Geiger is the home of the Marine Corps, School of Infantry-East. Marine Week included tours of various facilities, including some of the logistics motor pools, and exhibitions by different units, like Amphibious Assault Battalion. I ate up every minute of it. We ran PT, did obstacle and confidence courses, had combat conditioning, and some hand-to-hand combat training with a Marine Corps martial arts instructor. Guns weren't a part of my upbringing, so firing an M-16 for the first time was a pretty big deal—I had never fired a weapon before.

The thing that impressed me the most about Marine Week, though, was the way the Marines carried themselves. Every single Marine we interacted with, from the senior lieutenant colonels briefly introducing themselves to the privates doing maintenance in the motor pool, carried themselves in a certain way. They had an easy swagger. Their uniforms were neat, their hair was always freshly cut, and they spoke with confidence. I wanted to be like them.

Back at school the next year, ROTC was back in full swing and I was no longer a freshman. I was a squad leader with a small squad of freshman midshipmen to lead. My focus, though, was Marine PT. I had gone to a few of the Marine Physical Training sessions freshman year "to prove that I could," but all I had really proven was that I could show up. The Marine PT was harder than anything I had ever done. As a cross country runner in high school, I could run, but I was not prepared for five mile runs in boots and combat utility trousers.

"Pull ups!" Sergeant Roberts would yell. "Four sets of twenty!"

I was lucky if I could get twenty pull ups total, in short little sets of twos and threes. Four sets of twenty was out of the question. I started to feel that I had something to prove. Always the nerdy kid in school, running was about the only physical thing I was any good at. I started to work out, to try to prove something to the Marines in the unit. To prove that I could hack it just as well as they could. All the while, I still didn't realize that deep down I already wanted to be a Marine.

"Why do you want to be a Marine, Clement?" Sergeant Roberts sneered, halfway through a five mile run. We had just crested Georgia Tech's Freshman

Hill, notorious for its steep grade, and so named because all of the freshman dorms are at the base of the hill, while all classes and campus facilities are at the top.

"I don't want to be a Marine, Sergeant."

"Then *why* are you here?"

"To prove that I can hack it."

"Whatever. What do you want to do in the Navy?"

"Drive ships." A textbook answer, but I couldn't articulate a better one. Not at the pace we were running anyway.

"If you feel you have something to prove, that means that deep down you want to be a Marine. You *have* to be a Marine, you just don't know it yet. You won't be happy if you don't try." Sergeant Roberts laughed. "Who cares? I don't. It's your life. Prove it, don't prove it."

I kept telling myself I had just gone out there to prove that a Navy midshipman could PT just as well as a Marine. I needed someone to push me over the edge, and that someone was Sergeant Mike Wehner.

Sergeant Wehner was also a MECEP, and was one of the most down-to-earth guys I had ever met.

"Look, man," he said to me. We were in the wardroom of the NROTC building near the football stadium. "You gotta ask yourself what you want to do."

"I like teaching, I guess." We were talking about long-term plans. I loved being an engineering student and studying engineering, but I didn't want to actually *do* engineering as a career.

"Teaching, leading, mentoring, that's all the same thing. You will not have an opportunity to do as much of that anywhere else except in the Marine Corps. The young Marines need officers who can do that."

Sergeant Wehner wouldn't leave me alone. He would ask when I was switching to be a Marine Option midshipman.

"Not yet," I would respond.

"We'll see."

NOVEMBER 2005: 8TH ST DORM, GEORGIA INSTITUTE OF TECHNOLOGY, ATLANTA, GA

After a few hours of deliberating how exactly to tell my parents that I had decided to join the Marine Corps, I finally just picked up the phone and called. I didn't remember there being much to the conversation, but I didn't remember it right. It was a pretty intense conversation according to my Mom.

"Uh, hi, Mom. I have something to tell you."

"Oh, hi. Ok?" She later told me that she was thinking, "great, he got some girl pregnant."

"I've decided to become a Marine."

"We are in two ground wars right now, and you want to join the Marines?" She said she was thinking, "I wish he had said that he'd gotten someone pregnant." "Is this permanent? Can you change your mind later?"

I still don't remember there being that much to the conversation, but my Mom swears there was more to it. In hindsight, I can see how emotional it was for her. Nobody wants to send their kid off to war. But like me, she was also thinking, "It's just sophomore year . . . the wars would have to last another four years for him to get sent there. There's no way the wars will last that long. They would have to be longer than World War II for that to be the case."

I submitted the application to switch from Navy Option to Marine Option shortly before the end of the fall semester. Then came the waiting game. I wouldn't get an answer as to whether my request was approved or not until spring.

FEBRUARY 2006: GEORGIA TECH ROTC BUILDING, ATLANTA, GA

I was walking through the hall on my way to my Naval Science class one morning the next semester. I was still waiting to hear back from the board about my change of option from Navy to Marines, so I had to continue with the Navy classes. That semester was marine navigation (for ships), which was actually a pretty interesting class, using maneuvering boards and charting bearings.

Lieutenant Colonel Robert Weinkle, the executive officer of the ROTC unit, popped out of his office. "Hey Clement, congrats!"

"Excuse me, sir?"

"Your change of option was approved. Didn't anybody tell you?"

"I guess you just did, sir. That's great."

"Sorry, I thought you knew." He called out to the unit's Assistant Marine Officer Instructor or AMOI. "Gunny Hobbs, I thought we were going to call Midshipman Clement to tell him about his Change of Option?" Lieutenant Colonel Weinkle continued, "Well, now you know. Get yourself over to supply and get that uniform fixed, Clement."

I was wearing the insignia of a Navy Option midshipman, and raced to supply to switch it out for the Eagle, Globe and Anchor of the Marine Corps before my next class started.

JUNE 2006: CENTRAL ISSUE FACILITY, CAMP LEJEUNE, NC

There had been a lot of uncertainty about what I would be doing for "summer cruise" after my sophomore year, because I had just switched from Navy to Marine Option and missed the deadline for the Marine Option Cruise at the Marine Corps Mountain Warfare School in the High Sierras of California. I was visiting my girlfriend (and later wife), Alison, up in Syracuse when I got a phone call.

"Midshipman Clement, Major McCormick. It's all set. You leave for Mountain Warfare in a week. Can you get down to Camp Lejeune to draw gear?"

The ROTC unit had already issued me most of gear that I needed, like an ALICE Pack, Camelbak, cammies, boots, but there were a few things I needed that the ROTC unit didn't have, like helmets. Camp Lejeune was about a two-hour drive from my home in Cary, NC. After I got back from Syracuse a few days later, I made the drive down to Camp Lejeune. I got horribly lost on MCAS New River which was adjacent to Lejeune but on the wrong side of the river. I finally found the CIF, or Central Issue Facility on Lejeune.

Walking in wearing the Marine Option midshipman uniform, which consists of a US Navy khaki officer's uniform with some Marine Corps insignia on the collars, I completely baffled the supply clerk at the desk.

"Good morning, corporal. My name is Midshipman Clement. Gunnery Sergeant Hobbs talked to your supply chief about my drawing some gear."

"Uh, yeah, he mentioned something about it . . . sir? Do I call you sir?"

"You don't have to. It's this whole thing . . . "

"Is that really the uniform you all are supposed to wear?"

"It is. Pretty silly, I know."

I got the gear I needed, except that the only Kevlar cover they had was a desert pattern, which would later cause me some grief with one of my sergeant instructors at Mountain Warfare School. But I had the gear, and headed out to Mountain Warfare School in Bridgeport, CA by way of Reno, NV.

JUNE 2006: MARINE CORPS MOUNTAIN WARFARE TRAINING CENTER, BRIDGEPORT, CA

The next few weeks were exactly what I had hoped they would be. Filled with classes and practical exercises, we learned about mountain survival, leadership and unit planning factors for mountain operations, and weapons employment in the mountains. The altitude was a kicker too; tasks that were easy down at sea level took a toll at 7,000 feet, the base elevation at Mountain Warfare School.

Rock climbing is different when done in combat boots instead of light, pointy specialized shoes. We spent several days learning how to employ ropes on the mountain. Rappelling and top roping had to be mastered, first without combat equipment, then with heavy packs.

Due to the anticipated hasty nature of the combat activities that would require these assaults, the amount of specialized equipment was limited. No climbing harnesses were used; instead, we tied a Swiss seat of rope around our waists and legs. While it gave me some confidence that I could tie a rope that would arrest my fall, the damn thing cut off the blood to the legs and bit into my thigh. The function of the Swiss seat might be the same, but it was infinitely less comfortable than a commercial climbing harness.

My platoon patrols in the High Sierras of California. At altitudes around 11,000 feet, some of the snow never melts.

Suspension traverses, also known as "zip lines," were taught and used to safely raise and lower casualties or heavy equipment up steep slopes and cliffs. We also learned how to construct a high-tension one-rope bridge to cross streams or gorges. If we did it wrong, we would fall and die. Literally.

The second phase of Mountain Warfare School was a company-level exercise involving hundreds of Marines. Given a basic scheme of maneuver, each platoon would patrol a given route over a period of about a week, requiring hiking, climbing, rappelling, one-rope bridging, and traversing, essentially all of the skills covered during the previous week's instruction into a real-life situation.

We covered dozens of miles and climbed up and down thousands of feet in the High Sierras. Extreme changes in weather were the norm, with temperatures at night near freezing, and highs of nearly 100 degrees during the day. At one point, we were walking on frozen snowpack, but sweating from the heat. Because of Bridgeport's deep snowfall in the winter, there were places on the mountains where the snow never quite melted completely during the summer months.

Mountain Warfare School was one of the best experiences that I ever had in the Corps. Leaving Bridgeport, I felt like I had accomplished something. I was good enough to be here. I could handle the hardest rigors of being a Marine, and I was ready for the challenge of OCS the next summer. For the midshipmen at MWTC, we knew that the next time we would see each other again would be in the summer of 2007 as candidates at OCS.

CHAPTER TWO

DUCTUS EXEMPLO—*LEAD BY EXAMPLE*

We must remember that one man is much the same as another, and he is best who is trained in the severest school. —Thucydides (460–395 BC)

Marine Corps drill instructors are surely among the most creative and fast-thinking comedians in the world. For hours upon days upon weeks upon months upon years on end, they perform to both train and stress out their audience. They hone their craft while encouraging recruits to do one more pushup. They sharpen their wit while expertly cultivating panic in a recruit's mind when his rifle is not clean enough.

Marine officer candidates are trained by "Sergeant Instructors," mostly staff sergeants and gunnery sergeants, all of whom have had a successful tour training new recruits at either Parris Island or San Diego. Sergeant instructors are masters of their craft, and the candidates at OCS are rightly afraid of them. They hold the destiny of the candidates in their hands. A candidate can be dropped solely based on the recommendation of his sergeant instructors.

For all that, they are some of the funniest people you will ever meet. And when they were yelling at me, in the back of my mind, I couldn't help but think, "This is actually some pretty funny shit." It was hard not to laugh a lot of the time. A lot of the humor is situational, and only funny to other Marines who have been in that situation or were physically there. I'll do the best I can to illustrate this part of the drill instructors' character, but any lack of comedic value is due to my inability as a storyteller.

"Well, isn't this a tragedy? Wouldn't you say this is a tragedy there, Daniels?"

"YES, GUNNERY SERGEANT! A TRAGEDY!"

"Do you agree with Daniels there, Clement?" Gunnery Sergeant McKenney asked.

"Yes, Sergeant Instructor Gunnery Sergeant McKenney, this candidate agrees with Candidate Daniels. This is a tragedy." Talk about a mouthful.

A frog had died. We weren't there when he died, but this frog was dead. Completely and thoroughly devoid of life, he was lying on the ground near the Confidence Course, an advanced obstacle course.

"Alright. Well, we're going to commemorate this frog's life. Who here is religious? And I don't mean the bullshit religious that everyone pretends to be so that they can go to church every Sunday to hide from me for an hour, I mean really religious." He looks around. "Who am I kidding? You are all morally corrupt and headed straight for hell. O'Rourke, you'll be the minister."

"Aye, aye, Gunnery Sergeant!" O'Rourke assumed his position at the frog's head.

"And give me seven candidates lined up over there to be the firing party. We're going to give this frog a twenty-one gun salute." Seven more candidates lined up. "I need somebody to say the eulogy. The rest of you turds are the choir."

The eulogy was something that would have fit right in with Monty Python's *Dead Parrots Don't Talk*. We sang *Amazing Grace*, and prayed over the frog. The platoon saluted for the twenty-one gun salute, which the firing party executed (without ammunition) with their M16A2 service rifles and a crisp verbal "bang." And that's the story of how Officer Candidate School, Golf Company, Third Platoon, First Increment, Summer 2007 gave a funeral for a frog. After the funeral, the frog was appropriately buried. The last handful of earth was patted down and a small cross made from twigs was placed as a grave marker. Suddenly, one of the other sergeant instructors ran up. Staff Sergeant Francini tore in on the platoon and, with his usual ferocity, started raising hell.

"What in the hell is going on here? Are we some kind of barbershop quartet? Maybe you should all run away and join the circus!"

Some of the stuff that is really funny in hindsight was actually a big pain at the time and accomplished its intended purpose of stressing us out. More specifically, the sergeant instructors would do things to occupy every last second of the day so that we never had a minute of downtime, or they would force us to work all night on some urgent task in order to be ready for the next day.

"Oh, okay, I see how it is. You're an expert. Write me an essay. 1000 words," the platoon sergeant, Gunnery Sergeant Kevin Wiss, would say. We all knew the rules. Words with three letters or less didn't count. Essays had to be written on loose-leaf paper, double-spaced, and with each word over three letters individually underlined. Over each word with three or more letters, its corresponding number was written, from 1 to exactly 1000, with each number circled. You knew every essay would cost you about an hour of sleep, and since the squad bay lights had to stay out except in the bathroom, you were going to be sitting on a toilet to write it. We knew they didn't read the essays. Usually, that is. Every now and then someone got brave and included a sarcastic comment in an essay, and every now and then the sergeant instructors would catch it. The offending author would have to read his essay aloud to the platoon.

"Oh, we got a comedian. Well, tell you what, you think you're a regular ar-teest. Isn't that how the Frenchies say artist? Ar-teest? Tell you what, you're going to give us a Goddamned poetry reading. Let's hear your work of art."

The poetry readings were hilarious. Even the sergeant instructors had trouble keeping a straight face.

As important as leadership and academic knowledge was at OCS, the quickest way to get skylined, that is, singled out as a candidate, was to fall short in physical fitness. Marine officers are expected to lead from the front in intensely demanding combat situations, and the OCS staff made it a point to separate those who could hack it from those who couldn't.

Not a day passed without a PT event. Some days, the sergeant instructors would run us for miles, seeing who would drop off the back. Other days, the platoon would run the obstacle course over and over, running from the end back to the beginning, climbing up ropes and over high wooden beams.

Candidates weren't allowed to wear watches, so we lost all sense of time during PT, and the rest of the day for that matter. Without any knowledge of how long the workout would last, it was a game of survival, hanging on until the end. Survival wasn't enough, though. Marine officers are expected to inspire confidence, to betray no weakness. No matter the effort, no matter the pain, candidates were expected to stand up straight, to have an indifferent facial expression.

The evaluation was not merely subjective. Marine Officer Candidate School is renowned for its physicality. Many candidates who thought they were in shape were dropped, having been found wanting after failing one of the graded physical fitness tests. The evaluation began almost immediately.

After checking in on the first day and being kept awake for nearly 48 hours straight with in-processing and medical exams, the standard Marine

Corps Physical Fitness Test was the order of the day. Less than 18 pull-ups, and you were skylined, drawing negative attention from the instructors—most candidates could max out the test with 20 or more pull-ups. The second exercise was sit-ups—woe unto him who could not do the prescribed 100 in two minutes. The last part of the test was a three-mile run—most candidates finished in around 19 minutes.

Physical preparation before OCS was essential to meeting the rigors of the endurance course, a three-mile course through the woods that must be run in boots carrying a cartridge belt, canteens of water, and a rifle. The grading continued with the standard Marine Corps obstacle course, an exhausting sprint of muscular endurance demanding running, jumping, swinging onto logs, flipping over a ten-foot high bar and climbing a rope. Conditioning hikes with heavy packs went all night over rough terrain, and the daily grind of training wore on us. Sores, scrapes and scabs were commonplace. Few candidates did not rise before reveille to put moleskin and tape on already blistered toes and cracked feet.

"Foot rot" and ringworm were our constant companions. But we knew it was nothing compared to the torment of the Marines at the Chosin Reservoir in Korea or on Okinawa in World War II. We had to prove we could hack it, that we were worthy successors of their legacy.

Just about the worst thing that could happen to you was to have your footlocker or wall locker "dumped." Every object a candidate owned was required to be cleaned and neatly folded and organized in a specific way in our footlocker and wall locker. Furthermore, they were to be secured with a combination lock at all times. If we went to PT or class and forgot to lock up, our footlocker would be dumped and all of our stuff would be strewn about the squad bay. The sergeant instructors would usually cover everything with foot powder or laundry detergent to make clean up more difficult. The worst was when more than one person would forget to lock up and two or three candidates' gear was intermixed. You would never get all of your stuff back, but I suppose you got some of everybody else's stuff at the same time, so it all sort of worked out.

AUGUST 2008: FORT MYER ID CARD CENTER, ARLINGTON, VA

I was in the seating area at the ID Card Center on Fort Myer, waiting to get a new ID card. There was a single vacant seat, just to my right. A brusque, older gentleman walked into the room, paused, and looked around. Surveying his lone choice, he sat down next to me.

He looked familiar, but I couldn't place him immediately. He was dressed like many Marine retirees, wearing jeans and a polo shirt. His goatee was mostly gray.

"So, when did you go through OCS, Lieutenant?" he asked without introduction.

As soon as I heard the voice, I knew who he was. A chill went up my spine and I sat up perfectly straight, almost at attention.

"Relax, you're fine." He had noticed me stiffen up. "You must know me, then."

The commanding officer of Officer Candidate School during my time there was Colonel Robert Chase; he personally decided whether you would graduate and become a Marine officer, or be dropped like nearly 50% of those who tried.

"Yes, sir. I was in Golf Co, 1st Increment, Summer '07. You were my CO," I said. This was Colonel Robert Chase. He was truly a man that inspired fear, but who you would follow anywhere.

"Sounds right. What was the attrition rate for your platoon? Swag it, approximate?" he asked.

"Off the top of my head, sir, probably about 40%. I think we started with right around 55 and graduated just about 34 or so."

He laughed. "Oh yeah, that had to be one of my platoons. You know I got a lot of flak from the higher-ups about how many candidates I dropped? What do you think about it?"

It was funny to hear a colonel talk about "higher-ups" in the same way that lieutenants talked about them. I was a little more at ease now. "Honestly, sir, I don't think that anybody who was dropped should have been a Marine officer. The general reaction in the squad bay after somebody left was 'it was only a matter of time for him.'"

"I don't know if you're just telling me that, but I'll assume that you honestly feel that way. You know, I stand firmly by what I did then. I told you about my son, right?"

"Yes, sir, at our initial in-briefing." He had. We were sitting in the classroom at OCS and he told us that his mission was not to drop as many candidates as possible, but neither was his mission to pass a certain number of candidates. He told us that his son was an enlisted infantryman, and that he would not pass any candidate who he did not trust to lead his son in combat.

"Well, you know that's what it's all about. It was a great ride, and I stand by everything I did. My edges are a little too rough for this game anymore.

You get to be a colonel and it's all political. Things went downhill for me at my last job after I quoted Napoleon to a general. Or at least, I told him that the quote was from Napoleon. Maybe it was, or maybe it was just something I heard somewhere. I was tasked to put together a plan for the way ahead for training. I knew I couldn't do it; I got a group of captains and lieutenants and sergeants and gunnys, and they wrote the thing. All based on their recent experiences, the truth on the ground. I read it, and it was brilliant. I could never have come up with it; I'm too old and my experience is no longer relevant. But these kids, they nailed it. The General hated it. So I told this General, 'Napoleon said that by the time you are old enough to be a general you're too old to recognize innovation.'"

We both laughed. "You really said that to him, sir?"

"Damn straight, lieutenant. I could never play politics well enough to be a general. What are they going to do to me? I got a gig lined up at SOCOM down in Florida. I'll be working with innovators and warriors and get away from this Beltway nonsense."

My number was called. I started to stand up.

"It was good talking to you, sir," I said.

"Hey, you too, lieutenant." I could tell he really meant it. One of the things that he told us at OCS was that the best part of his job was mentoring young candidates and Marines and hopefully having an impact on the future of the Corps. "Enjoy being a platoon commander. It's the best time you'll have in the Marine Corps, and you only get one shot at it."

Mentorship aside, he was still a terrifying individual when he wanted to be. It was a persona that he had carefully crafted for the express purpose of effectively screening and training candidates at OCS. An inspiring leader, he didn't always give us what we wanted, but even in my brief interactions with him, he always gave us what we needed.

The attrition rate at OCS in 2006 and 2007 was no joke. The first few got dropped on the second or third day, and then everyone was left wondering until the third week. About seven candidates in the platoon got summoned to the colonel's office at the end of that third week. They would sit at attention, perched on their camp stools, in a line waiting for their turn to stand before Colonel Chase. From our platoon, at least, nobody who went into one of those meetings came out without being dropped from OCS. Their years of preparation and dreams of becoming a Marine officer ended in a five minute meeting.

It wasn't personal, and those of us who remained pretty much agreed that every candidate who was dropped should have been dropped. Some were not physically fit enough and couldn't handle the endurance course or the hikes. Others couldn't cut it academically, unable to master the wide variety of knowledge we were expected to know. Most, however, were dropped for poor performance and assessments in the somewhat subjective intangible leadership abilities; these candidates were called "leadership failures." Performance on the graded field events, as a platoon billet holder, issuing orders, and military bearing, all went into the leadership grade. More than anything else, the types of things that contributed to the leadership grade are essential to Marine officers, and deficiencies in these areas will quickly cause you to lose the respect of your Marines.

Every week, another list of candidates would be summoned to the Colonel's office, and every week another few would pack their bags. In general, the leadership tried to have the dismissed candidates pack their bags and leave the squad bay while we were gone.

"Whelp, looks like another of your friends is gone. Just like that. They didn't even wait for you all to say goodbye," Staff Sergeant Francini would gleefully yell, laughing heartily. "Colonel Chase told him to get the fuck out of here. He ran back here and packed his bags and is on his way to the airport, all while you all were eating lunch."

"It's funny how fast Vincent ran to get his bags packed. He had never run that fast before. Maybe if he would have run like that before, like he *cared,* he wouldn't have been dropped." This was from the platoon sergeant, Gunnery Sergeant Wiss. "Look how quickly we can be rid of you. I wonder who's next?"

I knew I could hack it, that I should be a Marine officer, but I had to prove it first. I didn't fail any of the graded events and I was always near the front at PT, but we all held our breath as they announced the list of names who had to go see Colonel Chase. After every round of interviews with the colonel and subsequent empty racks that we found in our squad bay, I was glad to have escaped that fate.

JULY 2007: OCS TRAINING AREAS, QUANTICO, VA
Perhaps the two most important graded events at OCS were the Leadership Reaction Course (LRC) and the Small Unit Leadership Exercise (SULE). The LRC was essentially an obstacle course or task that was executed by small squads, and the candidate leading the squad was graded on his performance. To complicate matters, many of the tasks were not physically possible, and

were instead an exercise in leadership when things aren't going right. An obstacle might be a wooden wall about twenty feet high with a window fifteen feet off the ground, and a five-foot wide moat with water in front of the wall. The task would be to move the squad through the window using nothing more than a twenty-foot long 3" diameter pipe and a four-foot length of rope. The tasks required physical strength, mental agility and leadership skills. The candidate being tested had only a few minutes to formulate a plan, sketch out an order, and brief his fellow candidates. Successfully completing the task was not a guarantee of receiving a good grade. Some candidates completed their LRC mission and received an average passing grade, whereas other candidates who were unable to complete the task received a higher grade.

The SULE was a little more involved. Executed in larger groups of twelve to fifteen candidates, the SULE required several kilometers of movement and took longer than the ten minutes of an LRC challenge. Again, the candidate being evaluated would be given a task and have several minutes to formulate a plan.

I was given my task by the evaluator, a captain. "You will move from our current location to this enemy communications node approximately two kilometers to our north." She pointed to the map. "There are no restrictions on your movement and you may use anything the squad currently has with it."

"Before you begin your planning," she continued, "you must plot on the map the following two grid coordinates."

I copied them down and plotted the first one on the map, drawing a dot on our current location.

"Wrong," she stated bluntly.

It was right, and I was sure of it. I plotted the second one.

"Wrong again." I knew she was just telling me that I was wrong to make me second-guess myself. It was one of their games; they tried to shake our confidence. Nothing to do but to press on.

I formulated my five-paragraph order, the standard briefing template used throughout the Marine Corps and, in fact, all of NATO, and issued the order to my squad. We moved out. I had the squad in a fire team wedge (four men in a diamond formation), squad column (with three fire team wedges, one behind the other). We were about halfway to our destination when the captain tapped me on the shoulder and said, "Bang bang."

"Excuse me, ma'am?" I asked.

She repeated it louder. "BANG BANG."

"Ma'am, with all due respect, this candidate does not know what scenario is being simulated here to direct a reaction from the squad." No personal pronouns allowed.

"Fair enough. You are being shot at from your left flank."

That was all I needed. "Contact Left! Prepare to buddy rush. Execute!"

Buddy rushing is the most basic, fundamental tenet of Marine Corps maneuver warfare. "Fire and movement" means that one Marine is engaging targets to prevent the enemy from shooting while his battle buddy moves forward. Once his battle buddy is set, he will begin firing at the enemy to allow the first Marine to leapfrog past him. Nobody should move without being covered by friendly fire.

My squad started pushing into the woods, buddy rushing toward the imaginary enemy. We had blanks for our M16A2 rifles, and were firing to "cover" each other's movement, though there were still no targets in sight. After a few dozen shots were fired, two Marines playing "aggressors" popped up out of their hole 100 meters to our front and pulled an M249 SAW up. They began to fire at us with blanks. I buddy rushed the squad through their position, redirecting some of the fire teams to focus on the aggressors.

I consolidated my squad on the "enemy" position, prepared to repel a simulated counterattack when I overheard the captain talking to the two Marines, OCS staff members, who had shot at us. "Don't ever let me catch you falling asleep on post again."

The whole incident was a little silly, our would-be attackers falling asleep while waiting for us, and our attack waking them up. When ENDEX (the end of the exercise) was called, the captain asked if I had any questions on how I would be evaluated, or tactical questions that were unclear.

"Yes, ma'am, this candidate does have a question. Given the confusion, what was this candidate's final grade?" That was all that mattered.

"You passed." And she walked away, leaving me to wonder if that was really my grade or if that statement was some kind of misinformation, too, just part of the game they were playing with us.

The games continued. "You think we're done? Oh, we're not done. Just because there's nothing on the training schedule we got the day off? HELL-LLLLLL NO!" Staff Sergeant Francini bellowed. "Hey there, Rice, what's your favorite restaurant?"

"This candidate's favorite restaurant is McDonald's, staff sergeant!"

"It would be, you nasty. Well, when's the last time you got to eat there? It's been a few weeks since you've been here at OCS. I bet you miss it. Do you miss it?"

"Yes, staff sergeant!"

"Well, alright then, we're going to give you a taste of home. Build me a McDonald's."

We all stood there in the squad bay, dumbfounded.

"This candidate requests permission to ask sergeant instructor Staff Sergeant Francini a question," Rice stated.

"Permission granted."

"How should these candidates build a McDonald's, staff sergeant?" No personal pronouns allowed, remember.

"Well, you all want to be Marine officers, right? Improvise, adapt, overcome. You've got racks, foot lockers, wall lockers, and candidates. Use what you've got."

"Aye, aye, staff sergeant."

We spent the next thirty or forty-five minutes building a "McDonald's" with our bunk beds and foot lockers. Candidates were tasked as fry cooks and cashiers, and worked the register at the drive-through.

The platoon sergeant came in right about then.

"What in the hell is going on here? Why are the racks out of place? Put my house back together now!"

"AYE, AYE, GUNNERY SERGEANT!" the platoon yelled as one. We put everything back in place, trying not to laugh.

One of the things we were taught in OCS was that a good Marine always has a notebook and an "ink stick" available. We were always taking notes to avoid getting yelled at, but if nothing else, taking notes helped keep us awake through the fatigue. The habit stuck though, and I've tried to save most of my notebooks because sometimes I'll catch a good nugget when I go back and read through them years later. OCS was a constant on-off cycle between leadership seminars, drill, PT and classes. In the haze of OCS, though, the leadership training really stuck with me. The leadership training notes are the only ones from OCS that really have any meaning.

Our company commander was Major Trent Gibson, the Marine Officer Instructor from Virginia Tech. He had been Corporal Jason Dunham's company commander in Iraq when Corporal Dunham saved the lives of his fellow Marines by throwing his helmet onto an insurgent grenade, and holding the helmet down with his body in an attempt to contain the deadly blast.

Hearing the story from Major Gibson was awe-inspiring, and drove my desire to be a part of the Marine Corps. Before the incident, Corporal Dunham had debated the strength of the Kevlar helmet with some squadmates and his platoon commander. Dunham theorized that even if the Kevlar might not protect the Marine holding it down from the blast of a grenade, it would definitely save the other Marines around him. His squadmates doubted that somebody could get their helmet off in time to get it on top of the grenade and hold it down with their body.

Corporal Dunham practiced this maneuver. He would unfasten his helmet, throw it down and jump on top of it. There was no way he could have known he would later use this same technique to save the lives of his fellow Marines in Kilo Company, 3rd Battalion, 7th Marines.

While attempting to detain an insurgent in Al-Karabilah, Iraq, a hand-to-hand struggle ensued. The insurgent pulled out a grenade intending to kill himself, Corporal Dunham, and two other Marines. Corporal Dunham disengaged from fighting the man, unclipped his chin strap, covered the grenade with his helmet and pressed his body atop it. He saved the lives of his two comrades, but was mortally wounded in the process. It was a sacrifice he made without hesitation, and for this he was posthumously awarded the Medal of Honor.

Major Gibson told this story with tears in his eyes. "Ownership," he said, "is the touchstone of leadership. There are three rules of leadership that I have learned over the years, and Corporal Dunham exemplified all three with this one act. First, leadership by example.

"Second, self-sacrifice for the greater good. Be willing to do anything for your Marines. Give everything you have, and then give some more. Tear yourself to the ground.

"Lastly, one man can make a difference."

There was no other organization in the world that I could think of whose members would do such things for each other. Once I knew about the Marines, how could I be a part of anything else?

OCS was not fun. Nearly the whole company got pink eye. We were living in close quarters, not really showering, not eating enough, being pushed physically, and getting only four or five hours of sleep a night, and they were rarely consecutive because every candidate would have an hour of firewatch (guard duty) at some point during the night. Everybody got sick. "The candidate crud" we called it. It was some kind of upper respiratory infection that made breathing hard, caused constant coughing, sore throats, and fever. Nobody would dare go to medical for it though, for fear of being dropped from OCS and ending our dreams of ever being Marines. We swore to ourselves that we would gut it out.

I would eat everything I could get my hands on, but it was never enough. Every trip through the chow line, I would pile extra peanut butter and jelly on my bread and cover my salads in ranch dressing for the extra calories. It was a numbers game; how many calories can you eat in five minutes? Never enough. Not for the level of activity we were putting out.

I showed up at OCS weighing about 165 pounds. I graduated from OCS six weeks later weighing 150 pounds. The "candidate crud" lasted for a good month and a half after I got back from OCS, and I was always coughing. Weeks of food and sleep were required to finally kick it.

But it was all worth it. On the day before graduation, we marched across the damned bridge over the railroad tracks that we had crossed six times a day to go to the chow hall, and formed up on the bank of the Potomac River, and our platoon commander, Captain Fleming, pressed a black Eagle, Globe and Anchor into my hand. It was the symbol that we had worked so hard for.

On the last day of OCS, the sergeant instructors pulled us out of our racks and told us to line up on the "highway" or center aisle of the squad bay.

"Do you think we enjoyed doing this to you? Do you think we find this funny?" Staff Sergeant Francini demanded. That morning we had found out he would be awarded the "sergeant instructor of the increment" honor—the instructor who had done the most to shape and mold the candidates. It was reserved for the hardest, loudest, most stressful sergeant instructor, and he was ours.

"So, do you?" Staff Sergeant Francini continued. We all hesitated. "Shit yeah, I enjoyed it. It was hella fun."

The next day, we got dressed for graduation. For the first time, I put on a pair of "cammies," the slang we used for our camouflaged utility uniform. The nametapes on the blouse said "Clement" and "U.S. Marines." I don't think I have ever been so proud of anything else in my life as when I put those cammies on.

After OCS, I returned to Georgia Tech to complete my mechanical engineering degree, required for commissioning. Senior year was filled with daily mentorship from Lieutenant Colonel Ronald Peterson, the Marine Officer Instructor for Georgia Tech and Morehouse from 2006 to 2008. His lessons were in mental toughness, fortitude and in bearing.

Lieutenant Colonel Peterson taught us well, and I appreciated everything that he had to say. One of the mantras I have internalized is, as he put it, "Always look cool. If you look cool, calm and composed, like you've 'been here before,' people will trust you. You can be freaking out on the inside, but if you look cool on the outside, people will rest assured that you have it all under control and follow you confidently."

At daily PT sessions and classes, he instilled these traits in us, preparing us to step in front of our first platoons. The last semester was a race to the end, to graduation and commissioning.

MAY 2008: GEORGIA TECH BALLROOM, ATLANTA, GA

I, Jeffrey Clement, do solemnly swear that I will support and defend the Constitution of the United States against all enemies, foreign and domestic; that I will bear true faith and allegiance to the same; that I take this obligation freely, without any mental reservation or purpose of evasion; and that I will well and faithfully discharge the duties of the office on which I am about to enter. So help me God.

The 2008 commissioning ceremony at Georgia Tech was a joint ceremony for all of the new Marine, Navy, Army and Air Force officers. The guest speaker was the chief of staff of Southern Command, who was an Army brigadier general at the time. I don't remember his name or much of what was said that day. There are, however, two moments from that day that I remember distinctly.

The first was the actual swearing in, the oath of office, and the corresponding "pinning on." I felt pretty powerful, like I had finally made it. It was gratifying to finally have four years of work culminate in this.

Almost more significant, and definitely more sobering, was the first salute. Long a tradition, Marine lieutenants select an enlisted Marine who has had a significant impact on their education and training to give them their first salute. The first Marine to salute me was Sergeant Jeptha Johnson (later commissioned and promoted to first lieutenant).

Sergeant Johnson was a MECEP (Marine Enlisted Commissioning Education Program) Option. He originally enlisted in the Marine Corps as an admin clerk in 2002, and went on to attend Georgia State University to study history. The Georgia State students were members of the Georgia Tech ROTC unit, so I was privileged to receive frequent doses of Sergeant Johnson's leadership. He stepped in front of me, and saluted.

"Good afternoon, Sir."

I returned the salute. "Good afternoon, Sergeant."

I handed him a silver dollar, the traditional token of appreciation given by new officers to enlisted advisors. I'm not a sappy guy, but the weight of the responsibilities that I would eventually have hit me. My Marines were counting on me. I couldn't escape or side-step the responsibility. Some people see the salute as a symbol of flattery or old-fashioned "classism." For officers, it signifies the responsibility that you owe your Marines.

Alison and I pose for a photo near Georgia Tech's Student Center on our commissioning day.

CHAPTER THREE

THE LIEUTENANT DON'T KNOW

MAY 2008

After I was commissioned, I was sent home. Without pay. Because so many lieutenants were being commissioned as part of the Corps' plus-up to 202,000 active-duty Marines in support of Operations Iraqi Freedom and Enduring Freedom (OEF), The Basic School was backed up. I got a job as a maintenance engineer at the Jurys Doyle Hotel, on Dupont Circle in Washington, DC from May to August of 2009, fixing toilets and doing wallpaper. In August, the Marine Corps decided that they were ready for me to start working. Still without pay.

Or rather, they should have been paying me, but due to a clerical error I didn't get paid for the first two months of work. When the paycheck with all my back pay finally did come through, it was large, to say the least. I worked at the Officer Selection Office in College Park, MD.

Every day, a few other new lieutenants and I would go to various college campuses, trying to recruit college students to become Marine officers. It really wasn't a bad gig, but we all were ready to begin our careers for real. We could not wait to start The Basic School.

OCTOBER 2008: O'BANNON HALL, THE BASIC SCHOOL, QUANTICO, VA

"Every Marine a rifleman, every Marine Officer a rifle platoon commander."
I was assigned to Basic Officer Course 1-09, Alpha Company. Dubbed "Arctic Alpha," we would train through the winter from October 2008 to April 2009. The Marine Corps provides its officers with better training than any other branch, and more of it. At the time, a typical US Navy Surface Warfare Officer received only a few weeks of training after commissioning, and was required to learn everything "on-the-job" at his first ship. Army infantry

officers completed a branch-specific Basic Officer Leadership Course that is about four months long.

Every Marine Corps officer, from pilots to logisticians to infantrymen, first goes to The Basic School. TBS is six months of training to prepare an officer to be an infantry platoon commander. Every Marine is a rifleman, and every Marine officer has to be prepared to be a provisional infantry platoon commander. The Marines take that seriously—in Iraq and Afghanistan, artillery units, in particular, found themselves leaving their M777 howitzers behind and conducting dismounted infantry patrols.

Officers are not assigned a Military Occupational Specialty (MOS) until the end of TBS. After TBS, every officer completes a follow-on school in their particular specialty, averaging about three months (although the pilots' flight school was usually about two years). It is pretty amazing when you get right down to it—a Marine adjutant had two more months of infantry platoon commander training than an Army infantry platoon commander. This was a considerable investment in time and money, but worth it in the long run. The combat focus of TBS was essential for all officers, because even the non-combat arms Marines could be called to operate in the most intense of combat zones.

Everything at TBS was graded. Just like OCS, academics comprised 25% of the final grade, and military skills (like rifle and pistol scores and physical fitness) were another 25%. Fully 50% of our TBS grades assessed "leadership skills," based on both objective testing and subjective evaluations of leadership in field exercises.

A component of the leadership grade was the dreaded peer evaluation or "spear eval." Several times during TBS, we evaluated the other lieutenants in our squad and platoon. Based on the ranking (say, 1st out of 15 in the squad, or 27th out of 50 in the platoon) we would get a certain number of points toward our leadership grade. Perhaps the most significant factor in the leadership grade was the staff platoon commander (SPC) ranking. My platoon's SPC was Captain Declan Lynch, a logistics officer. He spent nearly every minute of six months with the platoon, and was the individual primarily responsible for our training and evaluation.

Since I was already married, I was a "brown bagger"—I lived in town and commuted to TBS every day. Alison and I were living in Arlington, VA, a good 48 miles away. I was commuting south in the morning away from DC and north in the evening, so at least I didn't have to fight DC rush hour traffic. I wouldn't have had to anyway, since I normally left the house by 0400 and didn't get home until after 1900.

The unmarried Marines lived in one of several barracks aboard TBS. Our company was assigned to O'Bannon Hall, which was later demolished in 2012. With the surge of lieutenants at TBS, living conditions were tight. I was assigned, along with five other Marines, to a room intended for four Marines. Since I didn't usually sleep there, I didn't have a bed, but I did have a desk for studying and a gear closet to store all of my tactical equipment—pack, flak jacket, and helmet. We were in tight quarters during the day when I was there—and my roommates were glad that I didn't stay there at night.

The first phase of TBS began with instruction on individual combat skills. The first lesson was instructed by a compact, muscle-bound sergeant who was surprisingly quick and light on his feet.

"Good morning, ladies and gentlemen. This week will be dedicated to instruction and practical application of hand-to-hand combat skills." It sounded scripted. "The Marine Corps Martial Arts Program, or MCMAP, blends various martial arts to build a vocabulary of fighting techniques that are practical for Marines in combat. So these are techniques that you can use when you're tired, when you've got a flak jacket and Kevlar on. Flying round-house karate kicks are no good if you're wearing fifty pounds of gear."

He continued, "The strikes from taekwondo, punches from boxing, throws from judo, have all been blended together for the Marines' use. We need to build in the muscle memory so that if you need it, you've got it." We conducted thousands of repetitions to build that muscle memory. Strikes, punches, throws, on and on, until we were bruised and sore.

Next up was weapons training. I had not had any exposure to firearms before joining the Marine Corps—it just wasn't something that my family did growing up. At TBS, I learned to be comfortable with weapons. Two weeks were focused on the M9 9mm Beretta pistol and the M16A2 Service Rifle. The first week was called Grass Week, because it took place in a grass field, not on a firing range. We laid on the freezing cold ground of a field in front of O'Bannon Hall to "snap in," dry firing without bullets at a white barrel with small silhouettes painted on it. This was designed to help us focus our breathing, work on sight picture and get used to the rifle's trigger pull.

The second of the two Rifle Weeks required us to hike three miles every day to the rifle ranges on MCB Quantico over some pretty steep hills that we grew to hate. In the afternoons, we would hike the three miles back from Weapons Training Battalion to TBS. TBS required lieutenants to be in top physical condition, and though there were a few graded physical fitness events, mental and physical toughness were always being evaluated. Every day of Rifle Week included six miles of hiking with a moderate load (about 20 pounds) at high speed, and woe unto him who fell out of the hike.

I most distinctly remember being cold during that second week. We completed three rotations each day. Our first rotation was down in the target pits, pulling the targets down and putting them back up. We graded the shots of the shooters firing at the targets. The target pits were essentially a concrete caisson below ground level. In November in Quantico, VA, spending hours in a concrete box below ground level is a miserable experience. No matter how many thermal layers we put on, we could not seem to stay warm. A thermos of coffee wouldn't go very far, but everyone shared whatever they brought.

The second rotation for our platoon was on the rifle range, firing our rifles at distances from 300 meters out to 500 meters, using bare iron sights—back then, no scopes or optics were allowed. In the afternoons we fired on the pistol range at distances from 6 to 25 meters. I am convinced that something was wrong with the pistols that I was issued at both TBS and, later, CLB-6. They were old and worn and I could never hold a tight group of shots, never scoring higher than sharpshooter. But when I checked into 8th and I, the pistol assigned to me was brand new. I went to the range after not having shot in over a year, and ironically I held tight groups and scored high in the expert range without a problem. I know I didn't change—I didn't even practice. But someone who doesn't shoot expert always blames it on the gun, so assume I'm lying. The rest of the first phase of TBS passed quickly. It was all very exciting and novel, including putting on my uniform every morning with the shiny gold "butter bars" of a second lieutenant.

We had dozens of classes covering basic Marine Corps weapons and tactics, combat lifesaving medical skills, and doctrine. But the most high-tension training exercises were devoted to land navigation. The worst thing a leader can do is lose his cool; the second worst thing a leader can do is get his unit lost. As it works out, if the latter happens, the former tends to follow soon after. Land navigation was essential. We spent hours in the woods, working a map and compass, to find precious "red boxes," ammo cans painted red and designated with a number or letter. The task was to find eight, ten or twelve ammo cans, given nothing but the (often wrong) grid coordinates of their locations. We had to find the location and note the number or letter of each ammo can. If you were right, you got it right. If you were wrong, there was no partial credit.

I actually really enjoyed the land navigation exercises. They were an individual effort, spending hours alone in the woods, walking from point to point. I grew up playing in the woods, and my parents would let us roam for miles so I found that land navigation came very easily to me. I had been finding my way through the woods all my life. For some lieutenants, they either had bad luck or just couldn't quite visualize the process. It wasn't simple. Many of the legs between boxes were miles long, meaning there was a long hike through the woods with a pack and rifle. If you got a little off track, you could end up somewhere and have no idea where on the map you were. Scoring less than 80% on a land navigation assignment would get you put on "remedial land nav" on Saturday mornings—not a fun way to spend a weekend! Going into the final land navigation exercise, I hadn't yet missed a box—perfect grades on every land nav. On the second to last one, I had gotten a little cocky. With plenty of time left, I had found a little hollow in the woods and taken a nap.

The Friday before final land nav, I was called into the SPC's office.

"Clement, what are your plans this weekend?" Captain Lynch asked.

"Sir, my wife and I are going skiing up in Pennsylvania," I responded.

"Don't you think you should go to remedial land nav tomorrow to practice for Monday?"

"Honestly sir, no, I don't. I don't think that would be the best use of my time." And the hotel was already paid for!

"How have you done on land nav so far?" A question he definitely knew the answer to.

"All 100s, sir. I grew up in the woods."

He proceeded to rail on me about responsibility and dedication, but I had been warned by lieutenants who had gone to TBS before me. I figured there was about a 90% chance that this was a "mindfuck" game, an opportunity to screw with me to see how I reacted. It wasn't personal. He was testing my confidence in something both he and I knew I was good at.

I decided the worst thing I could do was change my mind and admit I was suddenly not confident in my land nav abilities. "Sir, are you ordering me to go to remedial land nav?"

"No."

"Then with all due respect, sir, I'm going skiing."

He smiled. "Good luck on Monday, Clement. Dismissed."

I raced through final land nav, covering close to 17 miles to hit all my points. It was an all-day affair. I was one of the first back to the rendezvous point, which I figured was either really good . . . or really bad.

"No time like the present," I thought to myself and walked up to Captain

Lynch, one of about five individuals I could have gone to for evaluation and the grading of my land navigation card.

"Alright, Clement, do or die." He looked at the card, and frowned. He kept switching between his score sheet and my card, frowning, and making tick marks. "Nah, I'm just fuckin' with you. 100. Good job."

"Thank you, sir." I headed for the bus that would take me back to Camp Barrett and TBS.

"Hey, Clement," Captain Lynch called after me.

I turned around. "Sir?"

"How was skiing?"

"Good, sir."

"Glad to hear it."

Sometimes you win one.

And sometimes you lose one.

The platoon had just completed FEX I, the capstone event of the second phase of TBS, focused on infantry squad operations. Incorporating all of the individual skills we had learned, the first field exercise required us to write squad orders, conduct land navigation, and patrol as a squad while tackling various simulated attacks, enemy patrols and ambushes. The event went well enough, but by the end of the afternoon on Friday we were ready to get back to Camp Barrett, turn in our weapons, and secure for weekend liberty. Amazingly, we weren't going to have to walk back from the training area—7-ton trucks had been dispatched to give us a ride back to Camp Barrett.

The platoon leadership billets would rotate from lieutenant to lieutenant every two weeks, and I was the platoon sergeant at the time, so I got everything organized for the trip back. Accountability of all weapons and other serialized equipment, like optics and radios, was more important than almost anything else—it is something that the Marine Corp stresses. I took the report from the three lieutenants playing squad leader, directing that they personally check each item—they had everything. When we got back to the barracks and began turning in equipment, one of the squad leaders grabbed me.

"Jeff, we're missing a set of binos." Leupold binoculars had been issued to each squad.

"What? We just had them at DZ Raven."

"I know. Wilson says they had to be on the truck, because he had them at the DZ."

"Ok." I grabbed the "platoon commander," another lieutenant. "Hey,

Chris, we're missing a set of binos. We had them at the DZ, but they're not here now. Wilson says he must have left them on the truck."

"Shit. Ok. I'll tell Captain Lynch."

Captain Lynch had overheard, and didn't need telling. He whirled on Chris Hanafin and me. "Who gave me a false report? I was told we had everything, and now we don't. So who gave me a false report?" he demanded.

"I did, sir." This was my bag. The platoon sergeant is responsible for accountability of weapons and equipment.

"Then you're fucking fired!" Captain Lynch shoved me down the hallway.

I took my place on line outside of my room at the position of attention. *Whelp . . . I'm probably getting dropped from this TBS class. This sucks.*

Lieutenant Hanafin yelled, "Get outside. Warming layers and a flashlight." The platoon assembled outside in formation with lights.

Captain Lynch was in front. "We're going to find those fucking binoculars if we're out here all night. Who had them?"

"I did, sir," Lieutenant Wilson said. "They must be in the truck. I had them in the DZ."

"We sent the company gunny to check the truck. He said they weren't there. Are you calling the company gunny a liar? Because either you are or he is." The company gunny was an enlisted Marine, permanently assigned to the TBS company staff.

"No, sir, they are in the truck."

"Well, you want to lie. Very well. Two ranks, march. We're going to find these binos."

The platoon set off into the darkness. By that time, it was well after 2000. We got to the trail the trucks had come back on and fanned out. All I could see was the ground in front of my flashlight and the little beams of the few dozen flashlights of the other lieutenants. Every few hundred meters, Captain Lynch would ask "Wilson, where are the binoculars?"

He would respond, "On the truck, sir."

We searched the first couple of miles of the trail. I was cold, miserable, and certain that I would be "dealt with" later. Around 2300, we turned back. We went into one of the classrooms. As we walked through the doors, the 500 eyes of the rest of the lieutenants in the company turned on us. They had been sitting there for hours, waiting on us, when they should have been home or on liberty.

"Tomorrow, Third Platoon will resume searching for the binoculars. We will not lose a single piece of serialized gear," the company commander, Major Barela, told us.

I drove home dejected and furious, only to wake up four hours later for a drive back to Quantico for what would surely be a miserable day.

The day lived up to expectations. The platoon followed the GPS trace that a few days of squad patrols had covered. On line, we covered every inch of about six miles through the woods. Having been fired, I had no choice but to resume my position as a "squad bod," a Marine in ranks. I played the game, and did whatever I was asked to do. I felt like a kicked puppy but I wasn't going to admit it.

A few key areas were searched four or five times by different sets of eyes. No sign of the binoculars. The sun set early, and it didn't make sense to search in the dark again. We set back for Camp Barrett, arriving just before dark.

One last time, Captain Lynch asked, "Where are the binoculars?"

Again, Wilson responded, "On the truck, sir."

Captain Lynch again said, "The company gunny said he checked the truck. Are you calling him a liar? Fine, check the truck. If they are on there, great. If not, I don't want to ever hear the word 'truck' again, and we will muster here at 0600 tomorrow morning to resume the search in the woods."

Most of the platoon walked the half mile to the motor pool, and the Officer of the Day let us in the locked gate. Wilson threw back the canvas on the MTVR, and sitting on the bench was a small, coyote brown case. Inside, a shiny pair of Leupold binoculars. Right where he had said they were all along. Nobody was really irritated with Lieutenant Wilson, only with the company gunny. Had he really checked the truck? We would never know.

The binoculars had been found. Well, at least we would get Sunday off. And we could complain to the rest of the company about how shitty our Saturday had been. Marines take great pleasure in having things worse than other Marines. At the time something might be unpleasant, but Marines will always brag about "how much more it sucked for us" after the fact.

I kept waiting for the hammer to fall. For days, it ate at me. Would I receive a negative evaluation? Would I be recycled to another company? Dropped from TBS completely? Finally, I got an answer.

Captain Lynch pulled me aside at the armory. "Hey, Lieutenant Clement, I uhhh, need to apologize for the way I responded the other night. I lost my bearing. You dealt with the adversity just fine, and a few people noticed. So it started out as a bad thing, but in the end it will probably be one of the best things for your evals."

It took a lot of guts for him to apologize like that, and I really respected him for it. So likewise, maybe he lost his bearing, but the fact that he apologized for it had a much greater impact on my impression of him.

The story is funny now, but I have thought of it whenever someone has asked me if I checked one thing or another. How easy it would be to say, "yeah, I checked." No matter how improbable it was that the binoculars were in the truck, if the Marine who said he had checked the truck truly checked the truck, a lot of pain and headache would have been avoided for a lot of people. Integrity meets the real world.

TBS continued. For months we rehearsed patrols and attacks, dug fighting holes in the snow and sat in trenches in the rain. We called for indirect fire from mortars and M777 howitzers, and built C4 breaching charges. We laid concertina wire and fired Claymore anti-personnel mines.

Second Lieutenants Bradley Fromm, Geoff Sanford and me in LZ 7 at The Basic School before a patrolling exercise.

One particularly funny story happened on a movement to contact exercise. The platoon's Third Squad got lost during the patrol, and while we were trying to link back up with them, simulated aggressors opened up with a M249 SAW on our right flank. The lieutenant assigned as platoon commander decided to suppress and bypass, and went to give the signal to break contact. I wasn't aware of that, though.

I was the platoon radio operator, talking to the lost squad, trying to help them navigate back to our position. I had assumed a kneeling position behind a tree to get some cover, when the platoon commander signaled "break contact" with a green pop-up flare, a hand-held pyrotechnic rocket. Normally, these are launched by slamming the bottom of the 14-inch-long tube against the heel of your hand. The recoil knocks your hand out of the way, and the rocket shoots up. The platoon commander, however, slammed the base of the rocket against my Kevlar helmet. I was immediately knocked unconscious. One second I was kneeling talking on the radio, and the next thing I knew, I was lying on the ground with no idea how I'd gotten there and why I wasn't talking on the radio anymore. It hurt at the time, but I recovered okay. If nothing else it gave me a story to tell, and a pretty funny one at that. TBS continued.

Live-fire machine gun ranges and grenade ranges were a staple. The platoon shot rockets and ran convoys. And we were somewhat competent!

The attrition rate was not nearly as high as it was at OCS, but quite a few lieutenants were dropped from the platoon. Most would be "recycled" to another company, and repeat most or all of TBS after a period of remedial one-on-one coaching with one of the instructors. A few, though, had already been recycled or were found to be unsuited for life as a Marine officer and were drummed out of the Corps—"drumming out" is a harsh term, but that's how it was. The Corps is a machine that chewed people up and spit them out if they couldn't hack it. On the one hand, it seemed a shame that they had put so much time into something, but on the other hand, the Marine Corps has high standards to maintain—it's who we are.

Through all the training and long nights in the field, we bonded as a platoon. Everything was shared. We connected with the Marines around us in a way that I had never experienced before and am quite confident I will not find outside the Marine Corps.

"Oh hey, I found your M&Ms," Second Lieutenant Sanders said to me. I had been on patrol during a training exercise and had just returned to our bivouac site.

"Oh. Where were they?"

"In your pack. Near the bottom."

"Indeed. I put them there."

"Well, I ate them."

Second Lieutenant Scott Sanders was an asshole. I need to be perfectly clear on that point. But he was one of the most competent assholes that I have ever met, a superb Marine Corps officer, and a good friend. The back-and-forth, push-and-shove banter between Marines is one of the greatest things about the Marine Corps. It lowers the barriers between Marines, and they let their guard down. The result is a unit full of people who know each other better than they know their families and who are willing to do anything for each other.

Marines would drink out of each other's Camelbak hoses and water bottles, forgetting the usual germs and cooties, and taking a bite of somebody else's candy bar was commonplace. Such an action was often preceded by a statement like, "Hey, can I get most of that?" It was phrased like a question, but wasn't really one. Even this early in a Marine's career, the camaraderie was unique and unlike anything I have found anywhere else.

The time finally came for MOS assignment. The Marine Corps assigned officers their specialty using a method called a "quality spread" in which the best officers, the middle officers, and the lower-ranked officers all got spread across all of the communities and job fields to ensure that no one community got all the talent. If they had assigned officers based purely on class rank, the best officers would have picked infantry, engineers and tanks, while communications, low-altitude air defense and aviation supply would be left with the dregs of the officer pool.

The MOS selection process was done a few weeks before the end of TBS using the class standings at that particular point in time. The contracts for pilots and lawyers were already in place, so this really only applied to ground officers, but everyone had to fill out the form anyway. Each lieutenant ranked every possible MOS choice by order of preference, and a computer did the rest. The company was broken into thirds by class rank, and the computer assigned the number one guy his MOS first, based on his personal preferences. The second person assigned was not the second in the class, but the first guy in the *second third* of the class. The third person to choose was the lieutenant at the top of the *bottom third* of the class. The fourth was the second guy in the class. Only a certain number of people were allowed to select a given MOS, so once your first choice was full, the computer would try your second, then third choice, and so on. After the computer results were developed, the company staff could jockey the final roster around, doing one-for-one swaps, horse-trading with lieutenants and their futures. Such shuffling around was based on largely subjective criteria, but was for the betterment of the Corps. For example, the computer could place someone who had no business as an infantryman in a 0302 Infantry Officer spot. The final list was scrutinized and stamped by humans, not the computer.

The results were announced after the final pugil stick match, a combative event that pitted lieutenant against lieutenant in a literal cage match using padded sticks. It was held in an eight-sided enclosure dubbed "The Octagon." Captain Lynch pulled the platoon aside. Tensions were high. The moment of truth had arrived.

Captain Lynch announced the results in class rank order. "Mueller, 1803. Clement, 0402."

I didn't hear anything after that. I had gotten 0402, Logistics Officer, my first choice. I had studied engineering in college and felt logistics offered the best chance to use my problem solving and analytical skills while still getting a chance to lead Marines. At the time, I was certain I wanted to lead Marines in combat, so logistics was the best of both worlds—I could do a "problem solving" job with a broad impact and still hopefully get a chance to be a platoon commander.

A few of my friends didn't get what they wanted. Some of them had played games with the numbers, trying to beat the system by ranking low-density MOSs higher than a high-density MOS they would be happier with. I couldn't really do anything to help them, but I was happy. I was going to be a logistics officer.

APRIL 2009: LOGISTICS OFFICERS COURSE, CAMP JOHNSON, NC

Two days after I graduated from TBS, I moved to Richlands, NC. One of my TBS platoon-mates and I rented a log house in the woods we dubbed The Cabin. We were there to attend Logistics Officers Course at Camp Johnson, NC, across the river from Camp Lejeune. Logistics is one of the broadest MOS fields, and the instructors only had 55 training days to cover the breadth and depth of combat service and support.

"Look, we're not going to teach you everything you need to know. Some of you are going to be truck platoon commanders, some of you will be maintenance management officers, some will be air delivery, some will be assistant S4s, etc.," Captain Efran Manzanet, our class advisor, began on the first day.

"We can't hope to teach you everything, or really anything. What we can teach is how to learn, where to look for information, and the types of things that Log-Os need to watch out for."

He was spot on. The Logistics Officers Course was taught primarily by staff NCOs, staff sergeants, and gunnys who were experts in their fields. Most of the instruction was classroom-based, with readings assigned from various Marine Corps publications.

The most valuable training came at the end of LOC, a one-week field exercise dubbed "Operation Blue Devil." The class was organized into a miniature combat logistics battalion and went to a training area several miles south of Camp Lejeune.

This exercise proved to be a good representation of what training exercises would be like at CLB-6. Once in the field, training convoys went out several times a day with notional or imagined objectives and came under simulation attacks by an opposition "Red Cell" force with blank ammunition and IED simulators that exploded in a cloud of baby powder. The process of planning, sourcing equipment, loading vehicles, and developing manifests gave us new lieutenants confidence in our abilities to get things done—we were actually competent. (Sort of.)

While the three months of LOC gave us a good introduction to logistics by the book, there was still a lot we didn't know. I felt that I wasn't quite sure what my day-to-day responsibilities would be as a platoon commander. I wondered if I was ready. There was a lot the lieutenant didn't know.

CHAPTER FOUR

CHECKING IN

"Your job is to be the hardest motherfucker in your platoon," he said while pointing at me across the desk. "Do that, and everything else will fall into place."—Nathaniel Fick, "One Bullet Away"

MARCH 2010: B STREET, CAMP LEATHERNECK, HELMAND PROVINCE, AFGHANISTAN

"The key to being successful as a lieutenant," Major Peterson, my NROTC Marine instructor, had told me, "is to ask questions. Ask questions of everyone, from the lowest ranking PFC to your company commander. Second only to asking questions, lieutenants should read voraciously. Read everything that you can get your hands on. Your Marines drive trucks? Read the 500-page technical manual for every truck that your platoon has. Your Marines shoot machine guns? Read every one of the 400 pages in the Machine Gun Bible. It sounds tedious. It is."

He went on, "For everything that you do as a lieutenant, there will be three things that you didn't even think to do, or nobody told you, or you could never even conceive of. These things will hit you when you least expect them, when they have significant consequences, and when everyone, from the lowest ranking PFC to your company commander, is there to see your failure."

To be a lieutenant is a strange thing. In general, you are well trained, untested, young, physically fit, cocky, confident, unsure of yourself, arrogant, and any number of other contradictory adjectives. The lieutenant is at the bottom of the officer chain, but technically outranks all enlisted Marines, even staff non-commissioned officers, many of whom are not only a decade or more older than said lieutenant, but have been in the Marine Corps for over a decade or more.

The moment that best captured the relationship between new lieutenants and senior enlisted happened while I was walking along B Street in Camp Leatherneck, Afghanistan. A convoy of trucks from another unit was lined up along the street, clearly ready to leave the wire—machines guns mounted, Marines up in the turrets, wearing flaks, Kevlar helmets and gloves. A lance corporal was being yelled at by his platoon sergeant.

"Why in the name of God would you do that?!" the staff sergeant demanded.

"I ... I ... " the lance corporal stammered.

"What? What? Have we ever done it that way?"

"Well, no ... I guess not ... but ... "

"But WHAT? But but but WHAT?!"

"But staff sergeant, the lieutenant told me to."

"I don't care *what* the lieutenant said. THE LIEUTENANT DON'T KNOW."

That's all I really caught. I don't know what unit they were from. I don't know what the lance corporal did or didn't do. I don't know who this lieutenant was, or what his background was. And even though he went to TBS and MOS school, the chances are still good that *the lieutenant didn't know.*

In hindsight, I was extremely fortunate to be assigned to a Combat Logistics Battalion as a logistics officer, but only because I was assigned to the best two billets for a lieutenant—truck platoon commander and assistant operations officer. There really is no other pair of billets I would have rather had. It may have been a terrible place to be at times, but CLB-6 was a great place to be from.

I checked in to CLB-6 in September 2009, and was assigned to Alpha Company, the motor transport company, as a truck platoon commander.

SEPTEMBER 2009: CLB-6 ALPHA COMPANY OFFICE, CAMP LEJEUNE, NORTH CAROLINA

As I stepped in front of my platoon for the first time, I thought of the three keys for success that Major Gibson had told us at OCS.

"Know yourself. Self-awareness and humility combined yield selflessness," he had said.

"Know your Marines. Know who they are, look out for their welfare, and validate them as members of the team," he continued. I wrote this down word for word, and still have the notebook.

"Lastly, know your shit. Be technically and tactically proficient. Bold actions and ownership! Nobody will follow someone who is incompetent."

The pressure was tremendous. What did I know about leading a platoon? Twenty-three years old, fresh out of TBS, barely out of college . . . what did I know about anything?

The company's individual platoons were already formed and had a rough leadership structure in place. I checked into Alpha Company along with two other lieutenants, and we would each be assigned as platoon commanders. Captain John Gallagher, the company commander, waited a few weeks to do this, though. He wanted to try to find the best personality fit for each of us with each of the three platoon sergeants.

I think I would have worked well with any of the three platoon sergeants at Alpha Company, and I would later work extensively with Staff Sergeant D'Andre Gillon, of First Platoon, but I was assigned to Second Platoon.

Staff Sergeant Joseph Caravalho would be my platoon sergeant for the next year. I cannot say enough good things about him or how much he taught me, not just about motor transportation, logistics, or the Marine Corps, but about leadership in general. Staff Sergeant Caravalho's Marines loved him even when they hated him, and would follow him anywhere.

My father, a career naval officer, had told me to trust my senior enlisted advisor, stay in step with them, ask them questions. "As an officer, your job is to make sure they have everything they need to actually do the job . . . which includes clearly defining and planning the mission," he said. I thought of this advice often.

When I had first talked to the CLB-6 Battalion XO in April 2009, he told me that the battalion would deploy in March 2010. That was the plan, until the decision was made to execute a 30,000-plus troop surge in Afghanistan. We were one of the units that would be part of the surge, and would deploy about three months early. We were on the fast track.

Our first major training exercise was at Fort A. P. Hill, just north of Richmond, VA. One way to learn is to make every mistake in the book. We did the best we could, but sometimes it seemed that making every mistake was going to be our approach.

Captain Gallagher had his work cut out for him. He spent hours and hours at A. P. Hill mentoring the lieutenants, teaching us how to run live-fire ranges and how to develop training standards. He demanded perfection. Every detail had to be accounted for, no contingency was too small to overlook. As leaders, we had to think of everything.

I still had a lot to learn. TBS had left some things out. It's one thing to brief a platoon of fellow lieutenants; it's another to brief a platoon of enlisted

Marines who judge their officers even harder than we judged each other (and, as they should). I was feeling pretty good toward the end of the exercise. I had run a couple of live fire ranges that had gone well and taught some good classes. I felt the Marines were responding to me.

The last thing I had to do was lead the convoy back to Camp Lejeune, a distance of just over 300 miles. It was the longest convoy I had ever commanded before. The night before we were to head back, I briefed all the Marines. I had prepared for it, writing a NATO standard "five paragraph" order and drawing a map. But for all the practice I had briefing and the hours of preparation, I just couldn't get it right. I tripped over words, lost my train of thought, and failed to articulate what I needed the Marines to do. The Marines were disengaged and none-too-confident about this convoy or its commander.

Captain Gallagher pulled me aside afterward. "How did you think that went?"

"Terrible. I don't know what happened. I'm more mad at myself than anything else."

"You lost a lot of face with the Marines." He lingered on the phrase.

I didn't know what to say.

He continued, "You're going to lead these Marines in Afghanistan in just a few months. They need to trust you; you need to give them a reason to trust you, and that wasn't it."

Prior to that brief, I felt pretty good about how things were progressing. I felt somewhat competent, like I could do this job and lead the platoon. But now I had my doubts.

Captain Gallagher had one last thing to say on the matter as we walked to get dinner. "You have a chance tomorrow. You're going to lead the convoy, and if you do it well, confidently, decisively, the Marines will take more away from that than from one bad order. Figure it out tonight, and hit it hard tomorrow, and you'll be fine."

The next morning, I did my final checkout with him, and he wished us luck. It was as if nothing had happened the night before. Captain Gallagher was good that way. When I screwed up, he talked to me about it, figured out what the root of the problem was, and made sure that I knew where I had gone wrong. After that, he never mentioned it again—he didn't hold it against me.

To be the convoy commander of a massive military convoy on I-95 was a lot of fun, though I have no doubt that we were the bane of every driver on the road that day as we lumbered along at 45 mph. It was my first experience maintaining control of that many vehicles spread out over several miles traveling at high speed. Communication was essential, and contingencies popped up that the platoon leadership had to address. We had a few mechanical breakdowns but were able to get the trucks back up and running or rigged for tow behind the wrecker without too much trouble.

"All vehicles, this is Arawak 2," I called over the radio, "pull into the next exit and into the Exxon parking lot. We will refuel from our fuel tanker there." A convoy that long required refueling, but we had brought our own fuel with us. By refueling in the gas station parking lot we would not have to set up our own environmental protection measures to deal with a potential fuel spill.

The convoy went well. I gained a lot of confidence in the Marines and, I hoped, they had gained some in me. The convoy had included a rest plan, addressing mechanical breakdowns, and many more little things that I had never considered—everything that we would have to contend with in Afghanistan . . . except the enemy.

One convoy down, it seemed like hundreds more to go.

The most intense predeployment training experience for many of the Marines was a live tissue combat trauma medical course. After a week of classroom and practical application instruction, the final day was devoted to treating live pigs that had real wounds. Sedated and anesthetized, the pigs were wounded in various ways, with rifles and shotguns, with broken bones, and with vicious knife wounds. The bloody work of saving a life in a combat trauma case was made real. I felt bad for the pigs, but the training was better than any I had ever gone through in terms of learning and giving us confidence in our ability to save a life. It was just one of the skills we had to learn.

From the time I arrived at CLB-6 in September 2009 to when we deployed to Afghanistan four months later in January 2010, the unit was singularly focused on preparing for deployment. Training was focused on individual skills initially, like getting the Marines licensed to drive different vehicle types and qualified to use all of the various machine guns.

The platoon leadership spent hours in a simulated virtual environment calling for indirect fire, rehearsing the use of combined arms that could decisively turn the tide of a battle. Dozens of convoys were run in the training areas around Camp Lejeune, on Saturdays and in the middle of the night. The compressed deployment timeline left us without enough time to properly prepare for our Mojave Viper exercise, let alone for Afghanistan.

NOVEMBER 2009: CAMP WILSON, MCAGCC TWENTYNINE PALMS, CA

The final training exercise before deployment was Mojave Viper, conducted in the deserts of Marine Corps Air Ground Combat Center Twentynine Palms, about three hours east of Los Angeles.

We were not ready for Mojave Viper. I didn't even have a full platoon's worth of Marines. I can only surmise that once CLB-6 was at Mojave Viper, weeks from deployment, that someone controlling manpower at our higher headquarters decided that our impending deployment was really going to happen and CLB-6 actually did need the people we were requesting. I met the last five or six members of my platoon when they showed up at Mojave Viper a week into the exercise.

For five weeks, CLB-6 ran the full spectrum of combat service and support operations, running convoys, shooting machine guns. We were graded on everything—all major unit and individual skills. It was incredibly stressful. The individuals doing the grading and evaluation at Mojave Viper were part of the Tactical Training and Exercise Control Group and were commonly referred to as "Coyotes." They were always talking on their headset radios, and wore bright orange Camelbak hydration systems. Quiet and stoic, they were always watching, writing things down, grading, and criticizing without giving much feedback.

The Coyotes constantly monitored our radio traffic during the training events. Communicating with confidence and clarity on the radio was one of the most important skills to learn, but also one of the most difficult. Somehow it got harder to convey lucid thoughts and short concise commands as soon as I clicked the radio handset!

A few of my Marines made jokes about the frustration that our radio callsigns caused during one of the Mojave Viper training events. I liked my callsign "Arawak 2" well enough, but on the internal convoy radio net it caused confusion. The original plan was for platoon sergeants to add an "alpha" to their platoon callsign. Marines calling for me would say "Arawak 2, this is . . . ," and to talk to Staff Sergeant Caravalho they would say "Arawak 2 Alpha, this is . . . " When Staff Sergeant Caravalho and I were calling each other, it would be even worse: "Arawak 2 Alpha, this is Arawak 2 . . . " It wasn't just irritating; it could cause confusion on the battlefield. Anything that compounded the fog of war was just foolish if it could be avoided.

"Hey staff sergeant, what do you think about our callsigns?" I asked.

"Sir, they're okay or whatever, but it's confusing as hell." He was nothing if not honest.

"Okay, I agree. Let's just pick different ones. It'll make things easier."

"Thank God, I've been wanting to change mine for three weeks now." For the internal nets, we would use "personal callsigns."

As a Georgia Tech grad, I thought about "Ramblin' Wreck," but it had too many syllables. The Georgia Tech yellow jacket mascot is nicknamed "Buzz" though . . . and that was just one syllable. Short, and with just enough attitude. I adopted "Buzz" as my callsign and logo. Staff Sergeant Caravalho chose a handle that he had used for years while playing video games, "Smoke-check," slang for sniping someone from afar.

Marines grow to love and embody their callsigns, just as their personality creates a personality for the callsign. Logistics convoys are generally designated by the callsign of the convoy/mission commander. When Alpha Company, Second Platoon went out, the COC would refer to the whole element by my "official" callsign, Arawak 2.

Captain Gallagher, as Alpha Company commander, was Arawak 6. He referred to his callsign as "the jersey." On one occasion he was going to embed on a British convoy with two trucks to observe a new route; at the last minute, he had to pull out and the battalion operations officer went instead. Rather than do the paperwork to change the name of the unit, they retained the "Arawak 6" callsign. Captain Gallagher told the OPSO, "you can wear the jersey, but make sure it comes back washed."

From that point on, we referred to "Arawak 6" as "The Jersey," and for his going-away gift, we bought Captain Gallagher a framed football jersey instead of the traditional plaque. The name on the back of the jersey was "Arawak" and the number, of course, was 6.

The days at Mojave Viper were long. Late into the night, Captain Gallagher would grill us on tactics and convoy procedures. We needed this. The battalion was compressing nine months of pre-deployment training into three months. Coyotes graded the platoon every day. I was under even closer scrutiny than at TBS, and the weather was just as miserable. The Mojave Desert is cold in November and December—well below freezing at night, and we were sleeping outside in the training areas or in covered (but unheated) Quonset huts at Camp Wilson. The same dry wind that is like a hair dryer in the summer sucks the heat out of every surface in the winter.

The battalion was at Mojave Viper for Thanksgiving, sharing a meal of *processed, preformed* turkey *log* and *reconstituted* mashed potatoes. It was the first real holiday that I had ever missed. It was just the first of what would be many to come.

CHAPTER FIVE

WHAT WE WERE GETTING INTO

The American ground war in Afghanistan began on 19 October 2001, almost two years before the war in Iraq. An aerial bombardment campaign had begun about two weeks prior, on 7 October 2001, less than a month after 9/11. The military operation was initially successful, supporting the Northern Alliance and toppling the Taliban Regime by December 2001. Fighting continued, but with the support of the UN and NATO, US forces moved toward achieving a stable Afghanistan. On 1 May 2003, Secretary of Defense Donald Rumsfeld declared an end to major combat operations in Afghanistan, while President George W. Bush unveiled the "Mission Accomplished" sign for the Iraq Campaign.

From 2003 to 2006, the Afghan democracy led by President Hamid Karzai slowly took root in the capital city of Kabul, but failed to establish a strong hold on the country. 2006 showed violence surging stronger than ever in the Helmand and Kandahar Provinces in the south, and Kunar and Wardak Provinces to the east, drawing renewed attention. In 2009, newly-elected US President Barack Obama announced a troop surge, similar to the one that had been successful in Iraq. A major focus area of the surge was the Helmand Province. The Helmand had long been a base of power for the Taliban, and provided access to Pakistan. It was also the center of poppy growth, fueling the opium revenues the Taliban needed to fight the war. Twice as much poppy was grown in the Helmand Province than in all the other provinces combined—enough poppy to fill the entire world's demand for heroin.

Only a small percentage of the land in the Helmand is arable, but over 70% of the population is dependent on agriculture for its livelihood. Large areas are windswept desert, with sand as fine as baby powder, called moondust. Walking on dry moondust, the Marines would sink up to their knees sometimes. Trucks could be hopelessly bogged down in it, unable to get traction.

Other areas are hilly and rocky, pocked by mountains. Water and the lack of it are the defining features of the region. Without vegetation and topsoil, the land does not drain—water sits on the surface of the earth. During the rainy season and snowmelt after the winter, water carves deep channels called *wadis*, which are usually dry but can have swiftly flowing currents several feet deep after a January storm. Over the centuries, they have been carved ever deeper—some are a few dozen meters deep, and have entire villages built within them.

CLB-6 deployed to the Helmand Province just as Marine Expeditionary Brigade-Afghanistan (MEB-A) began to push to the north of the province, supporting the offensives for Marjah, Musa Qa'leh, and Sangin in 2010 and, during the second deployment a year later, the push to Kajaki in 2011. The tactics that had seemed to work successfully in Iraq were being applied in the Helmand Province. Small Patrol Bases (PBs) for platoons and Combat Outposts (COPs) for company-sized units were established in villages, bazaars and key population centers to provide security and try to win over the "hearts and minds" of the people. A number of larger Forward Operating Bases (FOBs) were established to provide a better platform for operations.

A Combat Logistics Battalion provides the lions' share of the heavy lifting to provide logistics support needed in combat zones. We were responsible for actually providing support to the infantry units at the front lines. Everyone is important, but the CLB drives the fuel in tankers to the end user, drops off bottles of water to the grunts who need them, and goes out to where the trucks got blown up to retrieve them. We had a lot of work to do and a lot of Marines depending on us. It would be dangerous, and it wouldn't be easy.

In the war in Afghanistan, the term "front lines" didn't exist. Units could be attacked anywhere, and large, slow moving logistics convoys were easy targets. And we knew it. So did our families.

JANUARY 2010: CLB-6 BARRACKS, CAMP LEJEUNE, NC

The hardest thing I had to do on my first deployment was to walk away from Alison's car with my bags. It was a very final act. It tore me apart to leave her, but I was an officer. I had an image to portray, and when all of my Marines were experiencing the same kind of loss from leaving their families behind, I had to be the stoic, composed one.

A few of the Marines had their families wait until the very last minute, standing with them and waiting until the buses finally departed. I was glad that Alison and I had said a final quick goodbye instead of dragging out the process. It was at about 2200 that we boarded chartered coach buses for the ride to Marine Corps Air Station Cherry Point.

CLB-6 Marines stand with family members on Camp Lejeune before departing for Afghanistan in January 2010.

Every time the Marine Corps saw fit to send me anywhere, it seemed to always involve leaving in the middle of the night, and the darkness always seemed to heighten the isolation of leaving.

The ride from Camp Lejeune to Marine Corps Air Station Cherry Point took about an hour, and the mood on the bus was mixed. Many of the Marines shared the excitement that their forebears felt as they shipped off throughout the history of the Corps; most of the excited ones talked eagerly and roughhoused on the bus. The rest wore headphones and were more somber, sad to leave their families behind. A few cried quietly.

Upon arrival at Cherry Point we loaded our baggage (well over 100 pounds per person considering that everyone was carrying 40 pounds of flak jacket, SAPI plates and helmet) onto a small truck—this was everything we would own for the next seven months. We would be loading our own bags onto the aircraft. The Marines filed into the waiting area for a six hour sit. It was nearly midnight; most of the Marines slept in chairs. The plane would not arrive until about 0500.

Shortly before sunrise, an Evergreen Air jetliner taxied across the tarmac. Before we could board, the standard TSA brief was given.

"No knives or edged weapons of any kind are allowed in the passenger compartment of the aircraft. They must be stowed in your baggage under the aircraft," the flightline Marine said. "You will all pass through the metal detector before boarding." The Marines had all heard it before, and they knew the drill. A sarcastic lance corporal at the back shouted out, "I accidentally brought this rifle! Is that allowed on the plane!?"

"Look," the flightline guy said, "I don't make the rules. It's stupid. No knives, but you can carry your rifles on the plane." Every Marine had an M16A4 or M4 rifle, and many of us also had 9mm pistols, but we didn't have our ammo yet. True to his word, any Marine who had thought he could sneak a knife onto the plane had it confiscated, but was allowed to carry his rifle on board.

The chartered Boeing 737 would carry us across the Atlantic Ocean to Bishkek, Kyrgyzstan, the US Transit Center for holding troops heading into and out of Afghanistan. After a layover in Bangor, Maine and Leipzig, Germany, the plane set down in the former Soviet Republic around midnight. I had lost all track of time, and didn't completely understand what day it was or how it had gotten to be the middle of the night again. We were assigned to a huge tent that could hold hundreds of Marines. Inside were rows of bunk beds. There was nothing to do now but wait for a flight to Afghanistan.

The US transit center was built adjacent to the Manas International Airport outside Bishkek, the capital of Kyrgyzstan. Designed as a waystation into and out of Afghanistan, the transit center had a gym, coffee shop, movie theater, bar, chapel, library, and other recreational activities to keep deploying servicemembers busy. Most of the amenities were staffed by Kyrgyz citizens—they seemed to always be smiling.

The Transit Center existed for two reasons. First, most of the planes doing the long flights to and from the US were contracted civilian planes that couldn't safely fly into Afghanistan for fear of getting shot down. And secondly, troops returning from Afghanistan needed a few days to decompress before heading back home. Manas really wasn't a bad place to be, and I felt like it would be a good place to chill out for a few days on the way back to the US after our seven-month deployment.

The architecture of some of the older buildings and the concrete barrier walls were distinctly Soviet—cubist shapes of poured concrete—but older Russian tile mosaics survived in a few places. Walking around under the gray clouds of a Kyrgyz winter, I thought about the Soviets and their defeat in Afghanistan years ago.

"How many 23-year-old Soviet lieutenants had walked along these walls on their way to go fight the Afghan insurgency? What was their story?" I wondered. What would my story be?

I didn't have an answer. "The lieutenant don't know."

Weather delayed our flight to Camp Leatherneck, the main hub in the Helmand Province and the largest US Marine base in Afghanistan. The USAF Transportation Command liaison rerouted most of CLB-6 through Bagram Airfield, a base in the northern part of Afghanistan near Kabul. After three days in Manas, we were to muster around noon the next day for a military transport flight to Bagram that night.

First and Second Platoons would fly in first; Third Platoon would have to wait a day or two. The plane landed in Bagram after a short two-hour flight and again, we landed in the middle of the night. As I walked down the ramp of the C-17 Globemaster, a light rain was falling. I was in Afghanistan—I felt incredibly exposed. Even though I was deep inside an allied position on a heavily fortified airstrip, I felt vulnerable. I gripped my M4 rifle tighter, happy that I had it if I needed it. In hindsight, I realized that we had not yet been issued ammunition, so it would have been next to useless. "Effective range: as far as you can throw it," as the saying goes. After two more days of waiting in Bagram, a C-130 was tasked with flying us to Camp Leatherneck.

JANUARY 2010: CAMP BASTION FLIGHTLINE, HELMAND PROVINCE, AFGHANISTAN

We had arrived at Camp Leatherneck (or rather, at Camp Bastion, which was connected to Leatherneck). In true Marine Corps' fashion, we had arrived in the middle of the night. I was greeted at the Camp Bastion airfield by our company gunnery sergeant, Gunnery Sergeant Ed Kretschmer, and Company XO, Second Lieutenant Bobby Fowler. After making sure the Marines were squared away, the three of us went to the DFAC 2, the 24-hour "sandwich shop." I was surprised at the quality of the food. Cold cuts, fresh fruits and vegetables were piled on the buffet line. This war was expensive, but at least it looked like they intended to take care of us. Rumor had it that every meal we ate cost the taxpayer about $24.

Bobby and I caught up on the latest battalion operational gossip. Much of the company was still stuck in Manas. There was no word on when they would arrive, but it didn't really matter.

"We still don't have any trucks," Lieutenant Fowler said. "Bravo Company was going to get some, but ended up getting stuck for, like, three days down by Camp Dwyer. Apparently it was a clown show, but the weather was pretty bad. Who knows?"

"We don't have *any* trucks?" I thought higher echelons had known we were coming. Didn't they have missions for us? We couldn't do much without any trucks.

"Well, Major Stophel has been working on it." Major Stophel was the battalion XO, and was truly the MVP of the battalion staff. "We have a few trucks, but they're in terrible shape. Missing wheels, bent axles, that sort of thing. We're just going to have to take what we can get to some degree."

"Well, I guess we're not going on any convoys any time soon." How long, I didn't know, but I didn't want to sit on Camp Leatherneck forever. I wanted to get in the fight.

"Actually, in about ten days we'll do a ride-along with GS Motor T. I went with them on a mission about a week ago. It was crazy. You'll see what I mean. But yeah, the next one isn't for a few days. We'll have to do the indoctrination and Afghanistan orientation training, some rules of engagement stuff and zero the weapons in the next few days." Zeroing weapons made sure that the sights accurately showed where your rounds would impact.

"When is the rest of the company getting here?" I asked.

"I don't know," Bobby responded, "I'm content to wait for Captain Gallagher to get here from Manas."

JANUARY 2010: CAMP LEATHERNECK TO COP CAFFERETTA, NOW ZAD, HELMAND AND NOW ZAD PROVINCES, AFGHANISTAN

Whenever possible, units conducted a "left seat/right seat" turnover when they replaced another unit in Afghanistan. CLB-6 was first sent to Afghanistan as part of the 2010 troop surge, so we were not doing a "one for one swap" with another unit, and at first, nobody quite knew what to do with us. About a week after we arrived at Camp Leatherneck, though, we got the first indication of what we would be doing.

Our left seat/right seat mission was with the General Support Motor Transport Company (GSMT) from 2d MEB. This would be a combat logistics patrol from Camp Leatherneck to COP Cafferetta in Now Zad, about 65km (40 miles) to the north. GSMT conducted this run about once a month, to bring supplies to a company of Marines from 1st Battalion, Second Marines. We were going to take over this route, but before we did it alone we would ride along with GSMT. I took about 15 Marines from my platoon and they spread out to ride in GSMT's trucks.

I was excited to finally "leave the wire," and I could feel my anticipation rising as I got dressed for the mission. Inside the wire, we wore the standard desert Marine Corps cammies in the desert digital pattern, but on missions outside the wire we wore the flame resistant "FROG" uniform, also in the desert digital pattern. We also wore the deceptively named "lightweight helmet," which weighed about 3.25 pounds. Those three pounds got pretty heavy after a few hours. Our "flak jacket" or modular tactical vest was bulky and hot. With the Enhanced Small Arms Protective Insert (ESAPI), ceramic plates designed to stop AK47 bullets, the total weight of the flak was over 32 pounds. The flak jacket forced Marines into contorted positions in the trucks, as the vehicle seats were not designed for people wearing flaks. The weight and duration of wear, combined with the poor support from vehicle seats, resulted in lower back injuries for a majority of the Marines in the truck platoons, though we didn't know that yet. We were just excited to finally be in combat.

The anticipation that we all felt before the mission was a combination of fear, excitement, the desire to use our training plus a desire for adventure, and a need to live up to the legacy of the Marines who came before us. Most of all, we all wanted to prove ourselves.

For the left-seat/right-seat, I rode with the platoon commander for the Main Body, who was doing all of the heavy hauling. The convoy also included a security element and a Route Clearance Platoon (RCP). The RCP went first, searching for IEDs. The security element followed, providing a buffer between the RCP and the Main Body (whose cargo trucks often broke down or got stuck). Once we reached the primary danger zone, the security element would establish near and far point security positions, essentially "holding" that piece of land so that insurgents could not emplace IEDs there, and for at least that small segment of the route, the return journey would, theoretically, be a little safer.

We DFL'd (departed friendly lines) early in the morning, around 0300. The trip northward was uneventful and slow going. That was one of the first things that struck me, something we really had not prepared for. We knew the approximate size of our AO (Area of Operations) and we knew about how far we'd have to travel, so we would do the math and figure that it would take no more than a few hours to get from place to place, maybe a day in the worst case scenario. How wrong we were.

The average pace was about three to five miles per hour. At that pace, the trip to Now Zad would take about eight hours. Except that there were breakdowns. And trucks that got stuck in moondust. About halfway through the trip, a truck struck an IED. The platoon commander pushed his truck up to the site and we dismounted. He began giving directions to the Marines, orchestrating the recovery. I took careful mental notes.

As the recovery vehicle operators were recovering the damaged truck, a faint dust trail in the desert was growing larger, approaching us from the west. As it got closer, I could see that the dust cloud was being kicked up by a man on a motorcycle. He stopped on a small hill about 400 meters from us, got off his motorcycle and stared at us, holding something. I took up a position on a truck, using the hood to establish a stable shooting position. I observed his actions closely.

He was holding a rifle, probably an AK-47, but that alone was not a hostile act. Through my telescopic rifle sight, I tracked him as he walked back and forth, keeping the crosshairs on his chest and adjusted for the range so that I could take a good center mass shot if I needed to. A few Marines next to me did the same. I didn't want to shoot him, but I would if I had to. The man reached for something.

"Don't do it, Goddammit," I whispered. I moved my thumb forward and clicked off the safety on my rifle. At 400 meters it was a long shot, but not unreasonable. Out in the open desert there was nowhere to hide, and there were enough of us that one of us was sure to hit him. He didn't stand a chance.

After about thirty minutes, he got back on his motorcycle and went back the way he came. I was grateful I hadn't had to shoot him, but I was confident that I wouldn't have hesitated if it came down to it. At the same time, I knew he was a bad guy—why couldn't we do something about him? Because our rules of engagement prohibited us from taking any real action.

The IED strike added about three hours to the trip. Twenty hours later, it was just getting dark but we were finally through the last danger zone on the Acolyte Wadi, just south of Now Zad. The security element set up their positions, and we pressed on to the destination.

The concept of holding a security position on a small segment of a route was not new, but it was pioneered and routinely implemented in our AO by the British Army, which was heavily engaged in the Helmand Province from 2006 onward. It became a tactic that CLB-6 used on occasion, but its effectiveness was limited. Oftentimes, the entire route was relatively "high threat" and securing more than a mile or so took multiple platoons, manpower resources that we didn't have.

We finally arrived at COP Cafferetta, squeezed all the trucks onto the small base, and prepared to bed down for the night. There were no beds or berthings available for the logistics Marines at the FOBs, so we would sleep in, on, and around our trucks. Some Marines found portable cots and would bring them on their trucks, while others preferred to sleep on the hood of their truck or in the driver's seat. The next day was dedicated to offloading all cargo, onloading equipment for backhaul and preparing for the return trip.

The return trip was relatively uneventful. I do remember being struck by how far away we could see Camp Leatherneck, its bright perimeter lights shining in the middle of the desert. When we got back, we were ready to do it on our own. Or rather, ready or not, we were eager to do it on our own. Equipment was slowly arriving for our battalion, and it would be our turn soon enough.

An LVS MK48/16 towing an M870 lowboy trailer through the base of a wadi. The wadi is at least 60 feet deep. A Ground-Based Operational Surveillance System (GBOSS) tower is loaded on the trailer. Essentially a tall mast with day and night cameras, the GBOSS was an important tool for warning friendly positions of approaching enemies.

CHAPTER SIX

CONVOY BRIEFING

Before every mission, I briefed the platoon on what we were going to do and what the plan was.

"Alright guys, another run up to Now Zad. We're gonna be bringing supplies, especially fuel, up to 1/2 at Cafferetta. We'll have the usual mix of trucks, about 70 in all, and close to 200 people. MTVRs will form the core of our fleet, mostly hauling cargo. We'll have a few MK31 tractors towing M870 lowboy trailers to move heavy equipment and two M970 tanker trailers, holding 5000 gallons of fuel each. We're bringing a few LVS vehicles, MK48/14/14 'Tandem Tows' with two 20' beds of cargo."

All of the LVSs were old, used and abused. They were horses just begging to be put out to pasture, and were not sufficiently armored or powerful enough for the strains of combat logistics patrols offroad in the Helmand Province of Afghanistan, but they would respond to a good operator. The best motor vehicle operators in my platoon were consistently put in the LVSs because they were the least powerful vehicles, the most likely to get stuck or flip over, and required the most skill to operate. They were also the least comfortable. I felt bad that the best Marines got punished for their skills in this manner, but the mission had to get accomplished.

I went on. "We have a few of LVSRs, brand new, so if you're a new driver, be careful . . . don't drive beyond your skills. You assholes know what I mean," I said in an affectionate, joking tone. Crude, derogatory language was the norm, and generally meant that Marines liked each other. "All of the security guntrucks will be either MRAPS or MATVs." The Mine-Resistant Ambush Protected Truck or MRAP describes a family of vehicles developed to be more survivable against IEDs than Humvees, which were used in Iraq and Afghanistan prior to the MRAP. MRAPs offered good protection, but were very heavy and had limited off-road capabilities. MATVs were developed especially for the war in Afghanistan, and were designed to remedy the shortcomings of the MRAP, at least in regards to weight and off-road maneuverability.

I was a huge fan of the MATV, though there was definitely a compromise in terms of survivability. The MATV was a great truck, and I used one exclusively. It gave me the speed to maneuver up and down my lines without getting stuck. The MATV was also far easier to recover than an MRAP should it become disabled or destroyed by an IED.

"The biggest enemy threat will be from IEDs. In our AO, the bad guys are mostly putting in pressure plate IEDs, set to detonate when a vehicle runs over them." Marines sat around a terrain model, string and rocks and index cards laid out to model the area and show our planned route.

I continued, "To help mitigate this threat, we've got support from a Route Clearance Platoon or RCP. The RCP is planning to bring 11 trucks, including security trucks, Husky Route Clearance Vehicles, a wrecker, and a cargo vehicle. It's gonna be an Army RCP this time."

A few of the Marines groaned, uncertain of how good the Army was or was not. We had RCP support about half the time, and worked with both Marine and Army RCPs. Over time, we learned that the Army was actually better to work with than the Marines. This is one of the only times that I will ever say that I would prefer working with the Army over the Marines. The Marine Route Clearance Platoons that were in the Helmand Province in 2010 were good, but the Army teams, from the Oregon National Guard's 162 Engineer Company, were fantastic. We worked with two platoons in particular: Thor 3-1 commanded by First Lieutenant Andrew Carlstrom and Thor 3-3 commanded by First Lieutenant Ben Selander.

Army RCP vehicles staged for a CLB-6 convoy. The front left vehicle is an RG-31 MRAP with a mineroller; the center truck is a Husky Route Clearance Vehicle with metal detection panels.

Lieutenant Selander jumped in and briefed their plan. "The most danger is posed to the first vehicle in line. We're gonna have either a Husky Route Clearance Vehicle or an MRAP with a mineroller. The Husky is a lightweight, one-man vehicle, and we've got two. One has a ground-penetrating radar or GPR and the other has a simple metal detector. The problem is we're gonna have to roll pretty slow so they can detect anything. Probably about three or five mph."

"JESUS CHRIST!" one of the Marines groaned and we all privately lamented how long the convoy would take at three mph.

"The GPR has a limited resolution, and to really work it has to be properly calibrated for each different type of terrain . . . which we don't have time for. The metal detector works, but it's gonna beep whenever it finds any kind of metal, often resulting in 'false positives.'" Further complicating matters, most of the IEDs in our AO had very little metal in them. The batteries powering the initiator were buried, sometimes as much as 6' deep, beyond the range of the metal detector. The pressure plates were "non-metallic," using graphite rods pulled from the center of alkaline batteries for the electrical contacts. They were hard to find.

"Thanks, Ben." I took over the briefing. "The number one defense we have is *track discipline.* Stay in the cleared tire tracks of the truck in front of you. If you stray even a few inches, you could hit something." The "cleared tracks" was a relative term. Theoretically, if the first vehicle had rolled over a spot without an explosion (or the Husky had not detected an IED), that path should be free of IEDs. There were times when this rule did not hold true though, either because the IEDs were set to detonate after a few vehicles had rolled over them; they were designed to detonate under only the heaviest of cargo trucks; or they were "command wire detonated" with a triggerman and a wire. By 2009, all vehicles in Afghanistan had Electronic Countermeasure systems that would defeat radio-controlled IED initiators and would also jam most enemy communication systems. Unfortunately, our ECMs also had an adverse impact on our radios, as well as on the ECM systems in US Army and British trucks.

"There are gonna be times where we can't quite follow the tracks or RCP can't get through. Same thing we do when we don't have RCP. Corporal Zeitz, myself, Staff Sergeant C will lead with a mineroller. Corporal Z, what've you got?"

Corporal Jesse Zeitz was a military policeman, and the platoon's scout vehicle commander. "Alright, I'm gonna be in the MATV up front. Like always, Lance Corporal Stimson will be driving and Rea will be up in the gun. We'll try to find terrain that is navigable by the big cargo trucks behind us, so sometimes we're gonna have to leave RCP's tracks. Rea will scan for indicators using binoculars." These guys were a crack team, and went by the callsign 'Peewee.' The scout team was the first line of defense against IEDs, and they were constantly aware that their truck was more likely to hit an IED than any other truck in the convoy.

If there were no indicators or Corporal Rea missed them, the truck would run over the IED, and it would be all down to the mineroller and armor to keep the Marines alive. A mineroller was a metal "sled" with 8 to 10 wheels that was mounted on the front of the truck. Minerollers weighed about 9000 pounds, about a third of what each truck weighed. Driving with a mineroller was like driving with a trailer on the *front* of the vehicle and required a certain degree of skill. They increased the total vehicle weight by 33%, making driving even harder, but if the vehicle ran over an IED, the explosion would go off under the mineroller, limiting damage to the truck and injury to the occupants.

I picked up with the brief again. "Alright, now's a good time to talk about minerollers. Minerollers are a pain in the ass to recover after an IED strike. Pieces fly everywhere, and the mounting pins attaching them to the truck get bent by the explosion, so we're gonna need sledgehammers to get them out. Corporal Z, Staff Sergeant C, myself, and Godfather will have minerollers for this convoy to let us maneuver around the battlefield outside of the cleared tracks. Minerollers save lives and trucks, so if you don't have one on your truck, don't leave the tracks.

"Godfather will be second in line, right behind Peewee." Sergeant Ryan Galante, "Godfather," was the security team leader (STL). He was a "combat cook," a food service Marine who had applied for a lateral transfer into the motor transport MOS. He was an outstanding NCO and a newly promoted sergeant, and the Marines trusted him. "Godfather is responsible for everything related to the security of the convoy, so he's gonna be briefing all the gunners, running the weapons placement, the weapons test-fire the day before the convoy, and other preparations. When we have an IED strike or recovery, he will establish security positions on both sides of the recovery site to screen the Marines working within it."

Sergeant Galante stepped up. "Yes, sir. What I want the guntrucks to do is to set up on both sides of the recovery. If insurgents attack, the guntrucks are gonna be a wall of armor for the guys on the ground. We're gonna have mostly M240 medium machine guns . . . the 7.62mm rounds are powerful, and the weapon system is way more reliable than the .50 cal or Mk19. We will have a few .50 cals for longer ranges, and if you've got one, pay attention and brush it out every couple of hours. They're gonna jam." The heavy rounds were effective for over a thousand meters with good optics, but even these rounds, 1/2" in diameter, were not able to penetrate the thick mud walls of most Afghan compounds.

Each platoon had a slightly different organization and TTPs (tactics, techniques and procedures). We developed them based on our experiences, missions, personnel and our collective and individual capabilities. This stuff was all learned by experience, and was drastically different from how units operated in Iraq, and even from how we were trained and evaluated before the deployment.

Most platoon commanders would position themselves near the front, to best navigate and assess the tactical situation. I explained this to the Marines. "Because of the obnoxious size of our convoys, with more than 70 vehicles, I can't gauge the progress of the convoy or how the vehicles are handling the terrain if I'm in the first or second vehicle." Because I had such a good scout team which could handle the navigation and a solid STL, I was freed up to be a little further back. "I'll be the 30th vehicle, with an MK36 wrecker right in front of me." Without a doubt, the most valuable vehicle in our inventory was the MK36 "wrecker." Equipped with dual rear winch cables, a front winch, a hydraulic vehicle lift (for towing) and a crane capable of lifting 22,000 pounds, the MK36 was a monster. Not only was it essential for recovering vehicles after a breakdown or IED strike, the crane on the MK36 was used for offload and onload of cargo. Many small FOBs did not have forklifts or cranes, so we had to use our wrecker to get the job done. Our wrecker was also a "low-density" capability; nobody else in the area had one. This meant that we were often tasked with follow-on missions as other units had vehicles go down or hit IEDs. Since we had the only wrecker, we would have to go do the recovery.

"If a vehicle hits an IED, or gets stuck, I'll hear about it on the radio, but I will probably be able to see what happened. I'll push up, escorting the wrecker with my mineroller. Staff Sergeant C is going to push up too, but if something happens up front it will take him longer to get there."

My truck team was a great team of Marines, but I'm pretty sure they were sick of me by the end of the deployment because we had spent so much time together in a confined space. They didn't say anything about it if they were, though. My driver was Lance Corporal Edwin Sedam. A redneck from Kansas, he was one of the best vehicle operators in the battalion, and could handle our MATV with impressive precision. My gunner was Corporal James Sena from Mississippi. He preferred the M240 over the .50 cal, and would spend hour after hour in the turret in 120-degree heat, somehow remaining vigilant. Courageous and calm under fire, I trusted him implicitly. My radio operator was Corporal Garrick Williams. The sole radio operator in the platoon, he did the job of three Marines without any assistance, and I was always yelling at him to fix the radios, though it wasn't his fault that they weren't working.

These briefings were long, lasting about an hour. I never felt that I could give the Marines enough information. I needed to make sure they had the information to keep themselves alive, to ensure mission success, and to try to help them understand why they were doing what they were doing. We kept everyone alive and got the mission done, so it worked, I guess? The lieutenant don't know.

I went on. "The tail end of the convoy has quite a few vital members. The trail maintenance officer, Sergeant Calvin Williams, is the best mechanic in the platoon. He's got an MTVR with everything he needs to repair trucks outside the wire, like chains, towbars, spare tires, tools, parts and fluids. If a truck has a mechanical issue, Sergeant Williams will push to the downed truck with Staff Sergeant C and either repair it or rig it for tow behind another truck.

"Last in line is the Trail Security vehicle, commanded by Corporal Jesse Schueder. He's going to make sure that no vehicles are left behind, and that any Afghan civilians following us stay a safe distance away. Corporal Schueder, anything to add?"

"Yeah, just, these Afghans will come at us at high speed just to see what we will do. The Brits call them dickers, okay, they're just trying to test exactly

A "dicker" on a motorcycle monitoring and trying to provoke a CLB-6 convoy. The green dishdash or "manjams" and white turban were found to be characteristic colors for insurgents in Helmand Province.

what our Rules of Engagement (ROE) and Escalation of Force (EOF) procedures are." Corporal Schueder handled these types of incidents extremely well. He went on. "Okay, it takes courage to *not* act. It takes balls to *not* respond to these guys on motorcycles and in cars. They're trying to lure us into a fight or into shooting at someone." This could be construed as the imperialist infidels killing an innocent civilian.

I wrapped up the order, "So you know where we're going. You know what we're doing. Do the right thing, prep your trucks. A Marine who doesn't do preventive maintenance on his truck and breaks down endangers the maintainers who will have to fix it outside the wire. They slow us all down. Get after it, trust each other, and we'll be the best platoon out here."

The most critical member of the platoon, its heart and soul, was the platoon sergeant Staff Sergeant Joseph Caravalho, a Hawaiian native. One of only three Marines in the platoon who had ever deployed before, he is the reason we were successful in our training and preparation, and the reason we succeeded in Afghanistan. His driver was Lance Corporal Samuel Gorton, and Lance Corporal Jonathon Neubauer was on his radios. Lance Corporal

Staff Sergeant Caravalho and the author outside of Now Zad
wearing the flame-resistant FROG combat uniform.

Neubauer was a heavy equipment operator by MOS, but was one of the smartest Marines in the company. Lance Corporal Joey Moore, a military policeman, was Staff Sergeant Caravalho's gunner.

Staff Sergeant Caravalho was the assistant convoy commander (ACC). He was responsible for all matters "internal" to the convoy during mission prep. He made sure that we had all the Marines and trucks we needed, that all loads were picked up and strapped down tight, and that all weapons were cleaned. His list of tasks was never-ending, and I truly didn't appreciate what he did at the time, because I wasn't aware of half of it. The reason that I wasn't aware of it was because it never went wrong, it was never an issue. He was a true professional and expert in the field of motor transportation. I would not have been successful without him.

He rode as the second to last vehicle in the convoy, so that he could push up to any potential issues. He courageously left the cleared tracks time and time again to free stuck vehicles, to resolve mechanical difficulties, to change tires, and to recover vehicles that had been damaged in IED strikes.

CHAPTER SEVEN

ROUTINE OPERATIONS

"Smoking had come to be an important punctuation mark in the long sentence of a day on the road."—F. Scott Fitzgerald, "Thank You for the Light."

The routine operations that we conducted on combat logistics patrols (CLPs) were the most nerve-wracking, fun, stressful, exhilarating, frustrating, high-tension things I have ever done. I didn't personally take up smoking or dipping tobacco, but I did become a second-hand smoker of Marlboro Reds (my driver, Lance Corporal Ed Sedam, was the first-hand smoker). The smell of those cigarettes was strangely calming, unusual as I normally can't stand smoke. That is one thing that stayed in Afghanistan . . . I never really felt the need to smoke or hang around inhaling smoke after I got back. Nevertheless, the smell of Marlboro Reds will bring me right back to Musa Qal'eh and Now Zad.

The first mission assigned to CLB-6 was Operation "Khundee Larha," which was Pashto for "Safe Passage." Missions all had Pashto names, as part of an effort to increase the focus on the counterinsurgency effort and the Afghan people. The purpose of Operation Khundee Larha was to transport about a month's worth of food and supplies to a company from 3rd Battalion, 4th Marines at a combat outpost, or COP, in the town of Now Zad.

COP Cafferetta was located next to the Now Zad bazaar. The town itself was located in the northern part of the Helmand Province, surrounded by mountains to the west, north and east. All of the villagers had been driven off in December 2009, as 3/4 kicked off Operation Cobra's Anger to retake Now Zad. Though the Marines had succeeded, they now controlled a ghost town—it was a long way yet from a counterinsurgency victory. So far, very few Afghans had come back to start rebuilding homes, open schools or shops, and plant new crops. There was little support for the local government. The

District Governor of Now Zad remained in the relative safety of Lashkar Gah, over 50 miles away, cut off from the daily plight of the people he was appointed to protect. There was a good chance he would be assassinated if he returned.

The Marines of 3/4 patrolled the area. The constant security they provided had convinced a few Afghans that it was safe enough to re-establish the bazaar in town, though commerce was hardly thriving. The Taliban had decreed that anyone who shopped there was subject to punishment—taxes, kidnappings, and executions were common. Insurgents ordered villagers to shop at the "Taliban-sanctioned" Salaam Bazaar near the Western Cluster, and many still did. Every mud compound and house in Now Zad still bore spray-painted symbols, indicating that it had been searched during the Cobra's Anger offensive. Few walls did not show the pockmarks of bullets, witness to the firefights from earlier months. The Marines at COP Cafferetta needed support, and we would bring it to them.

The mission would be challenging and dangerous, we were told. What an understatement that turned out to be. We had to take 40 trucks worth of cargo

Mandzaraki Ghar, one of the mountains that formed the Southern Terrain Belt, was a haven for enemy spotters and weapons caches. IED attacks were frequent around the mountain and in the passes between it and the other peaks of the Southern Terrain Belt.

from Camp Leatherneck to COP Cafferetta. The first danger zone we would come to was the Southern Terrain Belt, a small range of mountains that provided safe haven for insurgents who could attack us, with trenches and firing positions to hide in. I actually coined the name "Southern Terrain Belt" during a confirmation brief to Brigadier General Hudson, pointing to the mountains on the map and referring to "this southern terrain . . . belt." The name stuck.

Weapons caches littered the foothills, and enemy spotters could see us approach from miles away. Equipped with binoculars and radios, the jihadists would emplace IEDs in the few passes between the mountains.

Once we were past the mountains, the land opened up on the Wulgak Plain. If we strayed too far west the terrain would become impassable for our trucks. On the other hand, if we went too far east, we would come upon the town of Wulgak itself, full of hostile Afghans—either insurgents or at least those sympathetic to the insurgency, we didn't know which. IED attacks were certain if the convoy strayed too close to it.

Beyond the Wulgak Plain was the Acolyte Wadi. A shallow streamed that

LVS MK48/16s towing M870 trailers haul battle-damaged equipment across the Wulgak Plain south of Now Zad.

only had flowing water in the rainy season, it was an ideal position for an IED attack. The difficult terrain had only a few passable areas, and each would be laced with IEDs. The rocky bed of the wadi rendered our ground-penetrating radar near-worthless and made identifying visual IED indicators impossible.

A single large hill loomed nearby, and provided an ideal position for the enemy to surveil our movements and plan attacks. It had been named the Lucy Pinder Terrain Feature by the British soldiers who patrolled the area prior to 2009. The name stuck, though few Americans were familiar with Lucy Pinder, who was a famous British porn star. One can surmise that the hill resembled the bosom of Ms. Pinder to one poor, bored, Limey standing post.

Once past the Acolyte Wadi, it was generally a smooth trip into Now Zad, because locals regularly traveled that route. Local routes were a toss up, but we learned which ones we could use or drive parallel to and which ones to avoid. There were a few options, but we found that the town of Jalal ud Din, off to the west, was particularly hostile with a high chance of driving over an IED. "A good place to find an IED," we joked.

This information was learned over multiple trips throughout 2010. Before our first mission, we had but a small glimpse of this knowledge, possessing very little in the way of detailed threat analysis or suitability of the terrain for combat logistics patrols. We learned the ins and outs of this land through experience. Experience, as it turns out, is a brutal mistress. She punishes you for the things you don't know, and there is little reward for things that worked somewhere else. Very little in our pre-deployment training prepared us to operate in the open deserts of the Northern Helmand Province. Tactics and techniques developed for the roads of Iraq, like route blocking, with security teams racing alongside convoys, and similar urban tactics were nearly useless, but they had been the focus of TBS, Logistics Officers Course and, especially, Mojave Viper.

We knew very little of this when planning our first mission. I had ridden along with the GS Motor T platoon on their run up to Now Zad and had taken in as much as I could, but that mission had gone fairly smoothly so there was little opportunity to see how they dealt with adverse situations. I asked some of their Marines for more details, but had gotten little feedback.

This was a company operation, with three platoons carrying out specific parts of the mission. Our company commander, Captain John Gallagher, would be the overall mission commander. I would command the main body, while Second Lieutenant Stacy Wood would take the security element. Route Clearance would be provided by the US Army National Guard's Thor 3-3, commanded by First Lieutenant Ben Selander.

We only had a few days to do all the planning and mission coordination, so we dove in headfirst. My platoon sergeant had the less-than-glorious task of sourcing us trucks. As a new unit in Afghanistan, CLB-6 had nothing. The battalion's Bravo Company had done several runs down to Camp Dwyer, in the south of Helmand Province, to bring up equipment for us, but everything we acquired seemed to be in a dreadful state. We received trailers without wheels, trucks missing engines, and similarly non-functioning equipment. It's just how the Marine Corps works; if I have three trucks and higher headquarters tells me to give you two, I'm going to keep the best one for myself.

Staff Sergeant Caravalho had to figure out what trucks the company had, which ones were usable, which were repairable, and what we still needed to be able to move all of our loads. Amazingly he pulled it off, and to my knowledge, didn't even steal any trucks from other units. We definitely borrowed quite a few, but I think Staff Sergeant C kept everything above board. The trucks we had were old, but they looked like they would get the job done.

The Marines turned to maintenance and loading all the cargo. This had to be done outside, in the rain, in January. January in the south of Afghanistan is cold. Temperatures hovered around freezing and we all swore that we would not complain about the summer temperatures when they arrived. We could not wait to be warm again.

My main focus during the mission prep was route planning. I pored over maps and satellite imagery, trying to create a route that would minimize enemy threat, provide smooth passage for our heavy cargo trucks, and not duplicate any previous coalition tracks.

"Sir, I've gone over everything that I could find from the MLG and GS Motor T, and even 3/4, but there's not a lot to go on. This route is our best shot though, I think. The biggest thing is that it avoids all previous honesty traces," I said as I showed Captain Gallagher the draft route in Google Earth, a 3D mapping program.

This last point was crucial. Convoys rarely took exactly the route they had planned, as terrain would be impassable or enemy threat would cause a diversion. Every unit would record their actual track or "honesty trace," which would be uploaded and could be used for future planning. Overlaying numerous honesty traces helped identify chokepoints or places friendly forces usually went, indicating a higher likelihood of an enemy attack there. If the enemy determined patterns in our movements, they could more accurately emplace IEDs to hit our convoys.

"Okay, Jeff, looks good. Have we got GPS units to record our honesty traces?"

"Yes, sir, I'll have mine." I carried a simple Garmin Dakota to track our routes. Sometimes, simple is best.

I later met with the Route Clearance Platoon leader, Lieutenant Ben Selander, to go over the route.

"Ben, what would work best for you, as far as the route?"

"The hardest thing for us is that we're trying to clear a route and navigate at the same time. It's hard because there's no BFT or GPS in the Husky, the route clearance vehicle up front. The second or third vehicle has to navigate by telling the lead Husky to turn 'less left,' 'a hair right,' or 'more straight.'"

"Okay, so is more checkpoints better or fewer? Is it more helpful to nail you down to a route, or just throw down general guidelines?" I asked.

"We've tried sticking to a super-detailed route, but that just causes confusion and slows us down. Just give us checkpoints every few kilometers and we'll try to stick to them. If we end up in terrain that doesn't work for your cargo trucks, you'll have to let us know, and just clear a new path with your minerollers, and we'll pick back up clearing."

This was all part of the learning process and after a few missions we arrived at a good balance in the route. I would provide enough checkpoints and the right amount of detail to ensure we were on a route that supported the tactical scenario while giving the Route Clearance Platoon the freedom to maneuver.

To say that the final mission preparation was smooth would be a lie of the highest order. We were learning every little thing for the first time. Marines were running around like chickens with their heads cut off.

The things we carried came in all shapes and sizes. Repair parts were packed in oddly-sized wooden crates, while mail was usually carried in thick cardboard "triwall" boxes the size of warehouse pallets. Anything might be packed in 20-foot ISO shipping containers, while Meals Ready-To-Eat and bottled water were usually on the pallets they came on. Bottled water was the bane of our existence. Most FOBs could not purify their own drinking water, so it all had to be shipped in by truck—by us. Ten, twenty or sometimes even fifty percent of every convoy's "bedspaces" were used to haul bottled water. The water bottles were not sturdy, so strapping the pallets to the trucks was challenging. The bottles were also heavy and would crush the wooden pallets they sat on as the truck bounced over the rough desert terrain. Once the pallets collapsed, the load became unstable. Plastic water bottles would begin to fall out one at a time, and then by the dozen, a trail of breadcrumbs along our tire tracks.

The platoon loadmaster had the unenviable task of figuring out how to move all of our assigned loads as efficiently as possible. We never had all the resources needed—we were short on trucks, ratchet straps to tie down loads, chains to secure heavy machinery to trailers, and licensed Marines to drive the specialized fuel tankers. A lot of rules were bent. They had to be. It was our platoon's mission, but it was the battalion's mission, too. Certainly, we incurred the tactical risks at the platoon level—an overloaded truck was more likely to break down, a complication that would slow our movement and make us more vulnerable. But administratively, I felt the battalion forced me as the platoon commander to accept the responsibility of bending and breaking rules, even though many of the leaders knew exactly what they were forcing me to do to complete the mission. If something went wrong, it would be my fault.

"Where do we pick up MREs for the mission?" The mission preparation continued.

"Who has batteries for the NVGs?"

"The seatbelts on this truck are broken, and the tires on that one went flat overnight."

There was a problem getting ammunition for Third Platoon, the security element, twelve of the eighty trucks on the mission. The S4 swore that no request had been submitted, but it was later discovered that the main body (my platoon) and the security element (Stacy's platoon) had each submitted individual requests for ammo, and the clerk, seeing two requests for the same company for the same day for the same destination, had deleted one of the requests, thinking it was a duplicate. Unfortunately, we both needed ammo for our trucks.

The day before the mission, the shortage of guntrucks was remedied as our battalion got a handful of the new Mine Resistant Ambush Protected All Terrain Vehicles (MATVs). They still had that "new truck smell," and were a sight to behold. Staff Sergeant Caravalho and I would each be riding in one, in addition to most of Stacy's security element and my scout.

Eventually, everything was sorted out. The night before the mission, I gave a final brief to my Marines, detailing the mission and the timeline. They bedded down for one last good night's sleep before reveille well before sunrise the next morning. We would depart Camp Leatherneck at 0400.

We got out of the motor pool and went through the front gate of Camp Leatherneck. Talk about a rush. This was it. I was outside the wire, in a war zone, as a platoon commander. Weapons were loaded and we were on a mission.

The movement north was slow but steady. We arrived at the Southern Terrain Belt and Stacy's platoon established their security position on that section of the route. They would hold that ground for about two days until we returned south. We continued north across the Wulgak Plain. Things were quiet.

Then there was a sudden *THUD*, a deep percussive sound and shockwave that I would come to know and hate.

The radio crackled. "*IED IED IED!*"

I jumped on. "Roger, this is Buzz. Can anyone identify which vehicle was hit?" This was the first IED that I had experienced in a leadership role, and I immediately worried about my Marines up at the front of the convoy. Second Lieutenant Bobby Fowler, in the lead security truck popped up. "Roger, Buzz, it was in the RCP."

I switched radios so that I could talk to the RCP, using my external call-sign. "Thor, Arawak 2. What's the situation?" Juggling between my internal call sign "Buzz" and my external callsign "Arawak 2" became a kind of game; with Arawak 2 (me), Arawak 3 (Third platoon commander), Arawak 5 (Lieutenant Bobby Fowler, the company XO), and Arawak 6 (Company CO) all on the same convoy net, using it was just a recipe for confusion. My Marines much preferred just using "Buzz."

It took a minute, but Thor came online. "Yeah, Arawak, we had an IED up here. Hit one of the RG-31s. Not too bad, just some bruises. The truck's had it though." The RG-31 was a type of 4-wheeled MRAP. For the first of what was to be dozens of times, the convoy halted and waited while the area around the damaged vehicle was swept for secondary IEDs. "Secondaries" were emplaced by insurgents, intended to hit recovery assets or Marines rushing to aid the victims of the first strike.

The RCP platoon commander was coordinating the recovery with some assistance from our Marines. After the victims of the IED strike were tended to by the platoon's medic, the soldiers and Marines turned to the task of recovering the damaged RG-31 MRAP. Unlike the Russians, whose burned-out vehicle hulks still litter Afghanistan, Americans never left damaged or destroyed equipment in the desert. In order to prevent the enemy from scavenging valuable armor from it, we would recover all of our trucks and minerollers. These recoveries were arduous and technically challenging, requiring cranes, flatbed cargo trucks, trailers, and heavy-duty tactical tow trucks called "wreckers."

Often, many of the Marines at the back of the convoy would have no idea what was happening. Lance Corporal Briana Toepler, one of the drivers, later told me, "I didn't know what was happening most of the time during recoveries or whatever. We were just sitting in the trucks, waiting to move."

While some Marines sat in their trucks, bored and scared, others were running around frantically. That's how war is—you're either running at 110% or bored out of your mind. A wrecker was brought up to recover the Route Clearance Platoon's MRAP, in this case the M984 HEMTT wrecker that Thor had brought with them. After what seemed like three hours (because it was about three hours), the recovery was finally complete.

Every ten minutes during those three hours, the Battalion Combat Operations Center, or COC, would ping my Blue Force Tracker. The BFT was an onboard computer that stored maps and detailed satellite imagery of our AOs and let us do GPS navigation. More importantly, we could send two-way text messages via satellite—this was the primary means of communication between CLB-6 convoys and our COC.

Photo of me taken by Corporal Sena, my gunner. I am in my usual position in the passenger seat of our MATV. The BFT screen is mounted on the dashboard in front of me.

Each BFT had a "role name," like an email address, that allowed text messages to be sent to groups of BFTs or specific individuals. The BFT also displayed the location of every other BFT in the AO, a lot like something from a video game.

MEB-A-CLB-B-COC: *Arawak 2, this is Red Cloud COC. Status?*

MEB-A-CLB-B-COC was the rolename for the CLB-6 COC. The Marines in the COC had no idea what was going on, or why it could possibly be taking so long. I later found out that the operations officer was demanding details every few minutes, and so was the battalion commander. Part of the problem was that I didn't know what information to send them or how to phrase it. I was of the opinion that I was outside the wire and they could wait on me. I was busy. I would send them information when I was good and ready. This was the wrong attitude and it would change, but not until after a few more missions and I learned to better understand why they needed the information. I responded with the same message, cut and pasted every few minutes.

MEBA-CLB-B-MTPLT2: *Red Cloud COC, this is Arawak 2. Still waiting. Recovery not complete.*

In the future, I would send more detailed information about what was going on and how much longer I thought it would take. Finally my radio beeped. "Arawak 2, this is Thor. Recovery complete. We are Oscar Mike." Oscar Mike, from the phonetic alphabet, meant "OM" or "on the move." Finally, the convoy would start rolling again.

I sent a BFT message to the COC.

MEBA-CLB-B-MTPLT2: *Red Cloud COC, this is Arawak 2. Recovery complete. We are Oscar Mike.*

We continued north and arrived at the Acolyte Wadi. It took about two hours to clear through this danger area. The rocky bed of the wadi and its high threat meant that it needed to be cleared by hand, using handheld ground-penetrating radars and handheld CMDs (compact metal detectors). The engineers of the route clearance element could clear about 150 meters per hour dismounted, so it was a two hour process to get across the Acolyte.

As we got across, the pace picked up on the run into Now Zad, though suddenly the convoy stopped. I pushed ahead to find out what was going on. An MK48/16 LVS towing an 870 trailer was stopped at a wadi. The tractor was down in the wadi about ten feet ahead of the trailer. The wrong size kingpin had been installed on the trailer; with the too-small kingpin, the tractor had been able to pull the trailer but when the tractor dropped down about 18 inches into the wadi, the kingpin popped out of the hitch vertically. What would normally be a relatively easy fix was complicated by the fact that the pneumatic brake-lines had been ripped off the trailer in the process. Though the trailer was easily reconnected to the truck, the brakes on the trailer were now locked and the wheels wouldn't turn.

It's always the little things. The kingpin should have been checked, but it wasn't. Now the brakes were locked and needed to be caged before the truck could roll again. Unlike the hydraulic brakes in a passenger car, all Marine Corps trucks use pneumatic brakes. The brakes are applied with a heavy spring, and are actually automatically depressed. When the driver lets off the brake pedal, pneumatic pressure actually *releases the brakes*. If there is a brake failure, brake line rupture or loss of pressure, the brakes will be applied, stopping the truck. Normally this is a good thing, preventing further damage or an accident. In this case it meant we were dead in the water.

"Caging" pneumatic brakes is a fundamental task for any motor transport operator. By use of a special bolt and a wrench, the brake spring is compressed, freeing the wheel to spin. This was the first time we'd had to cage the brakes in Afghanistan.

The sun had set so we were working in the dark. We had to locate caging bolts and a 3/4-inch combination wrench before we could even begin. That task alone took almost 30 minutes. "Goddammit, I can't find any caging bolts," Corporal Minetti, one of the wrecker operators said.

Never again would I let that be the problem. Caging the brakes on the trailer took another 30 minutes. I kicked myself for not checking this in the Pre-Combat Inspections. How could I have overlooked this? After this incident, I personally made sure that these items were readily accessible; I carried a wrench on my flak for the rest of the deployment.

A pencil sketch of the 3/4" wrench that I always carried in the front pocket of my flak jacket. It became some-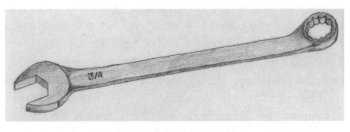
thing of a good luck charm. When grunts would snicker and ask, "What's the wrench for?" I would respond "So that us POGs can come recover your truck after you get it blown up or broken." "POGs" was a derogatory term levied against anyone who wasn't an infantryman— it stood for "Persons Other than Grunts."

By now, the front of the convoy had already pressed on to COP Cafferetta, just inside Now Zad. My scout vehicle commander had never been there, so even with the compound being only a few hundred meters into the city, there was not a clear route to follow. I pushed my truck up to the front. The convoy stretched about four miles back, so I waited to consolidate all of the vehicles before pushing into the COP. From the time the first vehicle entered the base, it would be almost an hour before the last vehicle entered.

The COP itself was pretty small, and barely large enough to fit all of our vehicles, but we made it happen. Twenty-one hours after we'd left Camp Leatherneck we were finally back in the relative safety of a friendly position. The next morning we met up with the company gunnery sergeant for 3/4's Lima Company. Responsible for all logistics and supply matters for the company and for COP Cafferetta as a whole, he was the go-to guy for all cargo offload.

"Alright, I need you guys to offload the fuel over there at the fuel farm. There should be a bulk fuel Marine hanging around over there to help you out. All the food goes by the chow hall. We've got a bunch of stuff that needs to be taken back to Camp Leatherneck on your return trip. I'll show you all that stuff." By 0900, trucks were going in every direction to offload and pick up cargo for backhaul.

Our primary fronthaul cargo was JP-8 fuel in 5000-gallon M970 tankers, pallets of MREs and other food, ammunition, and a postal team to support the "mailout" of 3/4's personal items. Marines redeploying back to the United States have the option to mail a footlocker back, reducing the amount of luggage they have to carry with them.

The backhaul cargo included hundreds of empty 55-gallon fuel drums. Earlier in the war, there was not enough ground logistics capacity so fuel had to be air-dropped out of C-130 cargo planes every few days. Drums of fuel dropping from the sky suspended by disposable (literally) parachutes was less than ideal. The company gunny was glad to be done with fuel drums, and even more glad to be sending back the empties, clearing out space.

The other cargo for backhaul was about a dozen Humvees, which were no longer allowed outside the wire because they did not provide adequate protection against IED explosions. Some of them could be placed on MTVR flatbed trucks, lifted into place with a TRAM, a type of heavy-duty forklift with a 10,000-pound capacity. Others had to be flat-towed behind other trucks, which would be troublesome freight, to say the least. Offload and onload took the better part of the day, and there were myriad other tasks to prepare for the return trip. Every vehicle needed a full maintenance inspection and all weapons needed to be cleaned.

Partly because it would be good for the local economy and perhaps help improve relations with the local populace, but mostly because it would give the Marines face-to-face exposure with Afghans, we arranged a short foot patrol from COP Cafferetta to the Now Zad bazaar. Their mission was to buy us some produce and livestock to diversify the Marines' diet.

The bazaar was only about 200 meters from the front entrance of the COP, but any time anybody left the wire, the same protocols were followed; any unit could be ambushed at any time. A manifest with everyone's information was compiled for accountability. The patrol leader, one of 3/4's experienced squad leaders, a sergeant, gave the patrol brief. Marines donned flaks and Kevlar helmets, and departed.

When they returned, they were all smiles. The shopping trip had been a success. I had sent only about ten Marines on the patrol because any more and the unit would get jammed up and be a liability for the 3/4 Marines. Everyone else was jealous, but they soon got over it. Corporal Sena, my gunner, had a live chicken in his dump pouch, a small bag worn on the hip used

CLB-6 Marines in the Now Zad Bazaar. Though the area was near COP Cafferetta, the possibility of enemy contact was ever present.

to deposit empty magazines. The drawstring on the dump pouch was drawn tight, but the chicken's head and neck were sticking out. The chicken looked around calmly.

Using HESCO, a construction material consisting of heavy steel mesh and burlap that is filled with dirt, the Marines fashioned a grill and cooked the chickens. It was the best meal I'd had in a month, and the only solid food I'd eaten in about two days. We had MREs and some snacks that I'd brought, but I couldn't really eat outside the wire. I was too busy, too nervous. I would snack on cookies and chips and eat cans of sardines sent by friends and family, but that stuff got old after a few days. And it wasn't really filling.

The night before we left, there was a fair amount of activity on the radio. Twenty-five miles south of Now Zad, Second Lieutenant Stacy Wood's platoon was still down at the Southern Terrain Belt, holding about a mile-long section of the route. This portion of the route was evaluated as being high-threat, and had taken a long time to clear on the way up, though no IEDs had been found. Stacy had set up two positions, one at each end of the route segment they were securing. She moved between the two positions every few hours to check on the Marines and the tactical situation. With the sun now set, she was making this trip in the dark.

Infrared chemlights, visible only with NVGs, were placed on either side of the route, but the MATV offered poor visibility and the moondust that was kicked up made the chemlights hard to see. While crossing one of the many wadis between the two security positions, the truck strayed just slightly out of the cleared tracks.

The ground exploded underneath Stacy's truck. The mineroller sustained the majority of the blast, but the Marines in the truck were rocked. The force of the explosion caused concussions and bruises.

Lieutenant Wood called in the IED report, and her Marines conducted the recovery. Since the MATV was disconnected from the mineroller, they backed it up, staying in the cleared tracks. The mineroller was destroyed and would have to be taken back to Camp Leatherneck on a flatbed truck. This required pulling the flatbed and a wrecker up to the destroyed mineroller, and hoisting it into place. The risk of doing this in the wadi near a known IED strike site was significant.

Sergeant Johnathon Rose thought of a better way to complete the most difficult part of the recovery—loading the mineroller onto the flatbed—and doing it outside the high danger area. Using the dual pulling winches on the back of the MK36 wrecker, he dragged the mineroller out of the wadi to a safer area, and loaded it for backhaul there. This type of "thinking around the problem" was something that he was known for, and was something that was desperately needed. Too often, the approach to getting around a "wall" was to crash against it until we broke through, no matter the cost.

With the mineroller recovered, the security Marines held tight and waited for us to come back south.

The next morning we managed to get everything ready to depart just as dawn was breaking. I wanted to maximize our use of daylight and get at least as far as the Southern Terrain Belt before the sun set. The smooth start to the day was not going to last long.

The eighth or ninth vehicle in line was an MK31 towing an 870 lowboy flatbed trailer. Just past the entry control point's serpentine barrier for COP Cafferetta there was a low wall made of HESCO, designed to make it difficult for a speeding suicide bomber to crash an explosives-laden car through the COP's gate. Coming around the corner, the driver cut too wide, and the rear axle of the 870 trailer clipped the HESCO, puncturing one of the trailer tires. We could have left it and run the trailer with a flat tire, but Staff Sergeant Caravalho recommended that we change it now, in the relatively safe area near the COP, rather than in an unknown danger area up ahead when we really needed to use the trailer. Our other 870 trailer was hauling a damaged LVS, so this one was our only free recovery asset. I agreed with Staff Sergeant Caravalho's assessment, and the maintenance Marines began to work on getting the tire changed.

Like everything else outside the wire, the first time we changed a tire on an 870 trailer took longer than it should have. In the ideal conditions of a garrison base with all the tools you need, it's a relatively simple task. We didn't have all the right tools though; the wrecker was missing a pneumatic impact wrench (it had been issued to us without one, and a new wrench was on order ... with an expected ship date of about a year), so all the bolts had to be "broken" by hand with a manual wrench and a breaker bar for leverage. The jacks and jackstands didn't work right, so we had to dig out a trench *under* the flat tire, letting the other tires support the weight of the trailer, and change the tire that way. Far from ideal. What should have been a twenty-minute job took over an hour and a half. We were learning, but not fast enough.

The entire time, the company CO was hitting me up for status updates every five minutes. I was mad at him for repeating the same question over and over and at the same time I was growing frustrated with my Marines. I tried not to let my frustration show. They would get better, I knew, and I had already heard quite a few comments about how they would do things differently "next time," but that didn't do a whole lot for me right then. I was growing concerned about the amount of daylight we were wasting.

The tire was changed, and we finally went Oscar Mike. The movement went smoothly across the Acolyte Wadi and past Lucy Pinder. The convoy trudged southwest across the Wulgak Plain, rough ground broken with wadis and frequent, shallow intermittent streams.

I was talking to Lieutenant Wood down at the security position on the Southern Terrain Belt over the BFT throughout the day. She had not seen anything to indicate an increased threat. Some Afghans were seen traveling through the area, and some of them came up to talk to her and the Marines. She had Ray with her, one of the company's interpreters. The sun set when we were about five kilometers from her position. Hands down, the most dangerous time of the day was the "evening transition period" between day and night. As the sun set, the enemy came out to play.

As we came closer to the security position, small lights started flickering and flashing on both sides of the convoy, some close and some far away up on the Mandzaraki Ghar, the small mountain immediately east of us. The lights looked like flashlights, but were undoubtedly being used as signals, flashing out messages in an improvised Morse Code. There was no way to know what they were saying, but I was sure it was about us. The radio erupted with traffic from the Marines talking about it.

"Buzz, I got blinking lights off the right side."

"I see them too, Buzz." The Marines were unnerved.

"All stations, this is Smokecheck." Staff Sergeant Caravalho jumped on the radio to restore order. "Roger, all, we see the lights, too. Just stay focused and keep pushing south. Nothing we can do about some little blinky lights."

The radio calls about the lights stopped, but I doubted that many of the Marines were at ease. We pressed on slowly, the RCP slowed by the onset of darkness.

The blinking lights had my adrenaline pumping; I was on high alert. I could see the same patterns of lights being blinked out on one side and then another. They were surely talking about us, and we were in a known danger area, vulnerable in the shadow of the Mandzaraki Gar. I hit Lieutenant Wood, "Slapshot," on the BFT again.

MEB-A-CLB-B-MTPLT2: *Slapshot, this is Buzz. Seeing a lot of activity back here. Several dozen signal lights, estimate at least 2 EN Squads worth. Be ready to push as soon as we get to your position. ETA is about 10 minutes.*

The front of the convoy got to her position, but her Marines were still doing final checks and accountability of all equipment and getting the trucks into the proper convoy order and so forth. My trucks were coming to a halt one by one.

WHUMP-CRACK.

Mortars make a very distinct sound when they are being fired—first, there is a "whump" of the mortar hitting the deck, followed by the sharp, percussive high-explosive charge detonating.

"Buzz, this is Blackout." Lance Corporal Randolph had driven the last five miles of the last leg of the convoy in the dark without headlights, earning the callsign, Blackout. "Some kind of explosion about 50 meters off the right side of my truck." He was toward the end of the convoy, maybe fourth or fifth from last. "Roger, Blackout. All stations, this is Buzz. Sounded like a mortar, probably an enemy 82mm. Stay buttoned up." We needed to get moving. The enemy was targeting mortars at us. I sent another BFT message.

MEB-A-CLB-B-MTPLT2: *Slapshot, this is Buzz. We need to get moving right now. Can't sit a minute longer!*

She jumped on her platoon's radio net. "All stations, Slapshot. Oscar Mike, now! Just get moving, we'll sort out the order later."

The trucks inched forward, and then started picking up speed. Another few mortar rounds fell near the tail of the convoy. They fell on alternate sides of the convoy, getting closer every time. The insurgents were bracketing us. The enemy mortar team had some training, with a somewhat competent observer, and posed a considerable threat to us.

Our rules of engagement limited us to only one real option—run. Without positive identification of an enemy displaying what we called a "hostile act," like firing on us, or "hostile intent," like pointing a weapon at us, we could not shoot at anyone. Even though the individuals with the blinking lights were most likely enemy fighters coordinating the fires on us, we could not shoot at them. We pushed through the final major danger zone, the Southern Terrain Belt, and continued our journey south back to Camp Leatherneck. We were still about ten miles away, but the Marines had already been awake for 20 hours.

It was right about then that we began to have a different problem. Or rather, it was a problem that we had seen all day; it only now began to become a serious problem. We were backhauling Humvees from Now Zad, and had placed a few on top of longbed MTVRs, LVSRs and M870 trailers, but most of them were being flat towed behind other trucks. The problem was that the towbars were snapping like toothpicks due to the rough terrain. We were still twenty miles or so from Camp Leatherneck when I heard someone call over the radio, "Uh, woah, someone just lost their Humvee."

"Say again, over?" I responded.

"The truck in front of me just had the Humvee that they were towing break away from them."

Staff Sergeant Caravalho jumped on the horn. "I'm on it, Buzz," and went to check it out. "Yeah, Buzz, we snapped another towbar. I don't think we have any left."

Sure enough, we were out of towbars. I can't even remember how many we broke, but it was a lot. We had broken all of the Humvee towbars early in the mission, and had switched to using the new lightweight composite universal towbars that were shipped with the new MATVs; these were supposed to be stronger, lighter, and better, but they, too, could not stand up to the terrain in Afghanistan.

With no towing capability and no room on any of the lowboys left, I saw only two options. I could call back to the COC and request that someone find towbars, which was no easy task . . . we had taken all that we could find before we left. We would have to sit out there, exposed, while someone brought them to us, prolonging the mission and increasing the danger to us. The other option was to put a Marine in the driver's seat of the Humvee and drive it the rest of the way back to Camp Leatherneck. While physically possible, this would be a significant risk for the individual driving, because Humvees have a flat bottom and only weigh about 30% of what an MRAP weighs, making them much less survivable in an IED strike.

The enthusiasm and courage of the Marines never flagged, and one of my guys eagerly said, "I'll do it. Just let me drive it back. It's the fastest way." He was right. After weighing the risks, I made a decision and we executed the plan. It was the best way to minimize the risk to the whole platoon. I never told the battalion about it, though.

One of the most dangerous things that a convoy could do was stop. If you are stopped, the enemy has time to prepare for you. IEDs can be emplaced just over the next hill, right in front of you, ready for you when you start to move again. Mortars can be dropped on you, or deliberate combined arms attacks can be orchestrated. Time and again, we learned the value of momentum. The faster we moved, the faster we continued to move. The slower we moved, the more problems and attacks we encountered.

We could see the lights of Camp Leatherneck from miles away, but we weren't back yet. Just north of Route 1, the Ring Road, there was a huge band of soft sand running east–west that was nearly impossible to avoid and would plague us again and again. This sand had the consistency of baby powder and was several feet deep. Lieutenant Wood dubbed these the "Sar Taizan Sand Pits" after the missions most often affected by them. Trucks were getting stuck right and left, and the Marines were growing tired and complacent. We needed to regroup for one last push back to Camp Leatherneck. Staff Sergeant Caravalho made it happen. Suddenly he was everywhere at once, riding up and down the line, jumping on the radio, yelling encouragement to Marines. The platoon snapped back and pushed across the sand pits. We made it back onto Route 1 and turned onto the Shorabok Road, the unimproved trail spur that led to Camp Leatherneck.

The first thing that we did upon arriving anywhere was to get accountability of every truck, Marine, and weapon system. The last thing we needed was to lose a truck or Marine somewhere outside the wire, and we could not let weapons fall into enemy hands. Every time the roster was read off, I was nervous that somebody's name would be followed by silence instead of a voice saying "here." This was, no kidding, my biggest fear in Afghanistan.

Thankfully, everyone and everything was accounted for. The first mission was complete.

CHAPTER EIGHT

THE QUEEN'S OWN GURKHA LOGISTICS REGIMENT

The city of Musa Qal'eh and the surrounding area in the northern Helmand Province was all British battlespace, but it was getting turned over to the US Marines, allowing the British to concentrate their efforts south of Sangin. As part of this turnover, or relief in place, all of the British equipment and supplies had to be backhauled from the Musa Qal'eh District Center, including several small bases in the area, to FOB Edinburgh, and from FOB Edinburgh (or "Edi") back to Camp Leatherneck. At the same time, American equipment and personnel had to be brought up from Camp Leatherneck to replace the British capabilities. The best way to accomplish this was to use all available trucks (both British and American) in both directions, full of American cargo on the front end and full of British gear on the return trip.

Befitting their long history as a military organization, the British Royal Army displayed a unique brand of professionalism. For better or worse, everything the Brits did was more methodical and deliberate than the way we did it. That's not to say it was lacking in tenacity, things just moved a little slower. For their logistics units, this meant that a lower percentage of their capabilities were employed at any given time. I envied the amount of time they allotted for preparation and the amount of equipment they had to throw at a mission. We always felt things were running down to the wire—turn around and go again—and we never had all the equipment we needed.

I was embedded with the British Royal Army's 10th Close Support Logistics Regiment for Operation Lava 29. We began the mission planning process almost two weeks before departure with an initial meeting at the British compound. I was struck by the refined civility of the soldiers. Rank seemed less important or, at least, less of a barrier than it was for Marines.

There appeared to be less of a division between British NCOs and officers, and Royal Army majors came up and introduced themselves by their first name.

"Eh, right, so this will be Operation Lava 29 going up to FOB Edinburgh," the British major began. "I'll be the mission commander, and Captain Gallagher will command the American contingent. We've done this run . . . well, it doesn't take a genius to figure it out . . . 28 times before."

"And it's called 'Lava' because the run gets hot," a particularly chippy NCO threw in. It wasn't named Lava because of the high enemy threat—it was just an ironic coincidence that this route, which had a particularly high enemy threat, happened to be named Lava. Every British convoy route in the Helmand Province was named for a type of stone or mineral. Other routes included "Loam" to Sangin and "Gypsum" down to Garmsir.

"Sergeant Jones is right, this run is a hot one. After we turn off Route 1, we have three primary danger zones that we have to cross. The first is the Mis Mas Wadi, just north of the Lone Hill. Second, we will get across the De Nowzad Rud, another wadi. Last and most treacherous is the Lande Nawah Wadi. Lande Nawah is so deep, in fact, that there are entire villages within the wadi. There should not be standing water this time of year, but the terrain canalizes us—it forces us into one area. The enemy knows that the terrain will force us onto this trail and we always find lots of IEDs in there," the major continued.

"Right. That's where the Foxtrot callsigns come in," added Lieutenant Andy Thackway. It took a little while to understand that the British units referred to each individual vehicle or squad as a "callsign," a term that we just used to refer to someone's radio nickname. I tried to keep up. The Foxtrot callsigns represented the security platoon. "It will take the route clearance troop, your American Thor callsigns, about three hours to get through the Lande Nawah. The risk of backlay is pretty bad, so we are going to sit on the wadi and hold the crossing point until the main body is headed back south." Being "backlaid" was always a threat. The insurgents would come in behind the convoy and lay IEDs on probable return routes, looking to hit the convoy on the inbound leg when our movements were much more predictable. It was tough to tell when convoys would leave the major logistics hub at Camp Leatherneck, but once we delivered our supplies to FOB Edinburgh, it was a sure bet that we would head back in a day or so.

The mission commander resumed the brief: "So Andy's boys will sit on the wadi, with the Thor callsigns, while we complete our offload at FOB

Edinburgh. Andy's platoon will push out about an hour before we get back to them, beginning to clear the route South so that we can maintain more momentum and get back quicker." The next three weeks would prove to be an interesting introduction to British culture. I had traveled to London briefly on spring break in 2005, but hadn't really spent much time up close and personal with any Brits.

One of the British sergeants had a list of words written above his desk on a whiteboard. Without any explanation, the list read "foresight, economy, flexibility, simplicity, cooperation." I wrote them down and Googled them later, and found out they were from the UK Ministry of Defense Joint Warfare Publication 4-00: *Logistics for Joint Operations*. We had plenty of publications in the Marine Corps, but we didn't have any principles like these. I liked that the British principles were much more general and applicable far beyond logistics.

I now have them printed and framed on my wall, and they accurately characterize what it's like working with a British logistics unit. The Principles of Logistics are, like them, calm, civilized and methodical. Notably absent from the list is "intensity" or "ferocity" or anything like that. The British way of waging war, from my perspective, was very realistic or down-to-earth, and was lacking some of the chaos that went along with the American intensity and bravado, even if sometimes it seemed a little slow. In any case there was a mutual respect between the British Army and the American Marines, and we worked well together.

One of the fundamentals of mission preparation is rehearsal. Rehearsals ensure that everyone knows what the unit will do if attacked with an IED, or if a truck rolls over, or somebody gets lost, or any one of a thousand different possibilities. Likely scenarios will be roleplayed, and key parts will be acted out. With forces from different countries working together, the rehearsals for Operation Lava 29 were absolutely critical.

We met at the British motor pool aboard Camp Bastion, which was adjacent to Camp Leatherneck. "British efficiency" was the name of the game. The rehearsals were set up in a round robin, with stations for vehicle recovery of American and British trucks, American and British rules of engagement, reactions to contact and IEDs, the mission brief and intelligence brief.

After the rehearsals, we had one last sync meeting with the British mission leadership, and completed final vehicle maintenance checks. The Marines were released for "convoy prep time," an opportunity to sleep, eat and rest up for the mission ahead. The next night, we went over to the British compound and lined up our vehicles on the road. They invited all of our Marines to fill a bag with "Class I" or "tiffins." The Marines appreciated the variety in British snacks, particularly the chocolate Yorkie bars, a plain Nestle chocolate with the inexplicable slogan "Not for Girls." I didn't then and don't now understand why that was the slogan (especially in post-feminist 2010). We traded MREs for the British Army Ration as well. I'm not convinced they are any better than our MREs, but they were something different, and, therefore, delicious.

Except for the mission planning, the rest of the preparation was no different than any other non-joint mission. Loads had to be placed on trucks, vehicles had to be maintained, weapons cleaned, and Marines assigned to trucks. For me, though, this mission would be something completely new. To help learn from the experiences that the Brits had in the area, I embedded with the Security Troop, the Foxtrot callsigns, learning how they did business.

I was assigned to ride in their second vehicle, a Mastiff, nearly identical to our six-wheeled MRAP. This vehicle was crewed by three soldiers, all Gurkhas, and the interpreter's nickname (and in fact, the only name I could get out of him) was "Lucky," so-called because he'd never been in a truck that hit an IED. I hoped that his luck (and, by extension, *mine*) would hold out.

The Gurkha soldiers who formed most of the 10th CSLR were recruited from Nepal. They were offered the chance to serve in the Royal Army, and in exchange for a certain period of service they could earn British citizenship and a pension. The United Kingdom was not the only nation to maintain a unit of Gurkhas—both India and Singapore continued to recruit Gurkhas after these countries were no longer British colonies. The brigade of Gurkhas included two regiments of infantry, an engineer regiment, a signals regiment, and a logistics regiment—the 10th Close Support Logistics Regiment, the Queens Own Gurkha Logistics Regiment, abbreviated 10 QOGLR.

Most of the officers and NCOs were from the United Kingdom, while the soldiers were from Nepal. The Nepalese soldiers seemed to always be smiling. I have rarely been among a group of people who were so consistently optimistic, cheerful and upbeat.

We got loaded and departed through the common entry control point that Camp Leatherneck and Camp Bastion shared, as we often did, in the middle of the night. Even departing on a dangerous mission at midnight could not dampen the spirits of the smiling Gurkhas.

The single most important piece of cargo the convoy was carrying was a Kalmar, a massive 100,000-pound machine used to move, load and stack shipping containers. The Kalmar would be essential for offloading and onloading the cargo at FOB Edinburgh, to support the logistics of switching out the Brits and Marines. The only truck capable of moving this piece of heavy machinery was the HET, a truck that the Marines didn't have, so a US Army HET platoon would be coming to haul this load.

The HET tractor and trailer system was originally designed to transport tanks at high speed on the Autobahn, in order to repel the Red Communists of the Soviet Union from invading Western Europe. With 40 wheels and weighing 50,000 pounds in its own right, the M1000 HET trailer was not designed for the terrain of Southern Afghanistan. Just after turning north off Route 1, the pace slowed to a crawl and then stopped completely.

The HETs could not handle the deep sands and side slopes, and the route was only going to get worse. The decision was made to keep moving, to tough it out. That only lasted for a few minutes. The HET trailer has hydraulic steering and suspension for each of its 10 wheel assemblies; because of the side slope and the heavy load, the hydraulics on the left side of the trailer blew out. As the left side of the trailer dropped, the Kalmar shifted and snapped a chain rated to withstand loads of over 20,000 pounds. Such was the challenge of the task. One of its tires was off the trailer completely, and the Kalmar was about to tip over.

A Kalmar Container Handler is slowly recovered after the HET trailer carrying it suffered a hydraulic blowout in the rough terrain of the Helmand deserts. Numerous US Army and British trucks were required.

Recovering from this incident took hours. Before we could recover the truck, we had to get the Kalmar off the HET trailer. The weight of the Kalmar and the precarious position meant special precautions needed to be taken. Three wreckers were brought up, and using their winch cables, held the Kalmar in place to keep it from falling over. All these movements were slow, because the ground had to be cleared for IEDs before the wreckers could be positioned. A Kalmar operator was located toward the rear of the convoy and brought forward. Because the convoy of over 150 vehicles was more than ten miles long and the max speed that could safely be accomplished in the terrain was about 20 mph, it took over 30 minutes to bring the Kalmar driver up from the rear of the convoy. Finally, everything was in place. The winches were slowly let out to match the pace as the driver slowly inched the machine back off the trailer.

Inch by inch, the fourth wheel of the Kalmar was pulled back onto the trailer, and then the Kalmar was driven off the rear of the trailer, onto the ground. The immediate danger of the Kalmar tipping over was resolved, but the convoy was sitting still, and hadn't moved in over six hours. By now, the enemy surely knew we were coming; any element of surprise was gone. We could not move until we did something with the Kalmar and the damaged HET.

A Quick Reaction Force had been called up from Camp Leatherneck to escort additional HETs to recover the Kalmar. Again, a seemingly simple matter, but something that took hours to execute. HETs were not just standing by, ready to roll. The convoy had departed Camp Leatherneck in the middle of the night, the Kalmar had tipped shortly after midnight, and the recovery was not completed until something like nine hours later. Not only was the enemy now alerted to our presence, we had burned four hours of precious daylight that we would need to get through the high threat zone near the Lande Nawah Wadi.

For me, this whole evolution was miserable. Embedded as an observer, I had to restrain myself from getting engaged or telling anybody what I thought. This was not my platoon or my mission. I watched the recovery while sitting on top of the British Mastiff I was riding in, drinking coffee with the interpreter, Lucky. He had a radio scanner and was keeping an ear out for enemy traffic.

"No, they are not saying anything. It is still too early for the Taliban," he smiled. "Not like us. They are too lazy."

Maybe so, but we were still south of the 60th Northing, which, at least for the western part of the AO, seemed to be the southernmost boundary for insurgent attacks. Finally, though, we started moving forward again. We knew the hard fighting would be up ahead.

The convoy arrived at the Mis Mas Wadi, which everyone pronounced "Mish Mash." This was a wide, shallow streambed that only had running water during the rainy season. The bed was littered with sharp broken rocks and gravel, washed down from the mountains off to the west.

There was movement near the Lone Hill. Several individuals on motorcycles had ridden to the top of the hill and remained there for a while, and had driven back down, leaving a small group of people at the top. Several of our vehicles reported pickup trucks with beds full of "military-aged males" headed north at high speed. Dressed in clean clothes and not rags, they weren't from around there. These were outsiders.

Meanwhile, we were moving at a walking pace. Dismounted route clearance was needed to effectively search the rockbed of the wadi for IEDs in this high-threat terrain. Using handheld metal detectors, the soldiers searched for the metal components found in IEDs, like batteries and wires. One of the soldiers got a hit, the telltale squelching of his metal detector instantly setting everyone on edge. He felt around with the metal detector, marking the zone of the hits with blue water bottle caps, an item in ready supply from the Dibba brand bottled water that we all drank. He had a circle about two feet in diameter marked with water bottle caps. He backed off.

The Route Clearance Platoon brought up the Buffalo. Weighing in at over 45,000 pounds, the Buffalo was a heavily armored vehicle designed for bomb disposal and was equipped with a large articulated arm to "interrogate" suspected IEDs. The fork on the arm poked and prodded at the rocks marked by the blue water bottle caps (with all passengers safely inside the vehicle). Slowly, they got through the first layer of rocks and earth, and uncovered an object wrapped in clear plastic and white tape.

It was rectangular, about four inches by fifteen inches. This was a pressure plate, part of the initiation system of an IED.

"Roger, stand by for BIP," Thor's platoon commander said.

BIP, or blow in place, was the standard method of destroying IEDs, and entailed placing a charge of C4 explosives atop the IED. More time passed. The engineers prepared the charges and fuses. The airspace in the area had to be cleared through higher headquarters, to ensure there were no aircraft in the area that could potentially be damaged by the debris kicked up in the explosion.

After nearly an hour, "Five minutes to BIP," over the radio. The countdown continued.

"Thirty seconds to BIP."

Whump. Different explosions have different types of sounds and sensations. The relatively "low velocity" homemade ammonium nitrate-aluminum explosives favored by the insurgents of the southern Helmand Province in 2010 had more of a *whump* than a *boom* or *crack*, if we want to get technical about it. This was the closest I had ever been to an IED detonating, about two hundred meters away. I would get closer (much closer), but at the time it was a rush. The force of the blast wave rocked the truck, hitting us right in the gut.

After the controlled detonation, the engineers got back out of the trucks, and finished clearing the Mis Mas Wadi. No more IEDs were found, but it took another half hour to get across the wadi. Finally, they were back in their trucks and the convoy began rolling at the breakneck pace of three to five miles per hour. The convoy arrived at the Rue De Now Zad, another shallow wadi that had to be cleared by hand. The engineers from the Route Clearance Platoon did their thing. Another two hours, but no IEDs this time. The convoy pressed on.

We were getting into much tighter terrain now, filled with small farms and compounds, with lots of places for enemy fighters to hide and take up firing positions. It was mid-afternoon, and the rear of the convoy started to receive small arms fire. Enemy fighters popped up over compound walls and fired off short bursts with their AK47s. As soon as the *clatta-clack* of their weapons went silent, they were on the move, safe behind the thick mud walls of the compound. Moments later, they popped up somewhere else and fired again. Shoot and scoot to stay alive. If they stayed still too long, we would get a fix on them, and our guns would beat theirs any day. Not to mention our jetfighters and helicopter gunships.

The convoy was so long (about six miles at this point), that up at the front we could only barely hear the sound of the guns behind us. The British Viking Troop, a maneuver element in high speed armored vehicles with tracks like a tank, came from several miles away to support the convoy, which would keep pressing forward. Maneuvering on the flanks of the convoy, the Vikings engaged the enemy from a second direction. Without enough Marines to kick in the doors of the compounds where the insurgents were firing from, suppressing the enemy fire was a short-term solution to a long-term problem, but we did not have a better option.

Our mission was to deliver our cargo, and we couldn't afford to dismount anyone to maneuver on the attackers. If we lost even one Marine, it would compromise our ability to move the trucks and their critical cargo. We pressed on, returning fire and suppressing the enemy as they popped up. A large number of vehicles at the rear of the convoy (all US Marine trucks) were under fire for over an hour. The rounds hit windows and pinged off armored doors. Cargo was damaged. The Marines stayed calm, even as their windshields shattered and their tires were filled with holes by enemy machine guns. We could press on with bullet holes in the tires—our trucks were equipped with a central air system that could pump air back into them to keep the pressure up a little. The tires were designed to be driven at least a kilometer when flat.

The front of the convoy arrived at the Lande Nawah Wadi. Over sixty feet deep and hundreds of yards across, the Lande Nawah is an imposing terrain feature. Villages were built in the wadi, and there were only a few ways to get across that were suitable for our large, heavy trucks.

When we left Camp Leatherneck, there were three potential crossing points. It was up to the mission commander to choose which one we would use once we got a little closer. The Route Clearance Platoon was drifting slightly to the east, trying to select good terrain for the trucks, so as we approached the Lande Nawah, the mission commander called across the radio, "We'll be going with the easternmost crossing, boys. Head for Checkpoint 51."

I had seen pictures of the wadi, but didn't appreciate the size of it and the threat it posed until I arrived in person. Our trucks would be descending on a winding path barely wide enough for them. The turns were tight . . . too tight for some of the trailers. These paths were cut by nature, the erosion in the rainy season carving out the cliffs, and the hills were steep. The MK31/970s with their fuel loads would have a hard time pulling them up the incline; fully loaded, the M970 fuel tanker weighed over 50,000 pounds. As if to increase the danger of the terrain, the landscape was all dirt and sand—not rock. The route could crumble and collapse under the weight of our trucks.

With only a few navigable paths across, we felt certain that there would be IEDs emplaced on whichever path we traveled, especially since we had moved so slowly and been attacked down south by the Rue De Now Zad. The enemy was active and alert. The Route Clearance Platoon began clearing down into the wadi. The path down on the near side was clear and no IEDs were found, but it took two hours to figure that out. They began to clear the far side.

After about an hour, they located a total of three IEDs. Over several hours they confirmed the location of the IEDs and blew them in place. It had been an exhausting day for Thor, the Route Clearance Platoon. Thankfully, it was almost over for them. A British security platoon had traveled the six kilometers from FOB Edinburgh and would escort the convoy the rest of the way. Thor established the security position on the "far side" north of the Lande Nawah.

Lieutenant Thackway's "Foxtrot Callsigns," the British security platoon I was with, remained on the "near side" south of the Lande Nawah. It had taken about five hours to clear the wadi and BIP the IEDs that had been found, and the enemy knew we would be coming back down. It made far more sense to leave a security element on the danger area, and keep it clear for the return trip south.

To further emphasize the security posture, British Longbow helicopters, callsign "Ugly," were doing nap-of-the-earth sorties, flying up and down the wadi as a show of force. Now that everyone knew we were there, we wanted to make it clear that we were not to be trifled with, and that if someone wanted to come fight us they had better bring an army.

The main body pressed on to FOB Edinburgh to complete their offload. By the time they arrived, it was nearly midnight, about 24 hours after the departure from Camp Leatherneck. They remained the whole next day and night, and departed at sunrise the following day. In the meantime, we held the wadi. The Gurkha soldiers whose truck I was in were very friendly, but made it clear that I was expected to take my turn in the turret while we held security on Lande Nawah.

The driver, Thapa, showed me the duty roster, written in immaculate, looping script. "Okay, sir, you are on from 1500 to 1600 and then again in the morning from 0100 to 0200. That will be okay?" He always called me sir. The Ghurkas were precisely polite.

"Sure. Can you show me how to work the GMG? It looks a lot like our Mk19, so I think I can manage it, but I just want to be sure." The Mastiff, basically the same as the American 6x6 MRAP, had a Heckler and Koch 40mm Automatic Grenade Machine Gun, or GMG. The platoon of Foxtrots had four security positions and established communications with each other and with the platoon commander over the British Personal Role Radios, which had a fairly limited range but were more intuitive and user-friendly than most of the American communications gear.

I was more than happy to take my turns on post. I had been a ride-along up to this point and hadn't actually contributed to the mission. By participating in the rotation, it meant one more person in the rotation, and one extra hour between shifts for everyone. I would have three shifts during the 30 or so hours that we planned to be there. The soldier (or Marine, in my case) standing post would keep a lookout for signs of movement or potential attack, using binoculars, a thermal sight, and NVGs. I saw very little on my shifts. There were some dogs running around at night, but nobody trying to sneak up on us.

The trucks of the platoon were set up in a circle, providing a relatively "shielded" position inside the circle. The Route Clearance Platoon had cleared the ground we were sitting on, so there was a relatively low threat of IEDs. Inside the circle, we could drop our flaks and helmets, and relax. Soldiers played cards and read magazines. I had brought my Kindle e-book reader and was reading *Atlas Shrugged*. Though we relaxed, the thought of the potential danger was never far from our minds. As soon as you stepped beyond the trucks, the ground was uncleared and could be littered with IEDs.

A picture of myself reading my Kindle at our security position on the Lande Nawah wadi. The Kindle had been a gift from some family friends before the deployment.

To help build relationships with the locals and to improve our overall security posture, the platoon detached a squad to patrol the village and the wadi around our position. There was another reason, though, that the Ghurkas were particularly eager to patrol—the prospect of buying some livestock to cook for dinner.

Lieutenant Andy Thackway, the platoon commander, was the patrol leader. About ten of us went, including three US Army soldiers from the Route Clearance Platoon. We descended into the wadi, staying in the tracks of the two lead soldiers who swept for IEDs with the handheld British Vallon metal detectors as they walked. We were wearing flak vests with heavy bullet-resistant ceramic plates, but not helmets. The British tactic, given the intent to build relations with the populace, required that we not wear our helmets (though I did choose to bring mine clipped to my flak in case we got attacked) and not wear sunglasses. It was amazing how much of a barrier sunglasses created between people—it dehumanized us to the Afghans, and we wanted to connect on a personal level, so no sunglasses.

We patrolled through the village, which was concentrated on the northern bank of the wadi. The farms here relied on the annual flooding at the beginning of the year, and were smaller than farms outside the wadi. As we approached each farm, the children would run in and alert the family. The women would disappear and the patriarch of the family would come greet us.

"As-Salaam alaikum," we would all say, and wave. Literally, "peace be upon you."

"Wa alaikum as-salaam." The traditional response. From here, all conversations were through Lucky, the interpreter.

Most people did not want to talk very long. Lieutenant Thackway would give it a shot anyway. "We are from NATO, and we are here to help secure your village. We do not want to fight. We are here to help you and your families. Have you seen many Taliban around here?"

Nobody ever saw Taliban. Pretty amazing. In fact, most Afghan civilians claimed that they had never seen, met or heard of any Taliban.

"He says 'No. Please leave,'" Lucky would tell us.

"Can you ask him why he wants us to leave?" Andy asked.

Lucky would. "He says 'Somebody might see me talking to you and hurt my family.'"

We wouldn't push the issue. The point was clear. The Taliban were in the area, and the people felt that interacting with ISAF Coalition forces, British or American, was a risk to themselves and their families.

One villager, though, was very warm and open. He brought his children out. Maybe nine or ten years old, one of the boys walked right up to us and shook all of our hands. He pointed to a black Sharpie marker that I had on my flak.

"What is that?" Lucky interpreted.

A group picture in the Lande Nawah village. Back Row (L-R): The author, CLB-6 S2 Staff Sergeant Pupillo; Center Row (L-R): US Army 162 Engineer Co RCP Platoon Commander Lieutenant Ben Selander, UK Platoon Leader LT Andy Thackway, unknown US Army medic, unknown UK Army Gurkha soldier; Front Row (L-R): Army RCP Sergeant Seeger, unknown Afghan boy, unknown Gurkha soldiers.

"Pen. Pen." I said slowly, and pulled it out. I uncapped it and scribbled in my notebook to show him how it worked. The boy's eyes lit up. I handed him the pen; I had plenty more, so I let him keep it.

We took a picture of our group with the boy, and continued talking to the man. He told us about the Taliban in the area, and that they knew we were coming. All the IEDs were planted at night, he claimed. Routine stuff. But then he said something that took us all by surprise.

Through Lucky, "Can you help us? I found a bomb and I am afraid my family will step on it."

Andy, Lieutenant Selander from the RCP and I talked for a minute. It could be a trap. On the other hand, it could be an IED that could hit one of our convoys in the future, and if true, it would be a great victory for the counterinsurgency and a way to build an ally in the village.

The farmer said that he had marked the spot with rocks, but that he would not go with us, because he might be seen leading us to the IED. He pointed to where these were, on another route out of the wadi that was trafficable for vehicles. That route had been our primary alternate route. We patrolled down the Lande Nawah on the way to the alleged spot, which was about 500 yards down the wadi, and then around a right hand bend that went up a steep incline. As we get closer, we could feel the tension rise. If this was an ambush, it would be initiated after we made the turn and there were high walls on both sides of us.

The threats were three-dimensional. IEDs could be planted in the ground. "Shotgun-like" IEDs full of shrapnel could be emplaced in the cliff walls, aimed to blow off legs and damage internal organs. Insurgents could shoot at us from compounds at ground level or down upon us from the high walls of the wadi. If an attack was coming, it would be initiated at any second. I adjusted the grip on my rifle.

We spotted the circle of piled rocks, right where the farmer said it would be. The Gurkha scout interrogated the site with his Vallon metal detector.

"Oh yeah, I got one. Righto." He spoke English with a British lilt on top of his Nepalese accent.

It was an anti-climactic end to the story, fortunately. One of First Lieutenant Ben Selander's US Army engineers conducted the BIP, blowing the IED in place. The stress of this kind of situation was just as bad as one where we actually got attacked. The anticipation raised heart rates, and put everyone on edge. The smallest glare or reflection immediately caught my eye. It was hard to relax or even breathe calmly for hours afterward.

We went back to the security position, stopping back at the farm to tell the farmer that he had been right and that our engineer took care of the IED for him. The farmer appreciated it. We considered it a small victory for the counterinsurgency, albeit an unsustainable one. We had destroyed a single IED, which would surely be replaced by the enemy.

We bought a goat from the farmer. It was delicious, cooked in a curried stew by the Gurkhas.

The next morning, just after sunrise, a young child and his younger brother brought us some flatbread, a traditional Pashtu offering of friendship and hospitality. We would be leaving that day, and were preparing to depart. The main body was on its way south from FOB Edinburgh, and were expected to arrive at the Lande Nawah midmorning. When they arrived, the trucks at the Security Position would be refueled by the refuelers with the main body, and continue south, led by the RCP and us, the Security Element.

The trip south was relatively smooth, as far as convoys went. There was an IED strike in the Rue De Now Zad wadi, damaging one of the RG-31 MRAPs of the RCP. As night began to fall, the convoy was once again engaged with heavy small arms fire. The British Viking Troop was again on the flanks, engaging the enemy, and we would later find out that they had gotten caught in some of our cross-fire with the insurgents. Fortunately nobody was injured, and no blame could be assessed; the British Vikings were running blacked out and could not communicate with the American trucks. We made sure this did not happen in the future. About 24 hours after departing the Lande Nawah Wadi, we arrived back at Camp Leatherneck.

Since I was riding in a British truck, we returned to the 10th CSLR's motor pool on Camp Bastion. I realized that I had not made plans to arrange a ride back to the American side on Camp Leatherneck. I really didn't want to walk the mile or so back to the CLB-6 compound, but I had no way to call anybody for a ride. I had my pack on. I took a deep breath, sighed, and resigned myself to walk. I took about four steps toward the American side when an MRAP rolled up. Captain Gallagher was in the turret.

"Ready to go, Jeff?"

"Hey, sir! Man, am I glad to see you."

"Yeah, I figured you would need a ride. I want to hear about the Brit side of the mission. It was a wild ride from our side. You heard about the firefight at the back?"

"Oh yeah, sir. I was watching the tracer rounds."

There was no reason to think that any other mission through that area would be any different, and this was just the first of many.

CLB-6 had two more of these missions to bring all of the 1st Battalion, 2d Marines' equipment and personnel to FOB Edinburgh and Musa Qal'eh. My platoon missed out on the second one because we had to do a "milk run" out to FOB Delaram II, about 60 miles west of Camp Leatherneck. The mission was a piece of cake, out and back on the only paved road in the region, Highway 1 or "The Ring Road." While there was always the potential for danger on the Delaram run, the platoon really wanted to be out on Operation Lava 30 with the rest of the company and the Brits. We wanted to be where the action was. We would get our chance, though.

With Operation Lava 30 and our Delaram run complete, my platoon would be on Operation Lava 31. While the Brits had led Operation Lava 29 and Lava 30, CLB-6 Alpha Company would lead Operation Lava 31. And not just Alpha Company, but Second Platoon. We were up. And these were the big leagues.

CHAPTER NINE

OPERATION LAVA 31

APRIL 2010: NORTH OF THE WESTERN CLUSTER, SOUTH OF MUSA QAL'EH, NOW ZAD PROVINCE, AFGHANISTAN

There is a common joke among Marines that "you will never look as cool as you did while you were deployed," and it's true. For me, I know that I will never be as cool as I was on one particular day in April 2010.

I looked cool, but I was terrified. What the hell was I doing there? I gave myself 50/50 odds of making it through without getting shot. I was dismounted, directing recovery operations and trying to avoid getting hit by the hail of gunfire pinging around me, while having this radio conversation with my company commander, Captain John Gallagher (Arawak 6).

Arawak 6: "Arawak 2, this is Arawak 6. Say again your situation, over."

Arawak 2: "Arawak 6, Arawak 2. Platoon sergeant's truck hit large IED, probably command wire det. No immediately life threatening injuries. I have pushed back to the blast site. Security cordon established, we are taking accurate small arms and medium machine gun fire from three positions to our North. We are also receiving mortar fire, 5 rounds impacting within 200 meters."

Arawak 6: "Roger, copy all. You said accurate fire?"

Arawak 2: "Affirmative."

Arawak 6: "How accurate is the fire?"

Arawak 2: "Well . . . they haven't hit me yet."

I can be pretty sarcastic when I want to be, and asking me "exactly how accurate enemy fire is," as it's pinging next to my head, is a good way to elicit that response. *Any more accurate and I wouldn't be talking to you . . .* I was terrified. My Marines, I later found out, just thought I was trying to be funny.

MISSION PREPARATIONS

Operation Lava 31 was a joint US-UK logistics mission from Camp Leatherneck to FOB Edinburgh and the Musa Qal'eh District Center. It was the third in a series of three joint logistics operations aimed at moving the US 1st Battalion, 2d Marines (1/2) into the Musa Qal'eh District, and bringing the Royal Army's Brigade Northwest (Bd. NW) back to Camp Leatherneck. This convoy would be the biggest one yet. Operation Lava 29 and Operation Lava 30 had clocked in with about 150 trucks each. Operation Lava 31 was a third again as large with 205 trucks and over 550 passengers, including US Marines, soldiers, sailors, airmen, DEA civilians, Afghan National Army soldiers, British Royal Army soldiers (including Gurkhas from Nepal), British Royal Marines, and one US Marine dog named Ringo (with his handler, Lance Corporal Green). The scale and scope of this operation cannot be overstated.

The turnaround from Operation Lava 30 to 31 was only about ten days, which is phenomenally fast for a multinational operation of this size. Captain Gallagher, the Alpha Company commander, was the mission commander. I commanded the US main body with about 140 vehicles, while a British counterpart commanded the British contingent.

The planning began while Operation Lava 30 was still outside the wire. Captain Gallagher and I had talked about the mission before he left on Operation Lava 30. My first task was to plan the route for the convoy. I looked at all the intelligence reports in both the American databases and the British J2 Intelligence Section, and overlaid the attacks and intel reports on a map with all the previous Operation Lava route honesty traces. Combined with the Ground Movement Target Indicator (GMTI) radar traces from JSTARS aircraft to show civilian patterns of life, I began to build the route. I pretty quickly came to the conclusion that there was no good route. That is, there were bad routes, and worse routes. Beyond worse, there were routes that were simply impassable. And there was not a route that would take us from Camp Leatherneck to FOB Edinburgh without exposing the convoy to high enemy threat or treacherous terrain . . . or both. Balancing these risks was the principal consideration in building a route. After about 12 hours, I think I had the best of (a very few) less-than-ideal options. The route was approved by the respective mission commanders for the US and British forces, and the planning continued.

Planning meetings with the British continued daily, and we moved closer to execution every day. After the near continuous enemy contact on Operation Lava 29 and 30, we were going to have unprecedented air support for

Operation Lava 31. Between the American ScanEagle UAV, FA-18s, and mixed "skids" (AH-1 and UH-1 helicopters) and the British Longbow "Ugly" and Lynx helicopters, we would have a lot of air support. Each request for an hour of air support required several hours of planning, laying out the specific tasks requested and the intelligence targets for the pilot, as well as syncing the movement with the convoy's timeline.

Once the planning was completed we had a large confirmation brief, with each element leader briefing the composition of his element and any key considerations for the mission. I had briefed my battalion commander before, and conducted dozens of briefings in training at TBS, but had never briefed senior ranking officers of a multinational coalition before. I was more nervous for the brief than for the mission itself. The training worked, and my portion of the brief went well.

A few trucks from the US Maintenance Support Battalion (MSB) truck platoon, callsign Warpig, embedded in the convoy. To protect the guilty, I'll just call their lieutenant "Lt Warpig," although the Marines of my truck team would tell you that he was often just referred to as "Dumbass." Working with him would prove trying. As we were about to head over from our motor pool to the British compound for the confirmation brief, Lt Warpig pulled up in his MATV (with a mineroller attached for an unknown reason) and asked if he could follow us over. Of course we obliged. We were less than a hundred yards down the road when the MATV suddenly veered off the graded road and was sideways in one of the drainage ditches along the side of the road. A set of wheels flew off the mineroller, while the mineroller itself came to rest at an awkward angle.

Captain Gallagher and I pulled a u-turn in our truck, one of the ubiquitous Toyota Hilux SUVs used on Camp Leatherneck, and drove back to make sure everything was alright.

"What do I do?" Lieutenant Warpig asked.

"Is everyone alright?" I countered.

"I think so," he stammered.

"Well, make sure so."

He did, and came back to his original question. The mineroller was badly damaged, while the MATV was stuck and would need a wrecker. "You're gonna need a wrecker for that. Call your COC and request one."

"Can you guys get one of yours? I don't want to tell my COC about this one."

Besides the fact that we were almost late to meet with the Brits and that his unit should support him before we task our Marines, there was no hiding the damage to his truck. He later told us that the mineroller was severely damaged and had to be rebuilt, while the truck had broken a tie rod, and that the driver just didn't know how to drive. If only I had seen this as the warning it was.

With a large group of Marines from 1/2 embedding in the main body to move from Camp Leatherneck to their new area of operations in Musa Qa'leh, which would include a different group of British soldiers from those in the previous missions, additional rehearsals were required. We once again planned for a "round robin" of rehearsals, with Marines and soldiers rotating from station to station, receiving a briefing or practicing a particular skill or maneuver for the mission. My station was the mission briefing station, so I briefed the scheme of maneuver to each individual who would be on the mission. After my brief, a junior Marine from 1st Battalion, 2d Marines came up to me and said, "Sir, I think you know my brother."

The Marine was Lance Corporal Christopher Drake, a 0331 machine-gunner from Burke, VA. I had indeed known his brother, Lance Corporal Daniel Drake, who was a good friend of mine from elementary school. It's amazing what a small world the Marine Corps is.

DAY ONE

The mission preparation was more hectic than ever. Because of the massive size of the convoy, we needed to mount an unprecedented number of machine guns in our trucks to maintain even a semblance of security. Even though every Marine carried a rifle, most Marines were occupied as drivers or assistant drivers and couldn't focus on gunning—we relied on putting dedicated Marines in truck turrets with machine guns.

Maintaining dispersion between the trucks was of paramount importance. If vehicles were closer than a few truck lengths, one IED might damage or disable multiple vehicles. On average, we tried to maintain between 25 to 50 yards distance between trucks. The trucks in this convoy ranged from 8 to 20 yards in length, depending on the type of truck and whether it was towing a trailer. With the huge number of vehicles we had to bring, each requiring a driver and an assistant driver, we only had enough Marines to put a gunner in one out of five trucks. Ideally, we would normally put a gunner in one out of every two or three trucks.

With a gunner in every fifth truck, considering the distance between trucks and the length of the trucks themselves, there was over 250 yards between gunners. On top of that, the gunners alternated which direction they were facing. The first gunner faced forward, covering our front, and the last gunner faced to the rear, covering our "six." The second gunner always faced to the right, covering our right flank. The third gunner faced left, covering the left flank, and so on down the line. There were over five football fields between a gunner and the "adjacent gunner" covering the same side of the convoy. It was less than ideal to say the least.

The hardware to mount the weapons in the trucks was in short supply, so we had to beg, borrow and steal to get enough of the critical universal mounts and universal pintle adapters to put the weapons in the turrets. We were short on traversing and elevation mechanisms that lock the weapon in place and allow for small, precise adjustments in aiming; without these, accurate engagement of targets at long distances was nearly impossible. We would have to make do.

There was never enough time. For the leadership, this inevitably meant there was very little sleeping in the days before a mission. Generally, we were able to get the majority of the junior Marines some sleep, but things were always popping up for unit leaders and NCOs. Before Operation Lava 31, which was set to depart around midnight, I was awake by 0500 the morning prior, after only a few hours of sleep. This schedule was the same one that circumstances forced upon the platoon sergeant, Staff Sergeant Caravalho, the trail maintenance officer, Sergeant Williams, and countless other Marines. For us, it meant that we had been awake for 19 hours before the mission even started.

The battalion leadership would always get on us about executing better rest plans, but did little to facilitate it. They demanded elaborate multi-hour, graphics-intensive PowerPoint briefs with 3D flyovers of the terrain, made last minute changes to the load plan, and only fulfilled equipment shortfalls at the last minute. These all had cascading effects that required attention from the platoon at the eleventh hour.

There was a definite feeling in Alpha Company that the rest of the battalion really didn't understand what it was that we did, or how to best support us (or support us at all, as the case was). Marines joked that the real enemy was not outside the wire, but in the battalion HQ.

As I was walking to the COC for what seemed to be the fifteenth time the evening before Operation Lava 31, I was stopped by Captain Driscoll, the H&S Company commander.

"So, you excited?!" she asked. "I really wish I was going with you."

"It is what it is, ma'am."

"What does that mean? Most of the Marines in H&S would be glad to be in Alpha and go on this mission. You don't know how lucky you are."

"I guess I'm a little more stoic about it or whatever. We just need to stay focused."

"But it's exciting!"

"You keep saying exciting, ma'am. But we know that we are going to get shot at."

"You don't know that . . ." she was as bubbly as ever, and it was annoying as hell.

"I do know that. This is Operation Lava 31. Lava 30 got in a fight. Lava 29 got in a fight. Every Lava between 1 and 28 got in a fight. We are going to get in a fight. So excited isn't the right word. Operation Lava 31 is going to get in a hell of a fight, and people are going to get hurt."

"Well, cheer up."

I walked away. What I wanted to say was, *"Go fuck yourself. Ma'am. You don't know who I am or what I have to do. So take your cheer up and go fuck yourself."*

I wasn't grumpy, I was busy. I wasn't depressed about the situation, I was realistic. I was steeling myself for the fight ahead. In the same way a runner prepares for the gun to go off or a boxer prepares to take a hit and hit back harder, I was mentally preparing myself. We felt that the concept of this was totally lost on most of the battalion outside of Alpha Company. We felt like it was Alpha Company versus the world.

The most stressful part of mission preparation was the convoy manifest. This document was an Excel spreadsheet that listed every vehicle, in order, by vehicle type and serial number, its cargo by serial number, along with each Marine or passenger. For each passenger, the manifest had to include their full name, rank, branch of service, social security number, blood type, rifle serial number, rifle optic serial number, and binocular or other optic serial number. While accountability was essential, there had to be a better way. Did UPS track packages and trucks with numbers manually punched into Excel? For the Operation Lava 31 convoy, with hundreds of passengers from dozens of different units, manifest preparation was a nightmare.

My manifest NCO was Sergeant Thomas Belcher, and he was a work-horse, but he was also the platoon loadmaster and had to supervise cargo loading. Every change came down to the last minute, and the operations officer required that manifest changes be made to the source document in Microsoft Excel, and resubmitted by us because his COC personnel refused to make the changes themselves. At the time, our motor pool on Camp Leatherneck was over a mile from the COC and company office, and I was stuck walking everywhere. Any manifest change required two miles of walking in 120-degree heat. It might seem trivial and like an idle complaint, but on the day before Operation Lava 31, I spent hours walking to the company office to use a computer to make minor manifest changes, and hours walking back to the motor pool to supervise final preparations.

"Lieutenant Clement, why isn't everything ready? We still need updated mission brief PowerPoint slides and Excel spreadsheets," the operations officer demanded.

"Oh, yes, *clearly*, it is *my* inability to manage my time that resulted in mission prep coming down to the last minute, and not ridiculous amounts of bureaucratic nonsense," I thought as I rolled my eyes and trudged off to try to finish things in time. Mission plans and Ground Transportation Requests, for example, had to be submitted in both the SIPR and CENTRIXS computer systems, and because of classification requirements, the requests had to be typed into each computer separately. I swore that if I was ever in the S3 shop, my Marines would bend over backwards to remove administrative restraints on the maneuver elements, the Marines who made CLB-6 a *combat logistics battalion*.

I was more stressed by and spent more time dealing with administrative bureaucratic requirements than with actual mission planning and preparation, and I know the other platoon commanders were, too. Why, exactly, did the commanding officer need a 3D flyover of the mission route in Google Earth? Wouldn't my time have been better spent supervising my Marines or getting sleep before a mission? The lieutenant don't know.

The battle with the chain of command finally ended and we suited up to go. The convoy would leave in the middle of the night, hoping to push east on Route 1 and well north into the desert before the sun came up and the enemy was aware of our presence. The idea was to get through the Mis Mas Wadi right after sunrise and race north, delaying the inevitable fight and keeping the momentum on our side.

With over 200 vehicles, the convoy stretched over 13 kilometers, or 8 miles. We were lined up in columns of ten in the British and American motor pools, with the smaller units who were embedding parked alongside the roads of Camp Leatherneck. Once the first vehicle pushed out the gate, it was over three hours until the last vehicle was outside the wire. As each vehicle left, we checked them off the list.

CLB-6's heavy cargo trucks (weighing 100,000 pounds or more) and armored security trucks on the Operation Lava 31 convoy stretch across the desert.

Our VHF radios were only reliable out to about 3 miles with the radio-controlled IED jammers on, so for this mission I would have three radio nets going—a satellite radio net back to the COC, a short-range VHF internal net (because most trucks only had VHF) and a long-range HF net for the convoy leadership, who would relay all calls on the VFH net to and from the trucks near them.

To further complicate matters, the encryption on the British radios was incompatible with the American radios. A British liaison officer rode with Captain Gallagher with a portable radio and magnetic antenna stuck to the top of the truck. All traffic to and from the Brits would be relayed through her, to Captain Gallagher, and on to us. Improvise, adapt and overcome . . . or something. The movement was steady, but I knew that the real challenge would not begin until the convoy was off the highway.

The convoy turned north. The Route Clearance Platoon, Thor 3–1, was up front, followed by our security element from Alpha Company, First Platoon, Arawak 1. The American contingent of the main body was next, and was under my command. The British main body cargo element was behind us. Last was a security contingent of three trucks led by our company operations chief, Gunnery Sergeant Mario Locklear, "Bad Boy."

About half of the convoy was off Route 1 when the first HET got stuck. The HET was a massive tractor trailer, capable of carrying loads exceeding 100,000 pounds. We had put them near the front of the convoy because they would set the pace—by putting the slowest trucks near the front, it helped ensure the front of the convoy didn't run off without them. They were simply not designed for use off road, and just as on previous missions, one of them had blown the hydraulics on the trailer. By then, it was about 0200 in the morning.

The front of the convoy was already within sight of the Lone Hill. As day began to break, Captain Gallagher pushed one of the security trucks to the top of the Lone Hill to keep watch and to provide a visible deterrent to any enemy fighters. The enemy knew we were there, surely. We might as well take the dominant terrain and deny it to them.

We sat. We waited. Daylight was burning, and we weren't moving yet. Six or seven hours passed while we waited, once again, for a QRF from Camp Leatherneck to return the damaged HET and allow the convoy to continue to FOB Edinburgh. By midmorning we were ready to get going again, but there was a new problem. The seven hours of idling had burned a lot of fuel. Most of our trucks were good for about 30 hours at our crawling pace between refueling, and we had killed seven of them. The trucks had enough fuel at the time, but I did the math in my head, and wasn't happy about where we would run out of fuel, somewhere near the Salaam Bazaar, which was not where I wanted to conduct refueling operations. More precisely, it was exactly where I *didn't* want to stop to refuel.

We began refueling each truck from one of several of the convoy's M970 fuel tankers. When I could, I would help with the refueling because it gave me a chance to get out of my truck and talk to the Marines. The attitude that morning was a frustrated one; even the most junior lance corporals knew how long we still had to go, and that the enemy was waiting for us. We had already seen a good number of dickers, Afghan fighters monitoring our actions, on motorcycles checking out the convoy and heading north. They would be waiting for us. We would see them again, we knew.

Progress. Slow movement forward. Through the heat, we pushed up to the Mis Mas Wadi. Of course, once again this meant dismounted clearance of the wadi by the engineers. As I recall, we didn't find or hit any IEDs in it that time, and there were no major delays at the Mis Mas or the Rue De Now Zad that I can remember. But then we got up to the Western Cluster, a region thick with poppy fields, mud compounds, and insurgent activity. Besides the enemy, the poppy fields and mud compounds made the area very dangerous due to the limited trafficability. Poppy flowers are grown in thick mud. The fields are, in fact, flooded with several inches of water during the growing season and trap even the most aggressive off-road vehicles. Our restricted mobility meant we were very easy to target with IEDs.

Poppy fields on the left (irrigated with several inches of water) and wheat fields on the right of this route limited the convoy's mobility to a single route. Insurgents could easily target the convoy by emplacing an IED several hundred meters ahead of us on the route they knew we were stuck on.

We stayed in the open desert as long as possible, where the freedom to maneuver limited the risk of IEDs, but we had to cut through the compounds at some point. The Route Clearance Platoon entered the compounds around 1600. The route was narrow, with barely enough space between the mud walls to fit our trucks through. Almost immediately, the RCP determined they would have to clear the route dismounted. The three kilometers to get through would take something like 15 hours to clear. And we knew it going in. 15 hours of painful, step-by-step minesweeping.

IEDs were found almost immediately. The first one was big, with a high metallic signature. It seemed almost too easy that the IED was found that quickly, and the ease of that find just added to the stress. Were we *supposed* to find that piece of metal, so that while dealing with it, a hidden, more deadly IED would explode or an ambush would erupt?

The engineers began interrogating the suspected IED, and unearthed three 120mm Russian mortars strung together with det cord and a pressure plate. This was the most sophisticated IED that had been seen in the area in a long time, and also one of the most deadly. We were up against the insurgent varsity squad, and they weren't messing around.

I had been awake for 38 hours by that time. The sun had begun to set, but there was nowhere to go. The convoy inched forward, moving only as fast as the soldiers up front could clear. Clearing with a metal detector is exhausting, especially while wearing body armor and under the intense stress of possibly being in a sniper's crosshairs. The Route Clearance Platoon soon asked for our Marines to rotate in and take turns on the metal detectors. Though our Marines were not engineers, everyone was trained on how to use the metal detectors to search for IEDs, and the truck drivers of CLB-6 did what they had to do.

IEDs were found every few dozen meters. The convoy would inch forward, and then halt while the IEDs were "BIP'd," deliberately exploded with C4 explosives. The sun was near the horizon.

The "evening transition period," the most dangerous time for us, was approaching. There was too much light for our infrared NVGs to provide good contrast and a distinct advantage, but too little light for ideal vision with human eyes alone. The relatively short range and limited visibility through our truck windows limited the effectiveness of our PVS-14 NVGs anyway. In other words, all our technology was nullified, and during the evening transition period, we were reduced to an even playing field with the insurgents.

On that day, as on so many others, we watched the sun dip below the horizon, and like the opening bars of a symphony, the enemy began pouring forth heavy, sustained, accurate small arms fire. The AK47 family of weapons is the most pervasive weapon in that region. Made of stamped metal parts, they were cheap, reliable, and deadly accurate at ranges under 300 to 400 meters. The AK47 makes a distinctive *clatta-clack* sound that is louder, rounder and somewhat more mechanical, and less surgical, less precise than the American M16s. We were in a cross-fire, being shot at from both sides. There was nowhere to go forward except at the pace that the route could be cleared, and nowhere to go back. Racing forward was a sure way to strike an IED, destroying a truck, injuring our people, and creating a blocked ambush for ourselves.

The bulk of the fire seemed to be concentrated on the middle of the con-voy, the main body. This was a relief, since the Route Clearance Platoon and our dismounted sweepers were outside the protective enclave of vehicle armor.

Our convoy was well armored. Every truck could stop AK47 bullets eas-ily, and even if our tires were targeted, most vehicles had a Central Tire Infla-tion System that could flood the tires with high-pressure air as fast as it would flow out through a small number of bullet holes. The key for us was to keep our gunners low in their turrets, returning fire and suppressing the enemy. With gunners in only one of every five trucks, most Marines were in trucks without an option. They had no choice but to sit there and listen to the rounds *ping* off their armor. The windows were bulletproof to a point—after a sustained hail of bullets, the windows could shatter and many did. No bullets got through the armor, but a few tires were hit and quite a bit of cargo was damaged.

I was especially concerned about the potential for rocket-propelled gren-ade fire. With mud buildings just a few meters from many of our trucks, an enemy fighter could pop out from around a corner and blast a truck broadside in one of the passenger doors.

We saw a few of the distinct smoke trails that an RPG-7 leaves behind as it is fired. The sound is unlike anything else. When fired, there is an initial explosion propelling the round forward sounding like a *KGH!*, immediately followed by the more directed rocket jet—*schew. KGHschew!*

I have thought a lot about this sound, and the sounds of all the weapons that were fired at us, as well as the ones that we fired back at the Afghans who were attacking. The word "onomatopoeia" is a noun that means, according to Webster, "the creation of words that imitate sounds." The onomatopoeia of the sound of each incoming weapon is important. The Marines who were being fired at will never forget it. When an RPG round hit its target, it would explode with the sharp punch and black smoke of high-explosives. *Boom.*

The RPG is a deadly Russian weapon designed to punch through armor, and would go cleanly through any of our trucks. There was just enough light from the moon to see the smoke trails of the RPGs' rocket motors. Except for the firefight, the night was quiet. *KGHschewBoom.*

Thankfully, the insurgents firing the RPGs at us were either unable or unaware of how to properly employ the RPG-7, and never set up a great shot. Only one vehicle was hit, a MATV, and the RPG struck the weight plate of its mineroller. The mineroller was loaded with about 5000 pounds of 8" steel plates to press down on the ground in front of the truck, so when the RPG round struck the plates, it exploded, doing no real damage to anything or anyone. The explosion from the relatively small warhead still created a tremendous, percussive blastwave.

The back and middle of the convoy repelled the enemy for about an hour. It was tactical whack-a-mole. Somebody would pop up and start shooting, we would shoot back. *Clatter-Clack*. Tracers were going in every direction. RPGs. *KGHschewBoom*. I was trying to keep everything together and keep the Marines calm. It was dangerous for me to bring my truck up on either of our flanks, because as our gunners fired, we could cross into the stream of their bullets. I was stuck in my truck, and my truck had to stay in its position in the convoy. I noted positions of enemy fighters and talked through the scenario on the radio as slowly and calmly as I could.

"Alright guys, this is Buzz. Stay cool as a cucumber. Identify targets as you see them, but don't shoot just to shoot."

Ammunition was always in short supply for the insurgents. After a while, having expended thousands of rounds, they would realize they were not going to have much impact on us, and they would retreat. The enemy "shoot and scoot" tactics of not lingering in any one position made it difficult to tell how many of the enemy we had injured or killed. Just because an enemy firing position had been silenced did not mean that the fighter was dead. We needed to recover and reset from the firefight, even though we didn't have any casualties. Primarily, we had to redistribute ammo between trucks, resupplying those that had been heavily engaged for most of the firefight.

It was completely dark now. The Marines at the front continued sweeping slowly, creeping onward throughout the night. More IEDs. More BIPs.

"Stand by for Blow In Place. Five minutes."

I could hear the fatigue in Lieutenant Selander's voice.

Through the night, we cleared the route. Inching forward. We dropped the convoy down to "50%," meaning that half of the Marines could go to sleep. One Marine in every truck needed to be awake, plus all the gunners. There was only one platoon commander though, and I was not comfortable going to sleep. I could not have slept if I tried. Captain Gallagher felt the same way. We checked in with each other on the radio every few minutes.

"Arawak 6, this is Buzz, radio check, over."

"Buzz, Arawak 6. Got you Lima Charlie," he responded, using the phonetic alphabet for the letters L and C, slang for loud and clear. "Interrogative, uhh, how is it back there?"

"Quiet, nothing going on, over."

"Roger, nothing up here. Slow progress. We really need the sun to start coming up. Stand by for something during the transition time."

"Solid copy, over."

The sun started to come up. I could see the BFT icons for the front trucks nearing the far end of the compounds. Something like a dozen IEDs had been found. It had been a long night.

DAY TWO

0500. I had been awake for 48 hours now. More RipIts. My truck team took care of me. In addition to bottled water and MREs, we could get Gatorade and RipIts through the supply system at Camp Leatherneck. RipIts are an off-brand energy drink, like a cheap Red Bull. Packed in squat little 8-ounce cans, they came in a few different flavors. Corporal Sena, my gunner, knew that my favorites were the red Power Punch and the yellow CitrusX flavors. I never asked him to, but he always got me a case of one or the other. I don't know how he did it, but I didn't ask. Forty-eight hours without sleep. More RipIts.

I was watching the little blue icon of the front truck on my BFT screen, overlaid on a satellite image of where we were. We finally got out of the compounds on the other side. We should start moving. There was a little wadi, an offshoot of the Lande Nawah, on the other side to clear through, and then it was back to three to five mph, which would feel like flying. The threat would go down, at least for a while, until we got to the Lande Nawah Wadi.

"Oscar Mike." We started inching forward, first one truck, then the one behind it, and the one behind it, and the one behind it. A slow rhythm, like a slinky.

BOOM. An LVSR was engulfed in a cloud of dust. It had only just shifted forward; I hadn't even seen it move forward. They hadn't left the tracks, but it was the heaviest truck that far forward. Some IEDs were set only to detonate under the heaviest trucks, an effort to make recoveries harder for us.

"IED IED IED!" I called on the radio.

"I'm rolling!" Lance Corporal Sedam, my driver, didn't wait to be told what to do. He knew what to do.

I clicked the radio. "Buzz is pushing up."

"Buzz, Arawak 6, come in," called Captain Gallagher, who was up toward the front. "What's the situation?"

"A6, Buzz. IED hit an LVSR. I'll be at the strike site in a sec, over."

"Alright, roger. Standing by."

"Roger. I think we should keep the front moving, and open up the dispersion in the security platoon to take up the space, keep it secure."

"Concur."

My truck pushed up to the damaged LVSR, and drove around it with the mineroller on our MATV. If there were any "secondary IEDs" designed to hit rescuers or medical personnel, the truck would hit them instead, a far preferable option. Lance Corporal Quinn Gordon and Corporal Jeremy Salsberry, the passengers of the LVSR, were conscious but shaken. Corporal Salsberry's leg was injured and he couldn't walk unassisted. Lance Corporal Gordon was rattled and only barely lucid, like a boxer who'd been hit one too many times this round.

Staff Sergeant Caravalho had pushed up to the downed truck as well, and we began debating the best way to recover the LVSR. An LVSR is a massive 10-wheeled heavy cargo vehicle, and since the front wheel had been damaged, knocking out steering, it would have to be lift-towed. We had two wrecker variants. The MK36 MTVR wrecker was rated to lift-tow 48,000 lbs. The MK48/15 LVS wrecker could only lift-tow 32,000 pounds and it had a complicated towing mechanism and a crane capacity of only 9,000 pounds. I didn't really like taking the LVS wreckers out, but sometimes it was the only option available. Since the LVSR weighed over 60,000 pounds, the LVS wrecker was just about useless in this situation.

I did have two more options that would present a better long-term option, but they would take longer to implement. The RCP had a M984 HEMMT wrecker, but it was three miles away on the other side of the danger zone that had just been cleared. To get it back to the downed LVSR, I would have to stop all traffic through the compounds to bring the wrecker back the other way. This would completely stop the convoy for close to an hour.

The other option was to use a British Man SV(R), a massive 8x8 wrecker far stronger than anything we had. The Marine Corps had given us the MKR18 LVSR cargo truck without an accompanying vehicle capable of recovering it—we finally got MKR15 LVSR wreckers a year later, so the Brits offered us the best choice. The closest SV(R) was near the back of the convoy with the rest of the British element, and would take over an hour to bring up to the front. We couldn't take the risk of bringing the wrecker, one of our most valuable assets, outside the cleared tracks, so I decided to drag the LVSR out of the way to allow the convoy to pass by. The SV(R) would stay in the tracks until it got up to the LVSR, and then pick it up.

My primary concern was to get the convoy moving again. We tried to use an MK48/15 LVS wrecker but it wasn't strong enough, so we had to get the LVSR out of the way with an MK36. After that, I could worry about setting up a sustainable option like the British SV(R) to recover the LVSR back to Camp Leatherneck. Had anyone ever done a front lift-tow of an LVSR with an MK36? We didn't have much choice in the short term. Inch by inch, the LVSR was pulled up. It wasn't the metal components of the hitch on the wrecker that I worried would fail, it was a catastrophic blowout of the main lifting cylinder, rendering the wrecker useless for the rest of the mission.

As the sun rises, an MK36 wrecker is hooked up to an LVSR whose front two axles had been destroyed by an IED.

The MK36 did it, though. Ask nicely, and your truck will do almost anything for you. As it started to pull forward, the front wheels of the MK36 were bouncing off the ground because of the heavy load on the back. The driver could only pull straight forward with the front wheels in the air, but it was enough. In less than thirty minutes, a quick turnaround that still felt like an eternity, the convoy was moving forward again, a new record for CLB-6. The Brits helped us out when they got their SV(R) up to the LVSR, snatching it up and towing it the rest of the way to FOB Edinburgh.

It was mid morning when my truck passed through the compounds and mud buildings to emerge on the other side. The front of the convoy was racing forward at about 8 mph. My BFT screen updated, and suddenly a gap appeared in the convoy. About 1000 meters long, there was a distinct lack of icons on a section of the convoy somewhere in the middle. I called Staff Sergeant Caravalho.

"Smokecheck, this is Buzz. Do you see that gap? Can you check it out?"

"Roger, Buzz, I'm on my way."

He got there, and found that an MTVR had stalled, and by the time the driver got the truck started, he had lost track of the convoy in front of him.

"Buzz, I'm bringing the convoy up." Staff Sergeant Caravalho, in his MATV, was now at the front of that line and was racing forward to close the gap.

The gap was down to about 500 meters. An explosion. The biggest we'd ever heard.

"IED IED IED!" We heard Lieutenant Warpig, our ridealong, on the radio. He was about thirty or forty trucks behind my position—almost two miles back.

My gunner leaned down and shouted into the truck, "Sir, we got red smoke."

TBS teaches lieutenants to always maintain an external focus; one of the harshest criticisms a lieutenant could receive was to be "internal." The point is to create a mindset where officers immediately focus on taking care of their Marines and defeating the enemy, instead of focusing "internally," on fear and self-preservation. The training worked.

"Go!" I shouted. I wasn't afraid, not at that moment anyway.

Red smoke grenades signaled that somebody had been seriously injured in an IED strike.

"I'm flipping this bitch around." Lance Corporal Sedam, the driver, pulled a U-turn and we raced toward the IED strike at high speed. "Hold on! This is gonna bounce." We flew over a small ditch, the MATV airborne.

Smoke grenades were used as a signal in an IED strike. Green smoke meant that everyone in the truck was okay, or at least not in need of immediate lifesaving medical attention. Red smoke meant the opposite. One of my Marines was dying. Massive hemorrhage can kill in just a few minutes, and I didn't have a corpsman anywhere near there.

"Smokecheck, this is Buzz, come in."

Silence.

"Smokecheck, Buzz, come in."

Silence. Finally, after what seemed like an eternity, "Buzz, Smokecheck, yeah, it was my truck." He was pretty shaken.

"Roger, I'm almost there." All traffic had stopped behind him.

I arrived at the spot where his truck had been hit and assessed the damage. The mineroller was destroyed, and the whole front end of the MATV had been gutted. The right front wheel was gone. He had kept all his Marines inside the truck until the area could be cleared. We pulled up alongside, running our mineroller beside the truck to clear the ground for secondary IEDs aimed at dismounted first responders. There were none.

I jumped out, grabbed my medical bag, and ran to the truck. I ripped open his door. "Who's hurt?" The red smoke had everyone amped up.

"Nobody, that bad, anyway."

"Oh, you guys didn't throw the red smoke?"

"No, Buzz, dunno."

"Huh. Ok." I later found out that it was Lieutenant Warpig, goon that he was, who had jumped the gun and thrown the red smoke unnecessarily. I made a point to tell him to sit back and shut up for the rest of the trip. We exposed ourselves to a lot of needless risk because of his foolishness, but it wasn't the first time and it wouldn't be the last. "Let's set up some security and get this convoy moving again."

Until we got more guntrucks in position, Marines would have to defend the position using their M4 rifles.

The first priority was to get the whole convoy moving again, which we couldn't do until the damaged truck and mineroller were recovered. We would need some wreckers, but the closest one was at the back of the convoy. There was an LVS MK48/15 wrecker at the front, and the trail maintenance officer, Sergeant Williams, was just a few trucks back. I pushed my MATV

From left to right, Lance Corporal Neubauer, Lance Corporal Gordon ("Delta") and Lance Corporal Gorton ("Tango") provide security for a recovery site. Their IED-damaged truck sits in the background.

back to his position and told him to follow me with his truck, but we couldn't get through on the left side of the convoy because of the poppy fields. There was already one MRAP stuck in the mud of the poppy fields—I didn't know whose it was but that wasn't my immediate problem. There was a mud compound wall on the other side of the convoy.

"Sedam, can you put this truck through that wall?" I asked my driver.

"Hell yeah, sir! For real?"

"Do it."

Lance Corporal Sedam backed the truck up and lined up his approach. He hit the gas and we were pressed against our seats as the truck accelerated. The mineroller plowed through the compound wall in a cloud of dust and rubble, leaving clumps of mud covering the mineroller and the hood of the truck. It was like something out of a movie. He had cleared enough space to bring Sergeant Williams' maintenance truck up to the site. Sergeant Williams then set to work disconnecting the mineroller and dragging it out of the way. Staff Sergeant Caravalho had set up dismounted security with a few Marines, but we needed more firepower. I called Sergeant Galante, the security team leader, on the radio.

"Godfather, this is Buzz. I need you to push back here to help with security." Staff Sergeant Caravalho was already running around, moving some of the trucks with guns. The children and women who had previously been watching us had scattered. This was not a good sign.

"Roger, Buzz. On my way."

Sergeant Williams had, by now, dragged Staff Sergeant Caravalho's damaged MATV out of the way with his truck and some chains, which allowed the convoy to get moving again. I started waving the trucks forward. We had to get the cargo trucks moving so that I could bring up the MK36 wrecker that was at the back of the American main body. I then turned my attention to the MRAP stuck in the poppy field. I raised them on the radio.

"Uh, yeah, Buzz, this is Warpig. We're stuck out here."

I had no idea what the hell he had been doing out there to begin with. I sent Sergeant Williams and his driver, Lance Corporal Renno, to drag them out with their MTVR. Less talented drivers would have gotten stuck themselves, but Lance Corporal Renno was a champ.

Snap. It sounded like someone had popped a bag of chips next to my foot. "What was that?" I asked.

"Uh, I wouldn't worry about it, sir. Just don't stand still too long," Staff Sergeant Caravalho said with a grin.

Small arms fire. We had security trucks all around, ready to return fire, and one of 1/2's machine gun teams had dismounted as well to provide more support. Every Marine on the ground began looking for targets, scanning the mud rooftops with the Rifle Combat Optic (RCO) gunsight on their rifle.

We were now taking heavy, accurate and sustained fire from the compounds to the north, about 100 meters away. The Marines started returning fire. The M240 snapped into action, and so did an Mk19. The Mk19 automatic grenade launcher is terrifying to be on the wrong end of. It emits a sharp explosion as it fires the grenades, followed by a short delay as they fly through the air, followed by the explosion of the 40mm grenades. *Bam bam bam bam . . . whump whump whump whump. Bam bam bam bam . . . whump whump whump whump.*

The desert sand frequently jammed the weapon and it required a special lubricant called "LSA" that was practically impossible to get ahold of, but this Marine seemed to be on top of his game. He kept his gun in the fight. *Bam bam bam bam . . . whump whump whump whump.* I took cover behind the damaged MATV, waiting for the MK36 from the back to pass by. I ran out and waved for an empty flatbed truck to pull in next to the damaged mineroller.

Enemy rounds were flying everywhere, pinging off the trucks, targeting Staff Sergeant Caravalho and me. I was terrified, just like everyone else. But I realized that the Marines were looking to see how I reacted and looking for direction; I couldn't afford to be paralyzed by fear. Finally, enough trucks had passed and the wrecker was there. I had started to doubt it would ever arrive, but waved it in next to the MATV.

Corporal James Prickett, callsign "Reaper," hopped out.

"Damn, sir, it had to be this one? Why you got this whack-ass adapter on your truck, staff sergeant?" The mineroller bracket on the front of the MATVs was a first-generation adapter, and did not have tow points on it. This was later identified as a critical flaw and fixed for future models, but for us there was no way to easily hitch it to the wrecker to recover the truck. "It's gonna take me a minute, but I can prolly snatch it with some chains," drawled Corporal Prickett. He set to work, wrapping chains through the hitch point on his wrecker and around the mineroller bracket. "It should lift, but steering's gonna be a bitch."

I stopped traffic once again because we needed another wrecker to recover the destroyed mineroller onto the flatbed we'd pulled over earlier. I sent Sergeant Galante to bring it back from the front of the convoy.

Again, another eternity. I crawled under the MATV to cage the brakes, really hoping that no bullets hit my feet that were sticking out from under the truck.

KGH-*schew!* An RPG. The enemy attack was intensifying. I was back behind the damaged MATV, peering through the RCO on my rifle trying to get positive identification on an enemy position. They kept bouncing around, popping up and firing once from one spot, and then moving to another spot within the mud compounds. *Whump-BOOM.* Black smoke. Mortars. The first one fell about 200 meters north of the recovery site. A minute passed. Everything was waiting on that MK48/15 to get the mineroller.

Corporal Prickett was still working on the MATV, struggling with the chains.

Whump-BOOM. Another mortar. This one closer, but from the compounds south of the convoy. This was bad. We were being bracketed. A reliable technique to adjust indirect fires like mortars or artillery, bracketing relies on dropping the first round on one side of the target, and the second on the other side, reducing the adjustment each time, walking the rounds onto the target. That the first mortar was short of us (from where I guessed the point of origin was), and the second was long, meant that the enemy mortar team knew what they were doing and had a spotter with a radio adjusting the rounds. While this was going on, I was on the radio with Captain Gallagher, relayed through one of the Army trucks since I was on a handheld PRC-152 with limited range.

Arawak 6: "Arawak 2, this is Arawak 6. Say again your situation, over."

Arawak 2: "Arawak 6, Arawak 2. Platoon sergeant's truck hit large IED, probably command wire det. No immediately life threatening injuries. I have pushed back to the blast site. Security cordon established, we are taking accurate small arms and medium machine gun fire from three positions to our North. We are also receiving mortar fire, 5 rounds impacting within 200 meters."

Arawak 6: "Roger, copy all. You said accurate fire?"

Arawak 2: "Affirmative."

Arawak 6: "How accurate is the fire?"

Arawak 2: "Well . . . they haven't hit me yet."

Sergeant Galante rolled back in with the MK48/15 wrecker. Sergeant Williams took charge, rounds impacting all around him. He paused just long enough to flip the bird to the attackers as he climbed over the damaged mineroller, strapping it to a flatbed truck for recovery. The rear of the convoy had been halted for almost ten minutes so that we could pull the wrecker from the front. The front of the convoy had kept moving, and once again there was a gap, probably about two kilometers long now. Not good, but the front of the convoy had to keep moving to pull the rear up. Stopping now was the worst thing we could do. I clapped Sergeant Galante on the back. "I need you to reconnect this convoy. Get them moving."

"Got it, Buzz."

He jumped up in his MRAP, hanging out the door, and waved for the rest of the trucks to follow him. He made it about 400 meters before there was a small explosion under his left front tire.

"This is Godfather, IED IED IED!"

A pause. The truck started rolling again.

"Buzz and Smokecheck, Godfather. We're a little shaken, but we're not hurt. I think we can limp the truck up to the convoy. We'll fix it later." The front tire was missing a big chunk, but he managed to reconnect the convoy and then pulled over, waiting for a wrecker to help him change the tire.

We finished recovering the MATV and the mineroller, taking fire the whole time. Staff Sergeant Caravalho and I double-checked that all of our Marines were back in the trucks, fist-bumped, and we jumped in trucks.

Terrifying. Exhilarating. I knew I would never look so cool or badass again. We pushed up to the convoy, and I finally took a breath. I was exhausted.

"Hey guys, do we have any water in here?"

Lance Corporal Williams, the radio operator, handed me one. "Sure thing, sir."

"Uh, can I have like …three more?" He laughed and handed them to me.

From the time the IED had hit Staff Sergeant Caravalho's truck, it was only 57 minutes to when the recovery was complete, which was actually a pretty good performance, given that we had to recover a MATV, a mineroller, free a vehicle from the mud of the poppy fields, get two wreckers to the site, take fire, and hit a secondary IED (when Godfather was relinking the convoy). When I got back in my truck and realized how little time had passed, I couldn't believe it.

The American half of the convoy was out of the compounds, but the British contingent at the rear was still back there. The enemy never broke contact, and continued firing and dropping mortar rounds on them. The convoy did not hit any more IEDS, though, and was able to push through.

Things were working exactly the way they were supposed to, given the circumstances. Captain Gallagher, as the overall mission commander, remained focused on the end objective, getting to FOB Edinburgh. I could focus on the details of the recovery and the firefight, the proverbial point of friction. When the main body (and my platoon, specifically) was heavily engaged with the blocked ambush, he continued driving the front of the convoy and the RCP, increasing dispersion in the security element to absorb any gaps. The end result was that the IED strike and ambush had not even slowed the convoy down in the slightest, because the Route Clearance Platoon, the slowest and most deliberate movers at the front of the convoy, had not slowed down. By the time I got up to the Lande Nawah Wadi, the front of the convoy had been there for nearly three hours. The RCP had cleared down into the wadi, and was working their way up the other side.

It was nearly dark. The last time most vehicles had refueled was at the Lone Hill, thirty-some-odd hours ago. Shutting down overnight had saved a lot of fuel, but almost everyone was on fumes. I organized a refueling operation to get everyone topped off before night fell and before they navigated the wadi. It was only a short drive from the Lande Nawah to FOB Edinburgh, six miles or so, but that could take hours or days. Nobody knew.

For every previous Operation Lava mission, the British had sent a security platoon south from FOB Edinburgh. But because of a heavy firefight up north of Musa Qal'eh, near Panda Ridge, there were no forces available to meet us down south. We would be on our own all the way in.

Staff Sergeant Caravalho was really not feeling well—the IED had hit him hard, and his truck had been destroyed. He was riding in one of the security guntrucks, so I dropped back to the end of the American main body to make sure that every truck and Marine got through. The descent into the wadi was steep and winding. The last thirty meters dropped down suddenly and curved sharply to the left.

The descent into the Lande Nawah wadi was treacherous. The wadi itself was more of a canyon—entire villages and farms were built within it. The zone was considered "high threat." We encountered dozens of IEDs in and around this danger area.

Most of the trucks were through the wadi. The second to last truck, one of the MK36 wreckers, started down the trail into the Lande Nawah, so I jumped in my truck and waved to the lead British vehicle, who would follow me.

We stopped moving. What was going on? It had just gotten dark, but visibility wasn't too bad. I stood on top of my truck to see what I could see. I couldn't see anything. A couple of my Marines came running up the hill.

"Hey sir, one of those guys from 1/2 flipped his MRAP."

"At the bottom?" Probably right on the left-hand curve.

"Yup. Right at the turn."

I jumped out and ran down the hill, trying to stay in the tire tracks so as to not step on an IED. Sure enough, the driver had not seen the turn until too late, and overshot the turn, rolling the MRAP onto its passenger side. The exhaust system and air intakes were torn up and cracked, but the driver was okay.

2100. I had been awake for 64 hours. The convoy was stopped. Another problem, just when we were almost there. I brought up a wrecker and we debated the best way to recover the truck.

"What if we use the crane to pull the truck up?" somebody said.

"No way. That truck weighs over 35,000 pounds. The crane on the 36 is only rated for 22,000."

"We're gonna have to roll it back up," I insisted.

"Alright, sir, I guess I could use the dual winches on the back."

It took about an hour, but we got the MRAP out and the platoon's mechanic, Sergeant Williams, gave the truck a once over.

"It's fine to drive, sir. The air intake is smashed, but the second filter will catch any dust for the short trip. It's safe." He turned to the Marine driving it. "Alright, killer, get moving."

"I'm not driving that truck. It could have been damaged," the lance corporal insisted.

Sergeant Galante, my security team leader, countered, "If anyone damaged it, it was you when you missed the turn."

"How could I have seen that turn?"

"The 150 drivers in front of you managed to make it. Get moving."

"No. You'll have to tow the truck." Who was this Marine and who did he think he was? His recklessness had already damaged equipment and endangered Marines, and now he was being insubordinate outside the wire in an area known to be full of IEDs. I'd had enough. I interjected.

Less than six inches from the Marine's face, I let him have it, waving my "knife hands" and aggressively gesturing at him. "That's enough. I'm not endangering anybody else by making them tow the truck that you rolled by your carelessness. We have waited here long enough. My TMO says the truck is safe to drive. You are *ordered* to drive that truck the last ten kilometers to FOB Edinburgh. If you refuse, I will charge you under Article 92? Any questions?"

"No." He looked sullen.

"No *whaaaat?*" Sergeant Galante smiled.

"No, *sir.*"

"Sergeant Galante, you got this?" I turned back toward my truck.

"Got it, sir." He turned to the lance corporal. "Get in your truck. Not another word."

We were finally moving again. It was completely dark, and took several hours to get over the rolling hills north of the Lande Nawah and up to the plateau that FOB Edinburgh sat on.

0200 in the morning. I was losing track of what day it was after 69 hours awake. My truck team was finally inside the wire. I found Captain Gallagher and briefed him on what had happened, and by the time I returned I found my Marines asleep around the truck. They had set up a cot for me and put my pack on it. They really went out of their way to take great care of me. I pulled out my iPod to put on some music as I fell asleep. I didn't make it through the first line of the first song before I was out.

DAY THREE

The British had decided to remain at the Lande Nawah to avoid navigating the treacherous trail in the dark. Their trucks started pouring in through the gate at the entry control point around 0900. I would have seen them, but I was still asleep. Captain Gallagher woke me.

"Hey, Jeff, you'll need to take some of the loads to the District Center."

"What? Oh, sorry sir, I didn't realize it was you. I thought everything was staying here?"

"Yeah, it was. But now it's not. Not much we can do about it, I'm afraid. Can you leave by noon?"

I looked at my watch. Three hours? "Should be okay, sir. I'll get 'em going. Who has a list of the loads that need to go?"

"Nobody, yet." He smirked. "Great, right. 'Take something! We don't know what yet, but we'll tell you at the last minute.'"

Nothing out of the ordinary, really. I started to get organized. Only about five miles from FOB Edinburgh, the Musa Qal'eh District Center, or MQDC, was in the heart of the city of Musa Qal'eh and was a critical coalition position, securing the seat of the district government and the Musa Qal'eh bazaar. The five miles to MQDC were not totally secured, and the route was easily IED'd. Further, there was a wadi as big as the Lande Nawah, and the Musa Qal'eh River to cross. With no bridge over the water, we would have to ford the river, expected to be about two feet deep.

Once we had the cargo list, I put together the convoy and briefed the Marines, US and British soldiers who would be coming. The convoy consisted of about twelve cargo trucks, two wreckers to help offload, and a handful of security vehicles. Corporal Zeitz, Second Platoon's scout, led the way. Fording the Musa Qal'eh River for the first time was not without some apprehension, but the scout, "Peewee," got the small convoy there without a hitch.

Arriving in the District Center, I got us checked in with the company gunny, and found out where they wanted the loads. We had only a few short hours to get unloaded and back to FOB Edinburgh before night fell . . . and I had a mission of my own to complete. I grabbed my interpreter, Raufi, an Afghan native from Kabul who was quiet, but friendly.

"Raufi, can you talk to some of the Afghan soldiers near here and ask them to run to the bazaar and find us two goats?"

"Goats?" He laughed.

"Yeah, goats." I laughed back. "How much for goats?"

"Oh, probably $80 for goats. It's not a good season."

"Ok, tell them I'll give them $90 each if they are back in two hours."

Two hours later Raufi turned up along with an Afghan who had two goats on a rope, one white and one black. I handed them the money and they handed me the rope, and for the next couple hours I walked around the Musa Qal'eh District Center supervising the offload of cargo with two goats in tow. My Marines took pictures and laughed. Anything to blow off steam for a few minutes.

"Hey Marine!" It was a voice I didn't recognize. I turned around.

"Yes?"

"Just who the hell are you?" It was 1/2's sergeant major or one of their first sergeants. *Brilliant*, I thought, sarcastically.

"I'm Lieutenant Clement, convoy commander of this unit. Can I help you?" I still had the goats on a leash.

"Yeah, you can help me. Help me understand what you're going to do with those goats."

"I'm going to eat them. Not by myself, but me and my Marines . . . we're gonna eat 'em."

"The hell you are. Whose goats are they?"

"They're my goats. I bought them. They're mine. And I'm gonna eat them."

"Nobody said you could eat goats."

"Nobody said I couldn't, either. Now if you'll excuse me, I have work to do." I made a *click-click* sound and pulled on the lead to bring the goats along. They were docile beasts, and I was starting to like them. I ruffled one on the head.

"I have one more question for you, looo-ten-at. Look at your trousers. What do you think your Marines think about an officer who wears unserviceable trousers?"

I looked down. Black oil stains were all over the front of my desert tan camouflage pants. There had been a pool of motor oil under Staff Sergeant Caravalho's MATV that I was laying in while I caged the brakes during the firefight in the Salaam Bazaar.

"I think they'll trust that I would come back for them in a firefight, just like I did when I got these stains on my trousers." I walked away. I didn't have time for this guy.

"If those goats shit on my FOB, you won't hear the end of it."

I didn't give him the pleasure of an answer. Raufi, the interpreter, along with one of my Marines who was a hunter, butchered the goats and packed the meat in a plastic bag so it could be brought back to FOB Edinburgh and shared with the rest of the Marines. We got back to FOB Edinburgh just as it was getting dark. Captain Gallagher came to find me.

"Jeff, uh, Staff Sergeant Caravalho isn't doing well. He started getting dizzy, vomiting, losing consciousness. We MEDEVAC'd him back to Bastion while you all did the Musa Qal'eh mission. You gonna be okay without him as ACC?" A MEDEVAC was a medical evacuation back to the hospital at Camp Bastion. This was a real blow. Staff Sergeant Caravalho was the platoon sergeant, the staff non-commissioned officer in charge, my mentor and assistant convoy commander. "We'll get by, sir. Sergeant Galante can do it." He could, I was confident, but I was worried about Staff Sergeant Caravalho.

Corporal Christopher Jacobs, a Louisiana native, and Lance Corporal Darius Jenkins took the lead on cooking dinner. A small campfire was built (using some wooden chock blocks purloined from an Army unit for fuel) and a grill was constructed out of HESCO mesh. The goat was delicious, but I was worried about the mission back. There was no way it would be any easier than the outbound trip.

DAY FOUR

We remained at FOB Edinburgh for the whole next day, resting and conducting vehicle maintenance, before heading back to Camp Leatherneck.

Thank God for that extra day of rest. We had not originally planned on it, but after looking at the Marines, many of whom had only gotten a few hours of sleep after the outbound leg, Captain Gallagher knew they needed it.

Corporal Salsberry, who had been in the LVSR struck by the IED on the second day of the mission, was getting worse. He could no longer bend his leg, and the swelling was bad. He would need to be MEDEVAC'd to the hospital at Camp Bastion. I requested a helicopter, and we put him on it about thirty minutes later.

Corporal Sena and Lance Corporal Sedam clean and repack .50 caliber ammunition at FOB Edinburgh before the convoy returns south to Camp Leatherneck.

I spent the rest of day checking on the Marines, reading and listening to music. Deep breaths. Got ready for the fight to come.

DAY FIVE

We were set to depart at 0600, but because of some bureaucratic issues with the COC, we didn't get cleared to depart until close to 0900. I never knew what those issues were; Captain Gallagher was working them, but was frustrated and thought they were ridiculous. More daylight burned. Didn't anybody at higher understand the tactical implications of this?

Captain Gallagher told me to start rolling, so I did. "Jeff, do you have accountability of every Marine?"

"Yes, sir." I don't know whether or not we ever actually got clearance to leave or not, but we left.

The trip back was just as painful as the trip up. The Lande Nawah wadi was held by First Platoon, Arawak 1, so it would not need to be cleared again. Three IEDs had been found on the way up, but the area was as safe as it could be because we had Marines sitting on it during our offload at FOB Edinburgh. We got down to the wadi, refueled the security element, and continued south. The delays and enemy contact started as the RCP began to clear through the compounds near the Salaam Bazaar. IEDs were being found right and left. A few trucks struck IEDs, damaging minerollers. A piece of shrapnel from an IED caught a Marine in the face. The corpsman could not get the bleeding under control, so a helicopter was requested for his MEDEVAC back to the hospital at Camp Bastion. The ground was cleared, and the US Air Force Pararescuemen of the Pedro Squadron were inbound. For the third of what would be many times, a CLB-6 Marine was put on a helicopter and raced back to the hospital to receive treatment for injuries received in battle.

As the RCP and the security element tried to make forward progress and pick a route through the compounds, we saw pickup trucks full of mili-

A USAF Pedro MEDEVAC helicopter takes off from a Landing Zone. CLB-6 trucks provide security for the MEDEVAC in between mud compounds and poppy fields.

tary-aged males and motorcycles streaming toward us at high speed from the east. Shir Ghazi was a small city south of Musa Qal'eh. It was a known enemy stronghold, and only five kilometers to our east. This was not good.

I pushed the information up, but we couldn't do much, except prepare for a fight. The sun dipped below the horizon.

Right on schedule, the enemy opened fire.

After over a dozen IED finds and a handful of strikes against both CLB-6 and the Route Clearance Platoon, we were finally moving. The fighting was heavy, exchanging small arms fire back and forth.

Whump-BOOM. Mortars were being fired on the trucks toward the rear of the convoy. We were being bracketed again, and this time the enemy got lucky. A British PLS cargo truck was disabled when a mortar hit the engine. Incredibly, they recovered the truck with a straight towbar and didn't suffer any casualties.

The energy in the convoy was at manic levels of terror and panic. This was a rare instance of not knowing if I would be able to get us out of a situation without casualties. We had encountered an unthinkable number of IEDs in the last hours. Close to dozens, each capable of destroying a truck and killing Marines. I was supposed to maintain control and keep everyone else calm, but I was no less scared than anyone else. I suppose it was sheer adrenaline and ingrained training that kept my fear in check and allowed me to stay in control. Around midnight, though, the momentum picked up. Captain Gallagher had picked out a route on the imagery that looked like a possibility. A "Hail Mary pass," it would bring us nearly into the heart of the enemy poppy industry, the Western Cluster. Nobody would go there on purpose. Which meant that the insurgents wouldn't put any IEDs on that route. It just might work.

It did. Suddenly, we were off any of the routes that the insurgents thought we would use, and on a route that didn't have any IEDs. It felt anti-climactic, but we knew it was something we could only do once—next time out, the enemy would put IEDs on this route too.

DAY SIX

After we got south of the danger zone, the convoy just kept moving, thankfully. Mercifully. Vehicles got stuck here and there, but nothing major. We sorely missed Staff Sergeant Caravalho, who was waiting for us when we got back to our motor pool midmorning. After getting the trucks secured, completing an intel debrief and making sure all serialized gear was accounted for, an exhausted Captain Gallagher, Lieutenant Fowler and I went back to the tent we shared with the company's SNCOs, and collapsed on our beds. The return trip had been short—only thirty hours or so.

We dragged ourselves off our cots long enough to take a quick shower and eat something, but we all fell asleep at the table after no more than a few bites of a sandwich.

CHAPTER TEN

INTO THE SWING OF THINGS

The Op Lava series of missions moved 1st Battalion, 2nd Marines into Musa Qal'eh, and they immediately began an intense series of offensives designed to clear and hold Musa Qal'eh and the surrounding areas. There were three logistics constraints that defined the pace of their movement and their counterinsurgency efforts. The first was a lack of building materials, essential to improving and fortifying the positions that they were establishing to help secure the area they cleared. Second was fuel. Fuel is heavy and difficult to transport. For an infantry unit in the offense, there is a limit to how much they could bring with them, but they always needed more to keep moving forward.

The MK31 Tractor was used to pull many different kinds of trailers, but the most important was the M970 5000 gallon fuel tanker. CLB-6 moved hundreds of thousands of gallons of fuel in these tankers. On many occasions, trailers hit IEDs or were struck by RPGs, but were remarkably survivable. The round shape of the tank tended to deflect explosions.

Lastly, 1st Battalion, 2nd Marines was constrained by limited quantities of ammunition, which was being used at a rapid pace in the heavy fighting to the north of the Musa Qal'eh District Center. In particular, shoulder-fired SMAW rockets and Anti-Personnel Obstacle Breaching Systems (APOBS) were needed. APOBS are essentially small rockets attached to a 150 foot-long sock filled with small explosive charges. The end of the socks are anchored to the ground on the "near side" of a minefield. The rockets are launched away from the Marines to the "far side," trailing the socks behind them. With the sock now lying on the ground, stretched out across the minefield, the explosives are detonated, safely destroying any landmines or IEDs in the path. The APOBS big brother, the MICLC, was launched by vehicles and could clear a 350-foot path wide enough for trucks and tanks.

So wood, fuel, and ammo were the priority cargo for my next run. Why couldn't I just take a nice, less volatile load of food and water instead? I had serious concerns about what would happen if one my trucks hit an IED. I went into the S3 to get an update one morning, several days before the mission and the operations chief grabbed me.

"Sir, the name for the next mission has changed. It won't be Operation Khundee Larha anymore. It's now Operation Oar Tupe."

"Oar Tupe? What's that mean?" I asked. All operations had Pashto names.

"Fireball." He laughed and thought it was great fun. "Because of the cargo list. Wood, ammo, fuel ... get it?"

"I got it. I just don't think it's funny."

I will admit that it's a pretty good story in hindsight and I can laugh about it now, but at the time it just seemed to add insult to injury. The incident illustrates one of my key frustrations at the time. Especially in the Marine Logistics Groups, Marines who were "in the rear with the gear" did not understand what it was, exactly, that we did outside the wire. We were willing to accept the risks that we took, but risks must be appropriately respected. What we expected from the CLB-6 staff was at least an appreciation for the dangers that we were facing. If a mortar hit the cargo bed of a truck carrying MREs, the Marines inside the armored cab would probably be fine; if the truck were carrying SMAW rockets and they detonated, it might not only kill those Marines but also the Marines in the truck in front of and behind it, depending on the blast radius. Of course we would move wood, fuel, and ammo to support the infantry. But someone who wasn't personally at risk shouldn't make jokes about those risks—especially not to the guy taking the risks.

There were no roads in the Helmand Province in 2010, except for the

Ring Road, which didn't go to any of the places we needed to get to. Operation Oar Tupe would follow a different route than Operation Lava, but it was not expected to be any less threatening. Now Zad was cut off from FOB Edinburgh and Musa Qal'eh by a string of mountains, impassable by our vehicles except through the Dehanna Pass east of Now Zad. Immediately to the east of the pass lay the fingers of the deep Lande Nawah wadi and the compounds of the Salaam Bazaar. Once through the Dehanna Pass, the route to FOB Edinburgh and Musa Qal'eh along Route Green was anything but smooth. It might be a better route than the Operation Lava route though, so we had to check it out.

After hours and hours of looking at imagery and maps, Captain Gallagher suggested we just request an aerial reconnaissance flight in UH-1 Hueys. "We could get a first-hand look at the terrain from above."

"That's a good idea. If we take enough pictures, we can compare them to areas that we know are trafficable."

The request was approved for the two of us plus one additional passenger—we brought our Joint Terminal Attack Controller, Captain Martinez, callsign Chosin 77, who would be on the ground with us coordinating all of the air assets available for the support of our operation.

After arriving at HMLA-369, the Marine helicopter squadron that would fly us on our aerial recon, we waited in the ready room for a while. One of the pilots who briefed us mentioned that there would probably be a few extra passengers coming along for the ride.

"They don't really care where they go. They just want to get a ride, take some pictures, that sort of thing. The focus will still be your recon, and we're going to spend all the time you need checking out your NAIs," he said, referring to our "named areas of interest," the key features and locations that we needed to see.

We soon found out who would be riding along with us. He walked in, clad in desert MARPAT camouflage trousers, a plain khaki shirt, an armor plate carrier, and carrying a unique brown helmet with a camera attached. His name tag said "North, Oliver" and below that he was wearing a Velcro name tape that said "Fox News." I was a little starstruck . . . Oliver North, on our helicopter.

He was very down to earth. "So we're gonna ride along, shoot some video. You guys are trying to find a route through the area we're checking out?"

"Yes, sir, we are. A better route, anyway. The convoys take days to push through the compounds and farms, so if we can get through one of the mountain passes, it could make the convoy a lot faster."

We walked out to the flightline and the crew chiefs strapped us into the UH-1Y Huey.

"Do you mind sitting on the side, instead of the center seat near the cockpit?" the Fox News cameraman said, referring to one of the seats along the open door of helicopter. "We'd like to be able to shoot some video of the pilots," he explained.

"Sure, that's fine," I responded. "The side will let me take photos of the landscape a little better anyway." And, I didn't mention, it would be a lot more fun.

We took off and gently "taxied" in a hover down the Camp Bastion flightline before rapidly ascending and flying a loop around the east side of Camp Leatherneck. A minute later, we were racing north at over 150mph. My feet were hanging out the left door of the bird as the pilots began flying slow, loping paths over our planned convoy route.

Aerial photograph of the Lande Nawah wadi from the recon flight. The dense farms restricted mobility to the paths between fields and provided insurgents dozens of hiding places to launch attacks.

Taking a few hundred photos that would take hours to analyze, we got the information that we needed. The only pass through the mountains that would work was the Dehanna Pass. Just as we thought, any other pass was either not trafficable for our vehicles or would dump us in the heart of the Salaam Bazaar, which we were trying to avoid. The Lande Nawah was deep, but if we cut north immediately after getting through the Dehanna, we could avoid the worst of the terrain. We had to try it. Anything was better than another Operation Lava.

There were a few things that were always in short supply for convoy operations, and though we would always try to find a work-around, there were certain items that were truly critical, for which there were no substitutes, like vehicle towbars. If a vehicle was mechanically disabled or minimally damaged by an IED, or even if we didn't have enough drivers, the best way to get that vehicle to the FOB or back to Leatherneck was to flat tow it. All military vehicles, from Humvees to tanks, could be towed, and most could be towed by another of the same kind of vehicle. To do this, though, a towbar was required. The towbar had two legs that connected to special lugs on each side of the front of the vehicle being towed. The two legs came together in a sort of V at a single point and connected to the pintle hitch on the back of the pulling vehicle.

The towbar shortage problem was not easily solved. I hammered the supply chief, Gunnery Sergeant Serpa, about this all the time. "Gunny, we ordered some towbars months ago, right at the beginning of our deployment."

"Sir, I hear you. The towbars that you ordered . . . literally do not exist yet. The expected ship date for that order is not for about two years . . . literally, years."

"Well, that's great. They'll be here when we come back on our next deployment."

Sure enough, when CLB-6 got back to Afghanistan in mid-2011, there were plenty of towbars. But in 2010, every convoy that went out had to scrape and scrounge to get enough towbars. We went out with about 60 vehicles on every run and could expect four or five breakdowns, which meant that we would need a minimum of four or five towbars, and that assumes that we didn't break any.

As we were preparing for Operation Oar Tupe, I went to do my pre-combat inspection of the trucks. I spot checked each truck, looking over a few critical items. Based on problems that we had seen before, I always ensured that each vehicle had food and water, that the pintle hook retaining pin was present, caging bolts were installed, the air filter was cleaned, the headlights worked, and so on down the checklist. Of course, I always checked the towbars. I only found three towbars; two on the trail maintenance officer's truck and one on the wrecker. I found the TMO's driver, who was responsible for checking the TMO gear list.

"Hey, Roberts, I could only find three towbars on the trucks. Do we have any more?"

"No, sir. I've looked everywhere. I even stole one from Bravo Company." We were always robbing Peter to pay Paul.

"Man. We really need those towbars."

This was go/no-go criteria. If we had a breakdown, without a towbar we were left with few options to get the truck back to base. Depending on the type of breakdown, it could be pulled with a chain, but that required leaving a Marine in the truck to steer, which was very hazardous. The truck could roll over or the brakes could fail, causing the disabled truck to crash into the truck towing it. I thought about it for a minute. "Alright, Lance Corporal Roberts. I need you to figure this one out. When the sun comes up tomorrow morning, this convoy needs to have five towbars." I might as well have given him a wink wink, nudge nudge.

"Tracking, sir. I've got an idea." A devious grin spread across his face.

The next morning I issued the final convoy order to my platoon. After the brief, I grabbed Lance Corporal Roberts. " Roberts, how many towbars do we have?"

Straight faced, he responded "Five, sir."

"Excellent." I smiled. "Are they, uh, are they ours?"

Roberts cracked a sideways grin. "Well, uh, they have CLB-6 painted on them."

"Is the, uh, is the paint dry?" I asked.

"Almost, sir. I'd give it a few more minutes, though."

There is a saying in the Marine Corps that there is only one thief—everyone else is just trying to get their stuff back. Organizational theft really was a problem, but nobody could crack down on it because every unit did it, and the intent was just to get the mission done. I don't know where or from whom Lance Corporal Roberts "acquired" those towbars, but we did end up needing them on that mission.

If I had ever doubted how important Staff Sergeant Caravalho was to the platoon and to me, his importance was reinforced as we prepared for Operation Oar Tupe, headed to COP Cafferetta in Now Zad where we would deliver supplies then rest for the night before continuing on to FOB Edinburgh. He was still recovering from his injuries on Operation Lava 31. It didn't help that the load plan kept changing until the last minute, but the biggest problem for us as a platoon was that we were missing our platoon sergeant, and neither I nor the sergeants had yet figured out how to operate efficiently without him.

Due to manifest and cargo loading issues, we left almost six hours late. It was one of my greatest failures in Afghanistan. Captain Gallagher was watching this unfold in the motor pool and he was furious. He wasn't going on the mission—I was the mission commander. I had to own it. I should have supervised better and known when to ask for help. I learned a lot from that failure. I was a little shaken up by it when we left Camp Leatherneck—getting yelled at every five minutes for several hours before a mission doesn't exactly put you in the right mindset for combat operations. Gunnery Sergeant Locklear, the company operations chief, was our saving grace. He grabbed Staff Sergeant Caravalho and the two of them helped finish the manifesting and organization of the convoy to get us out the door.

Once we were outside the wire, the mission went much more smoothly. The Marines were experienced, so the IED strikes and recoveries didn't slow us down as much. The most junior private first class was an expert vehicle operator by now, taught and trained by the challenging terrain.

We reached Now Zad in near record time (even making up the six hours that had been lost to manifesting before we left), and unloaded our cargo. In discussions with 1/2, we decided that it was too difficult to bring our whole convoy inside COP Cafferetta for the night. The convoy would establish a defensive position outside the city of Now Zad, about a kilometer from the COP. We would be in the "safe zone" watched by the GBOSS tower-mounted camera and a small outpost on ANP Hill, just south of Now Zad.

We arrived in Now Zad to be greeted by dozens of children and a few adults, all hoping to sell us things. We kept them back from the convoy while we got organized, established a perimeter and sent in the vehicles that needed to offload at Cafferetta. The Marines who did not have an urgent task began to play with the Afghan children. I bought a few pieces of flatbread and a local "Pebsi" soda from one of the kids. The bread was plain, but chewy and filling. The more entrepreneurial children went on their way after we had bought all we were going to buy, but quite a few remained behind. A game of soccer broke out. A bunch of Marines taught the Afghan kids how to play Red Rover.

Afghan girls hanging out around CLB-6's trucks encamped outside the town of Now Zad.

I saw one of my Navy corpsmen with a toddler riding on her shoulders. "Doc, whose kid is that?" I asked.

"I don't really know, sir, but this must be his older brother," Hospitalman Third Class Suzanne Fauci replied, gesturing to a boy of about seven. His clothes were immaculately clean; I don't know how his parents managed to keep them that way without running water. "He's ticklish, though."

She tickled the kid on her shoulders and he giggled, giving her head a hug. While one of these children could have potentially been a terrorist, I felt that these few hours with the Afghan children were worth the risk because it might help establish the Afghan people's humanity in the minds of my Marines. It also seemed to be a good way to reduce stress for my guys.

I walked through the outskirts of Now Zad to COP Cafferetta to talk to one of 1/2's platoon commanders, the only U.S. platoon known to have ever used the Dehanna Pass before then.

"You're gonna bring all these trucks through that pass? Even them big trailers?" he asked, somewhat incredulously.

"Yup. I think we'll be ok. But we are looking at a couple of different routes to get to the Pass. It looks like we can either go straight through the Now Zad Bazaar which is short, or swing way down south and skirt along the mountains."

"Yeah, man. You can go either way, but I would just drive through the city. It's fastest. The route was cleared by the civilian demining team."

"Okay, thanks."

One of the actual victories in Afghanistan was the civilian demining project. With support from U.S. Marines, the State Department, the United Nations, and several Afghan Non-Governmental Organizations, a community-based demining site was established in Now Zad, employing Afghans. They were trained and equipped to find and destroy IEDs. They began clearing the whole town of Now Zad of the hundreds of bombs left behind by insurgents who were pushed back by the Marines during Operation Cobra's Anger in December of 2009. These bombs were not only a threat to the Marines, but to the people and children of the village.

The civilian demining team painted rocks, white on one side and red on the other. If you were on the white side of the rocks, you were safe. The red side indicated an IED threat. There was no dedicated effort to necessarily keep the white zone clear, but I never encountered an IED in the white zone. However, there was ample opportunity to attack us in the red zone, so I assumed that any insurgents looking to attack us would just emplace IEDs south and east of the cleared zone around Now Zad.

I walked to COP Cafferetta to look at the GBOSS, a high-resolution camera with night vision mounted on a tall mast. I wanted to know how closely the Marines of COP Cafferetta could watch over us and alert us to somebody approaching our position while we remained encamped outside the city for the night. We would still maintain about six or eight guards through the night, with the whole contingent, over 120 Marines in total, ready to spring into action if the alarm was sounded. After gathering the information I needed, I walked back out through the entry control point (or gate) of COP Cafferetta and returned to the convoy. I pulled all of the Marines in.

"Alright, guys. I just got back from the COC, and the GBOSS has a good view of our position, but an enemy could approach and try something. Jalal ud Din is about five miles to the southwest, and there are a bunch of unfriendly dudes there. I think the most likely course of action is a mortar or rocket attack. If we start taking fire, everyone should stay where they are. If you can get in a truck, do that. If you can't get in something armored, get under something armored. If you can't get under something armored, curl up into a ball, lay low and think small thoughts."

A few Marines laughed.

"Stay low. For the guys on post, stay awake, and if something happens, stay low in the turrets and look for targets. The sergeant of the guard will come around checking on the posts every hour or so."

After an awful departure from Camp Leatherneck, the trip was going pretty well. I hoped the night would go smoothly. It had warmed up but wasn't scorching yet, and near Now Zad there was little water, so there were no mosquitos. Sleeping in the deserts of Afghanistan was stunning. Even the back-country of the United States is flooded with the light of our electrified civilization, but most of the Helmand Province suffers no such problem. I didn't think I would able to sleep well—after all, we were outside the wire, in enemy territory. I ended up sleeping just fine.

A gunner mans his .50 caliber machine gun equipped with a thermal sight as the sun begins to go down. CLB-6 convoys had too many trucks to fit inside some FOBs and were forced to spend many nights "outside the wire."

After I got in my sleeping bag, I was awake for only a minute or two. I got up every few hours, however, to check the lines, and consistently found the Marines on post to be alert.

In the early morning hours we got things moving again. As the sun came up, the front of the convoy pulled forward through the sleepy village of Now Zad. The route through the Bazaar was tight—it seemed far too tight for our trucks and trailers, but we managed to get all 75 trucks or so through. Operation Oar Tupe was a pretty typical size for one of our convoys, 75 trucks and about 200 Marines. We arrived at the Dehanna Pass and began to clear it. Dominating mountains stood on either side of us, allowing less than a few hundred meters of clearance. Shale and rock fragments, broken off the peaks over the centuries, formed a natural roadbed that was well suited for our trucks.

Nature favored our passage through the Dehanna Pass by giving us such a good route, so I expected the enemy planned on it. The enemy always planted IEDs on routes that were easy for us to drive on. In the coming weeks, 1/2 would establish a partnered Afghan National Police presence in the pass and the village of Dehanna, but none of that was in place yet. No logistics convoys had driven through the pass before then.

That turned out to be our biggest advantage. Operating in an area with a persistent enemy presence, I found that I could do just about anything *once* and get away with it. The enemy would adapt and react next time, but for today, we had gotten through Dehanna without a problem. We pushed north around the fingers of the Lande Nawah wadi (through an area that would later be heavily IED'd in response to our traffic) and arrived at FOB Edinburgh less than four hours after leaving Now Zad. I was ecstatic that we had covered the fourteen miles in so little time.

We remained at FOB Edinburgh for less than 24 hours, just long enough to offload our cargo, rest, and get set for the mission back to Camp Leatherneck. The return trip was filled with the usual mechanical breakdowns and vehicles getting stuck, but I kept pushing the momentum on the front, doing recoveries on the fly, and catching up. Sergeant Galante had stepped into the role of assistant convoy commander, and was doing a good job of it. In less than 24 hours, the convoy drove from FOB Edinburgh, back through the Dehanna Pass, through Now Zad, and back to Camp Leatherneck. We had averaged just over two miles per hour.

We never did it that fast again. The enemy adapted, and we hit a few IEDs on every subsequent trip up that route. The trips became more frequent as combat operations picked up for 1/2 in Musa Qal'eh. We were running to FOB Edinburgh every other week.

APRIL 2010: SHAH MIRZA VILLAGE, NOW ZAD PROVINCE, AFGHANISTAN

In April 2010, 3rd Battalion, 7th Marines was conducting security operations near the village of Shah Mirza, at the base of a mountain called Kuh E Khan Baba or "The Foot." One of their MATVs had struck an IED, blowing off the front axle. They had no ability to recover it, so the task fell to us, to respond with our "Quick Reaction Force" or QRF. With only one MK36 wrecker available, I didn't want to use it to tow the MATV all the way back to Camp Leatherneck. A wrecker towing something has to go fairly slow to ensure its load doesn't tip over, bringing the wrecker with it. It would also tie up my wrecker, so if something else was damaged or destroyed, I wouldn't have any recovery assets available.

We used to joke that nobody yet knew the capabilities of the new LVSR and that we would just keep trying things out to see if there was anything they could not do. I had done the math, and figured that we could get a MATV on top of an LVSR. I brought the idea to my Marines, the motor transport experts, and asked what they thought.

"Hell, sir. We put one on an LVSR a couple of weeks ago just to see if we could."

"And?"

"Works great, sir. We just didn't want to get in trouble so we took it off right away. But sure. Works just fine."

That settled it. The wrecker operators would recover the MATV on the MK36 and tow it to a safer area, where it could be loaded onto the LVSR. Once the MATV was on the LVSR, the convoy would be free to drive much faster than it could with it being towed by the wrecker. We left Camp Leatherneck with about eight trucks and linked up with 3/7's Weapons Company who had the damaged MATV. I left about four of the trucks at their company assembly area and took only the essential vehicles forward to where the platoon was guarding their damaged MATV. We arrived at their position and I jumped out of my truck and walked over to the platoon commander's truck. When he opened the door, I recognized him immediately.

"Schroeder?" I asked. "What the hell are you doing here?" I only had his callsign on my mission briefing; I hadn't known that the platoon commander was a platoon-mate of mine from Mountain Warfare School.

"Damn, dude. You know how it is."

"That I do. Well, it looks pretty gray off to the east. I'm going to try to recover this and start heading south before the rain blows in."

The wrecker operator hitched the MATV up to his MK36, its blasted and mangled engine compartment a mockery of its designers' vision.

We proceeded south a few kilometers then back to the Weapons Company assembly area, where I had left the other four trucks. The MATV was unhitched from the MK36 wrecker. Out there in the desert, the Marines, lance corporals and corporals, loaded the MATV onto the back of a flatbed

LVSR, something they were never taught to do. But they figured it out; their ingenuity and skills were admirable. We were back on our way. It was one of the fastest missions we had ever done, because the wrecker was free to travel without a load.

On the way back to Leatherneck our small convoy passed some Bedouins. A frequent sight, these nomads tended to their sheep and goats, moving from place to place to find water and what little vegetation they could for their flocks. They lived in round tents that could sleep at least ten people. For the most part, they seemed to avoid getting caught up in our war, and generally didn't get along with most of the villagers or the insurgents. I admired their perseverance to live in such a harsh environment, but wondered why they didn't just keep walking to less hostile environs.

I turned to my driver, "You know, Sedam, if I were them, I would look left, look right, and say, 'Damn, I'm just gonna keep walking until I find a place that is not so . . . deserty.'"

"Haha, I know what ya' mean, sir. Hell, why do *we* care about this place, anyway?" Lance Corporal Sedam replied. "I mean, it's not that great a place. Can't the hajis take care of it themselves? Or who even cares if there's insurgents out here?"

The lieutenant don't know, Marine. That's what I wanted to say. I had told them the party line, of course, that we were here to provide security and stability to the people of Afghanistan, and to establish a democratic government capable of providing for the people and ensuring their rights. But were we accomplishing that? Were we *capable* of that?

I always bristled when I overheard my Marines use the term *haji.* I had talked to them about the origin of the word and its meaning as a term of reverence and respect for a Muslim who had completed a *hajj,* or pilgrimage, to Mecca. The Marines, however, used it in a derogatory sense. I corrected them when I could, but I could only ask so much of them. The enemy they referred to as *hajis* were actively trying to kill us; how can you convince a nineteen year old not to hate somebody who's trying to kill him? In every war we have always found a denigrating term for our enemy—huns, Japs, gooks. Why would anyone expect this war to be different? What was I supposed to do about it? I hated the enemy, too. They tried to kill my Marines.

Nineteen years old or not, even the most junior Marines were incredibly insightful about the war. "Damn, sir, aren't they just fighting us because we're *here* to fight? If we just left, would they just stop fighting?" The Lieutenant don't know, but it sounds like a damn good question. This type of dialogue was typical during our missions. The long expanses of boredom and trepidation and waiting for the inevitable attacks gave us plenty of time to ponder the meaning of it all.

We drove back into the motor pool aboard Camp Leatherneck, only to get accosted for the manner in which we had recovered the MATV by loading it onto the LVSR.

"You can't do that!" one senior officer stormed at me, pointing to the truck.

Dressing me down when I'm tired, filthy, and haven't slept in a long time is a good way to not get what you want from me. "Well, I think we just did, sir. Fifty kilometers ago, I might have believed you. Might we shorten the life of the equipment? Sure. But so does an IED. I'm going to make the decision that makes the most sense tactically, not the one that administratively ekes out the last bit of life from equipment that will probably get blown up anyway."

Even though he saw battle-damaged equipment and IED strike reports every day and should have understood what it was that we were doing out there, that officer didn't get it. There wasn't anything that said you *could* do what we did, but more importantly there wasn't anything that said you *couldn't*. He spent a fair amount of effort unsuccessfully trying to make sure we never did it again, but the battalion commander loved the idea and we did it all the time after that. I can't prove it, but if anybody asks, I'll tell them that it was the Marines of CLB-6, Alpha Company, Second Platoon who first put a MATV on an LVSR early in 2010.

Every CLB-6 convoy left the wire to provide logistics support to the infantry, not to engage the enemy. Yet the jihadist insurgents in the Helmand Province sought us out. They saw us as a soft target, big and slow. Though some missions did not directly engage the enemy in firefights, every CLB-6 convoy faced IEDs—nearly every convoy struck at least one. Pre-mission briefings were not phrased "if we take enemy contact," it was "when we take enemy contact."

"Detailed puh-lllllannning is the hallmark of an officer," Lieutenant Fowler used to say, imitating Captain Gallagher. We would both laugh, but Captain Gallagher did not mess around when it came to mission planning. No plan was detailed enough for him and there was always a contingency that I hadn't considered. His questions never ceased, but he had a point. Mission planning was about increasing our odds, turning the battle in our favor. Seemingly insignificant intelligence and terrain considerations could mean the difference between a smooth convoy that rolls slowly but steadily and a "slogfest," where the convoy has breakdowns and IED strikes. Air support was one of the best ways to give us this kind of advantage.

Unmanned aerial vehicles (UAVs) were requested for every mission to provide an "eye in the sky." CLB-6 was supported by MQ-1 Predators, RQ-7 Shadows, MQ-9 Reapers and ScanEagles to provide Intelligence, Surveillance and Reconnaissance (ISR). Occasionally, manned platforms were used to provide non-traditional ISR (NTISR). Depending on the situation, these NTISR missions were run for CLB-6 by UH-1 Hueys, U2 Dragon Lady spy planes, F/A-18s and EA-6Bs. ISR reduced everyone's stress level during long convoys when we couldn't see what was going on ahead of our route. The pilots would search along our route and on specific target gridpoints for thermal hotspots on the ground, possibly revealing buried IEDs. Motorcycles and vehicles along the route were watched closely.

Consider this scene: *Four or five motorcycles all converge in a small wadi south of the village of Wulgak. The riders, eight in total, dismount and begin walking around and pointing. They then walk back to their motorcycles and remove several large parcels. Several of the men (the riders are always men) begin to dig holes along the most trafficable approach to the wadi. The parcels are then placed in the holes, and covered with dirt. The men remount their motorcycles and scatter.*

This is a scene that played out thousands of times in the deserts of the Helmand Province just a few miles ahead of every logistics convoy. When we had ISR watching our route, we would get advance warning and specific locations to avoid.

MEBA-CLB-B-COC: *Arawak 2, be advised, four motorcycles and military-aged males were loitering IVO 41SPR 27893 64512. They were seen digging and there is a hotspot on the thermal.*

Oftentimes, these messages would have a startling amount of detail. The optics capabilities of our aircraft were amazing. Nevertheless, there was only so much we could do. Sure, we could avoid one particular spot, but what if there was another IED ten feet away from that spot? If nothing else, it helped us to know where there was a fair amount of activity and where to pay particularly close attention.

Most radio traffic, reports and requests, had to follow a very specific format for clarity and efficiency, which had the effect of making many Marines nervous talking on the handset. There was even a (politically incorrect) slang term to describe the condition—a "radio retard" was someone who turned into a stuttering idiot as soon as he clicked the push-to-talk button. Talking to artillery units was particularly difficult, as they could be very nit-picky (admittedly, for good reason) about the way we would say things. Numbers had to be passed according to a strict format. 4300, for example, was pronounced "fo-wer tree hundred," and 329 was "tree too niner." Many people were even more nervous when talking to aircraft. Captain Lynch, my platoon's instructor at The Basic School gave me some great advice about talking to aircraft, and I have passed it on to other Marines verbatim.

"Listen, don't sweat talking to aircraft. There's a pilot up there, okay, and he thinks he's a sweet dude. Or she thinks she's a sweet dude. Either way, the pilot is going to try to sound cool as hell." He laughed. "So he's going to talk to you like a cool dude back on the block. Just tell him what you see, tell him what you need." He laughed again. "The real reason pilots just talk to you like a normal person is they're busy. They're scribbling on a kneeboard, looking at map, trying to look at what you're talking about, all while trying not to turn their plane into a lawn dart."

The pilots who worked with us were top notch. We usually would not know who they were before they checked on station, but occasionally we would head over to their hangers on Camp Bastion to coordinate particularly crucial parts of a mission. On one occasion, Captain Gallagher and I were meeting with some of the pilots from HMLA 369, a Marine Light Attack Helicopter Squadron. We would be supported by a section of "mixed skids," one AH-1W SuperCobra and one UH-1Y Huey. I was going over the standard convoy air support checklist with the two pilots who would support the mission.

"Right, so this area here," I pointed on the map, "is a typical hotspot. We always see IEDs and ambushes in that area. We laid out the timeline so that we will be about an hour away from there when you check on station." The idea was to have them patrol the route ahead of us. Anyone trying to take advantage of the advancing convoy would be confronted by the substantial armament of the helicopters.

"Yeah, definitely, man. We will have enough time on station to fly the whole route a few times, as well as the tracks leading to it. Do you want us to do any show of force?" the pilot asked.

"Yes, sir. The village of Wulgak seems to be an insurgent staging area, and the people seem more openly hostile there than in some other places."

"Okay, sure thing. We'll probably do a few low, slow passes and fire some flares."

The intent of a "show of force" was just that, to show force. Having aircraft hover over an area and fire flares was a way to say, "we know who you are and what you are doing . . . I could shoot at you, but I'm not going to . . . yet." The long-term counterinsurgency effects of "shows of force" are perhaps debatable, but in the short-term they seemed to reduce insurgent activity.

The mission briefing was about halfway over when loud music began blaring on speakers throughout the compound. . . . *Looking for you to start up a fight . . . Running, On our way, Hiding, You will pay.* . . . The strains of Metallica's rock anthem "Seek and Destroy" electrified the compound, the alarm-like rhythm of its baseline oscillating in my head. One of the pilots, Major James "Weasel" Weis, jumped out of his chair. He grabbed up his notebook and ran out of the room without a word. The second pilot explained, "Weasel is on standby today. Somebody must be in a TIC."

A TIC or Troops In Contact meant that somebody somewhere was in a firefight and needed immediate air support. Within minutes of the call coming in, Major Weis would be in the air. By the time he had run from the room, donned his gear and sprinted to his aircraft, the ground crew would have everything spinning.

Pilots were dedicated to us guys on the ground. They were so focused on providing close air support as quickly as possible that they wouldn't even pause to say goodbye before rushing into action. The seconds they spent talking to somebody could mean that their aerial guns are fired a few seconds too late for outnumbered Marines in a firefight. I was glad these guys were on my side, and grateful that they would support me. It gave me a lot of confidence.

JULY 2010: CLB-6 COMPOUND, CAMP LEATHERNECK, HELMAND PROVINCE, AFGHANISTAN

A few months and few missions later, Captain Gallagher pulled me aside. "Hey, uh, Jeff . . . Major Weis was killed today. They aren't saying anything yet, but his helicopter went down near Lash."

Lashkar Gah was the largest city in the southeastern part of the Helmand Province and was densely populated. News reports later said that his helicopter was shot down. Major Weis was the first person I had personally known who was killed while I was still in Afghanistan. Other Marines had been killed while I was there, quite a few in the same areas that I operated, but none who I had known personally—none whose face I could picture. I wasn't good friends with Major Weis and I hadn't known him for long, but that wasn't necessary for the loss to really hit me. He and his squadron had risked themselves flying in support of CLB-6, in support of my platoon. To support me.

CHAPTER ELEVEN

ROUTE RED RECON

MAY 2010

It took about a week to complete each round trip from Camp Leatherneck to FOB Edinburgh and back. The strenuous demands of the mission and the cost in damaged and destroyed equipment limited the frequency of the missions to no more than about two per month. Alpha Company was still supporting convoys to Now Zad, Marjeh and Delaram, which all required assets and Marines as well. There had to be a different route, better than either the Operation Lava route through the Salaam Bazaar or the western route through the Southern Terrain Belt, past Now Zad and through the Dehanna Pass. The civilian route straight to FOB Edinburgh, designated "Route Red," was laid full of IEDs, according to the intel reports. Still, the promise of a better route was alluring. We talked about this idea frequently.

Small trucks and compact Toyota sedans were often found parked beside the more prosperous farms in the Helmand Province. Routes popped up throughout the province, and though they were not paved, the routine traffic kept them generally free of moondust. Some villagers had built culverts and other improvements along the route. Some areas even had bridges built by non-governmental organizations, the US Agency for International Development, or a charity. Such routes were far better than a random track across the desert, and any path that an Afghan could handle in a late-model Toyota Corolla would be no problem for a trained operator in an LVSR. Unfortunately, many of these routes were heavily IED'd, laced with bombs. Civilians knew where the IEDs were—insurgents would post warnings in mosques and go door to door to warn villagers. We were not privy to their warnings, so rolling headlong down a route was a sure way to run over an IED.

The routes, not even wide enough for cars to pass side by side in many places, connected village to village, and small farms were built all along these small trade routes. With compounds right on the road, we could expect to get hit with command-wire detonated IEDs. These compounds posed another problem for us. The buildings gave insurgents lots of cupboards to cache weapons, escape routes to hide in, and firing positions to launch attacks from. The conditions were ripe for an enemy ambush.

"But how bad is the threat? It's taking us days to get there as it is," we asked each other.

We were hitting IEDs out in the open desert. At least on a highly trafficked route we might move a little faster and suffer fewer breakdowns. With air support and our heavily armed trucks we could fight through an ambush. Captain Gallagher, Lieutenant Wood and I had looked at maps and satellite imagery of the route, but there were unknowns. Exactly how wide were some sections of the route? Could we get trucks with trailers through the gaps? How easily could we be ambushed? To more accurately assess the threat and determine if our trucks could actually get through on Route Red, someone would have to drive the route.

Combat Logistics Battalions do not normally conduct pure ground reconnaissance missions, particularly not through "regimental security areas," a battlespace that is not really owned by anyone and lacks a persistent presence of friendly troops. Route Red, which cut through the heart of the Western Cluster, was in the "Wild West," but there were no other units available to conduct the recon. The Light Armored Reconnaissance Battalion, 1st LAR, was in a heavy fight down south by Khan Neshin Castle.

Alpha Company was assigned to do the ground reconnaissance. The tactical considerations for the mission were different than for a combat logistics patrol, but the rest of the preparation was the same. Though our Marines had the skills needed, it was still a little out of our usual repertoire. Captain Gallagher was going as the mission commander. "I wouldn't feel right dumping this on you. It's not that I don't trust you." I wasn't sure that I believed him at first. "You could do this, but I want to be there to provide you some top cover from the COC and battalion."

So, was I the "assistant mission commander"? "Convoy commander"? I didn't really know what my role was exactly, but I did a lot to prepare for the mission. My platoon was tasked with most of the support, including the scout vehicle and trail maintenance vehicle; a few trucks would come from the other platoons. I oversaw the detailed mission, administrative and personnel preparation.

Captain Gallagher and I drafted the route together. I respected him, but our interactions were awkward at times. It was tough to explain then, and is still hard to explain. He had a very Socratic way of doing things and talking to people—a lot of what he said was very succinct, or in the form of a question. A lot of people didn't really like Captain Gallagher; he certainly frustrated me at times, but I learned an incredible amount about tactical operations and combat from him. The assistant convoy commander was First Platoon's Staff Sergeant D'Andre Gillon, since Staff Sergeant Caravalho was still not cleared to leave the wire after his IED strike. A few days before the mission, we were walking through the motor pool going over the trucks.

"Hey sir, I don't like this one. I don't have a good feeling about this," Staff Sergeant Gillon said. We were talking quietly in the motor pool out of earshot of anyone else.

"Honestly, me neither. But we have to go."

"We don't have a choice?"

"Someone from CLB-6 has to go."

Staff Sergeant Gillon shrugged. "Alright, fuck it. We'll do it."

After about a week after the decision to launch the recon mission, we left Camp Leatherneck and drove east on Route 1 with a small element of about twelve trucks. We were going alone on this one, without any route clearance or attached security element. Traveling further east than any previous CLB-6 convoy, we entered the outskirts of the city of Gereshk. The green zone along the Helmand River, so named for its lush flora, was visible in the distance.

The villages just north of the Ring Road, the "suburbs" of Gereshk were full of people who were outwardly friendly. Here a group of children salute the passing CLB-6 convoy. We had crushed some of their family's crops on a tight turn. I found that a few cases of bottled water quickly settled almost any debt with the Afghan farmers. The kids loved the taste of clean, fresh water.

Unlike the relatively safe haven of the Iraqi Green Zone in Baghdad, this verdant area was a hotbed of insurgent activity. Our route took us north through the compounds and villages west of the river, to the base of the Table-top Ridge.

The convoy pushes north of the Ring Road and onto Route Red.

Route Red entered the Western Cluster a few kilometers north of Route 1. The convoy had made great progress thus far, but we lost all our momentum when one of the MRAPs died. We were just inside the Western Cluster, the most dangerous part of the route.

It was "Gnome," Sergeant Geising. "Buzz, this is Gnome. My truck just died. It's done this a few times and we were able to restart it, but no luck this time." He had adopted the callsign "Gnome" because of his diminutive stature.

"Roger, Gnome. Lollipop, can you check it out?" Lollipop was Sergeant Williams' callsign.

Sergeant Williams, mechanic-extraordinaire, was escorted up by Staff Sergeant Gillon who had a mineroller on his truck. Sergeant Williams determined that the MRAP's alternator had shorted out; the battery was now dead and with no alternator there was no way to power the fuel pump to keep the engine running. There was nothing to be done except tow the vehicle. Unfortunately this conclusion, and the process of rigging the MRAP for flat-tow, took approximately an hour. I could feel the clock ticking. I could feel dickers watching us and running off on their motorcycles, telling other people about us. I envisioned "trigger-men" positioning themselves in spotting positions to detonate command-wire IEDs under our trucks. We had lost momentum, speed, surprise.

At every culvert and bridge, we dismounted and swept for IEDs with metal detectors. Lieutenant Tony Rowley, a combat engineer from the battalion's Engineer Company, took pictures and measurements, assessing the ability of these improvised public works structures to bear the load of our heaviest cargo trucks. If they could not bear the 80,000 pounds of an MK31/970 full of JP-8 fuel or the 100,000-plus pound loads on our 870 trailers, Route Red wasn't any good to us. The assessments had to be done, but they slowed us down. At 1300 we approached the densest village in the Western Cluster, Garmeh Vassati. Every "little main street" in every village up till now had been full of people engaging in commerce, selling crops, and dispensing gasoline from yellow jugs. Children played and rode bikes. In every other town, everyone stared at us as we drove by. American forces never entered the Western Cluster—what were we doing here, they wondered? *Were we crazy?*

Garmeh Vassati was different from the other towns we had driven through. The buildings looked the same, but where were the people? The southern outskirts of the town were empty. Shops were closed. It was a ghost town. This was *not* good. The Marines, well attuned to the "normal" in the area, were on the radio immediately.

Corporal Zeitz, the scout, saw it as soon as we crested the sweeping left-hand turn into the village. "Buzz, this is Peewee. There's nobody here. Like... nobody. I got a funny feeling."

Abandoned buildings in the town of Garmeh Vassati.

Captain Gallagher's radio had perhaps shorted out, so the only way to talk to him was over the Blue Force Tracker. I was relaying everything to him that I received from the internal radio traffic.

"Peewee, this is Buzz. Roger. Just keep your eyes open and keep pushing. It might be prayer time." It wasn't prayer time—there hadn't been a call to prayer or *azan* over any loudspeakers. I needed the Marines to remain calm. I needed to remain calm.

Another hundred meters. Another ten meters. Another meter. Time stopped. *WHUMP.* The dust cloud of an IED at the front of the convoy, bigger and louder than any we'd ever heard.

The dust cloud kicked up by the command-wire detonated IED that struck our first vehicle in Garmeh Vassati.

"IED IED IED!" Corporal Sena, my gunner, shouted down into the truck.

No more than ten seconds passed and then *WHUMP.* Another mushroom cloud of dust, this one behind us.

"Fuck. IED IED IED!" Corporal Sena again.

A white cloud of smoke now appeared by the first truck, and my driver, Lance Corporal Sedam shouted, "Hey, sir, we got white smoke from Peewee. What the fuck does white smoke mean?" The signal plan called for green smoke if everyone in the vehicle was okay after a strike, red smoke if they needed immediate lifesaving medical treatment. White smoke grenades were carried to screen the convoy in a firefight.

"Fuck, if nothing else it means that at least one person in the truck is alive. With an IED that big, it's good news," I responded.

Over the radio, Lance Corporal Amanda Trombley's voice came on, "Buzz, this is Optimus Prime." She sounded shaky. "That second IED was us. Staff Sergeant is unconscious."

"Roger, Optimus. Try to see if you can revive him."

The truck in front of theirs, commanded by Corporal Bush, started backing up. "We've got a corpsman, we'll back up to you."

WHUMP. A third IED. It was odd that nobody had set off that IED before. It hit the back of a truck, and luckily didn't even blow off a wheel. I figured it was a command-wire IED and the trigger-man had hit it too early. The cargo bay of Corporal Bush's MATV was damaged, but the truck was drivable. The Marines in Corporal Bush's truck had concussions, but were otherwise okay. Not so in Corporal Zeitz's or in Staff Sergeant Gillon's trucks.

"Buzz, this is Peewee." Finally. "Yeah, we're okay, I guess, but Rea is bleeding pretty bad." Lance Corporal Thomas Rea, a military policeman, was the gunner in the front truck. "He smashed his face on the 240."

In the back, a corpsman was assessing Staff Sergeant Gillon. "Buzz, this is Optimus, he's in and out." The blast had knocked him unconscious and had probably caused other internal injuries.

"Okay, roger." I sent a BFT message to Captain Gallagher.

Captain Gallagher agreed that we needed an urgent MEDEVAC for these two Marines. "Yeah, Buzz, I concur. And with Staff Sergeant Gillon gone, you will take over all duties as ACC." I was now in charge of all movement, accountability and recoveries, but I had mostly been playing that role already.

"Roger, sir, solid copy on all." A nine-line MEDEVAC report was sent up via BFT. The "Nine-Line" was something that all Marines practiced ad nauseum; the goal was to have a casualty on an operating table within an hour of an injury. After this "golden hour" passed, the chances of survival declined precipitously.

MEBA-CLB-B-MTPLT2: *Red Cloud, this is Arawak 2. Stand by for Nine-Line MEDEVAC.*

Back at Camp Leatherneck, the watch officer, First Lieutenant Chris Graff, would be yelling "Attention in the COC" and mobilizing the COC watchstanders to support the MEDEVAC request. Notification would be given to the battalion's higher headquarters and to the MEDEVAC pilots.

MEBA-CLB-B-MTPLT2:   *Line 1: Location of Pick Up 41SPR 65275 35329*
                          Line 2: Radio Freq VH 402, Callsign Arawak 2

Line 3: # PTs/Precedence, 2 Urgent
Line 4: Special Equipment None
Line 5: # PTs by Type, 1 Litter, 1 Ambulatory
Line 6: Security: Possible Enemy Activity
Line 7: Method of Marking LZ Smoke
Line 8: PT Nationality US Military
Line 9: Chem/Bio/Radiation/Nuclear Threat None

Additional information was sent up for each casualty to help the combat medics in the pickup aircraft treat them, and to prepare the hospital at Camp Bastion. Each patient was identified by a "kill number," a unique combination of letters and numbers assigned based on their name and social security number; these were designed to streamline communication and to help limit unnecessary excitement that was inevitably caused by passing names of Marines injured or killed over the radio. The effect was perhaps negated by calling it a "kill number" or "zap number."

MEBA-CLB-B-MTPLT2: *PT 1: Kill# MLR8394*
Mechanism of Injury: IED
Injury: Trauma to face, shattered teeth, broken jaw
Signs: Headache, bleeding, extreme pain
Treatment: Bandages
MEBA-CLB-B-MTPLT2: *PT 2: Kill# MLG9283*
Mechanism of Injury: IED
Injury: Concussion
Signs: Unconscious, unresponsive
Treatment: None

The COC began sourcing the MEDEVAC. It usually took about fifteen or twenty minutes to get the bird in the air, and the flight would take about ten minutes each way.

MEBA-CLB-B-COC: *Arawak 2, this is Red Cloud COC. MEDEVAC bird will be Pedro 52. Estimate wheels up in ten minutes.*

MEBA-CLB-B-MTPLT2: *Red Cloud, this is A2. Rgr, standing by.*

From the looks of it, we would have our casualties at the hospital well within the golden hour, and began preparing for the MEDEVAC on our end. A landing zone needed to be cleared for the aircraft, an Air Force HH-60G Pave Hawk, callsign Pedro. The pararescuemen and pilots of the Pedro squadrons were true professionals who would land in the hottest LZs. They lived up to their motto, risking everything so "that others may live."

"Chosin 77, this is Buzz," I called over the radio to our JTAC, Captain Martinez, who was in our third or fourth vehicle. The Joint Terminal Attack Controller was a specially trained Marine, a pilot, whose sole job was controlling aircraft and indirect fire support. By having an expert, this not only improved results but also freed up the convoy commander to focus on the overall situation and not end up in "radio defilade," focusing so much on the fires or aircraft that the big picture is lost. "I'm going to clear an LZ with my mineroller and post up on the west side to provide security. Do you have smoke or do you need more?"

The radio beeped, "Buzz, this is Chosin. I'm good on smoke. We'll look for you."

I turned to Lance Corporal Sedam, my driver. "Clear that field."

"Got it." He began to drive back and forth over a fallow farm field, running over every square inch with the mineroller to make sure the MEDEVAC helicopter wouldn't land on an IED. Technically this wasn't "clearing," this was "proofing." To "clear" meant that IEDs would be found and removed—we were merely showing "proof" that there were no IEDs. What we were doing was sacrificing our MATV to any IEDs that might be in the field—it would be better to strike any IEDs with our $500,000 armored MATV than with the relatively unarmored $40 million Pave Hawk Helicopter.

MEBA-CLB-B-COC: *Arawak 2, this is Red Cloud COC. Pedro 52 is 5 miles from wheels down.*

The helicopter was an estimated five minutes away. Sedam finished proofing the field. He parked the truck facing west.

"Buzz, this is Chosin. I've got comm with Pedro 52. He has a visual on our position. One minute from smoke." The pilot could see us and was talking to the JTAC. Once he was close enough, he would tell us to pop a smoke grenade to precisely mark the LZ. I could see a pair of Pave Hawks off in the distance. One of them would be designated to pick up the casualties, the other would hover overhead to provide security with its .50 caliber machine guns. Unlike Army Dustoff helicopters, Air Force Pedro birds were armed and would provide their own security. The lead helicopter came in and swung around the LZ and surrounding areas, looking for any enemy forces. It was impossible to put an LZ out of RPG and AK47 range in this area.

The trailing Pave Hawk came in fast, flared the nose and made a surprisingly soft landing at the last second. The pilot kept the rotors spinning but adjusted the blade pitch so they provided no lift, and stopped kicking up dust. Time seemed to stop as the dust cloud died down.

MEBA-CLBB-MTPLT2: *Red Cloud, this is A2. Pedro 52 is wheels down.*

A few of the Marines carried Staff Sergeant Gillon to the bird. Lance Corporal Rea, broken face and all, ran to his own MEDEVAC; he was injured but not defeated. Every second the bird was on the deck was a second too long, and every second was a lifetime. I could feel the seconds ticking loudly. An attack became more likely. The smoke trail signature of an RPG was the thing I most hoped and prayed I wouldn't see just then; images from *Black Hawk Down* flashed through my mind. A minute passed. Then two. What was taking so long?

Finally, dust started blowing around the bird as the blade pitch angles were adjusted for takeoff. For half an instant, the airframe began to lift up, the wheels still touching the deck as the suspension adjusted. Time sped back up as the helicopter lifted itself. The nose tilted down as the bird picked up speed and took up a position by the wingman.

MEBA-CLB-B-MTPLT2: *Red Cloud, this is A2. Pedro 52 is wheels up.*

MEBA-CLB-B-COC: *Arawak 2, Red Cloud. Roger. Will advise you once they are wheels down at Bastion.*

The last piece of information wasn't necessarily tactically relevant to us, but it was something that the Marines would want to know. They could, at least temporarily, stop worrying about Staff Sergeant Gillon and Lance Corporal Rea, knowing they had made it to a hospital. In this regard, I guess it *was* tactically relevant; I hoped it would help "close the chapter" on the MEDEVAC and restore their focus to the moment.

Though our worst casualties were evacuated, the unit still couldn't move. We had two disabled vehicles and a destroyed mineroller, and our lone wrecker wouldn't be sufficient to recover this equipment—we also didn't have enough seats in the remaining vehicles to carry all of our passengers. Captain Gallagher requested a recovery mission through the COC. Our company's First Platoon would be coming to support us, with a few assets from the general support motor transport company and a MK48/15 wrecker from the Marine Wing Support Squadron. But they were hours away.

The MEDEVAC had been completed around 1430; the recovery wasn't expected until around 0200 the next morning. We would be here overnight and needed to improve the security of our situation. Some built-up compounds with mud buildings and high mud walls were immediately next to the convoy on the east, inches from our trucks. If we were going to sit here, leaving them uncleared was a liability. We had trained for this but never planned on actually doing it.

Corporal Zeitz and a few of the Marines discussed how they would clear the compound. The Marine Corps had become experts in military operations in urban terrain, or MOUT, during the campaign in Fallujah, but CLB-6 had never done it before except in training. With a fire team reinforced, about six in all, the Marines entered the compound. They stayed tight, clearing left and right, each maintaining their sector of fire. I was glad to have Corporal Zeitz, a highly trained designated marksman and military policeman by MOS, leading the clearance team.

Everyone held their breath while the Marines were in the small compounds. If they came under fire, we would essentially rush in—there was not a better plan, and we knew it could be a disaster. The platoon had not conducted MOUT rehearsals in months. We only had about 20 Marines total, but a few had pretty bad concussions, and we needed some to remain outside to maintain our overall security. The compounds were clear and had no occupants, though there were signs of current habitation. Whoever lived here had been warned to leave. No wonder we hadn't seen any Afghans around.

But then we started to see some. All males. In pickup trucks. I could see about five pickup trucks moving north at high speed on a route about 200 meters to our east. They seemed to be turning to enter the Western Cluster just to our north. There was a total of about 25 individuals, and they were maneuvering on the immovable CLB-6 convoy. As evening approached we continued to see people moving around, in particular some moving on foot off in the compounds to our west. A BFT message popped up on the screen.

9RW-5RS-ACFT1: *Arawak 2, this is U2 plane Bones 21. I have visual on your convoy.*

Was this for real? I didn't even know that we still had U2 spy planes flying. Captain Gallagher's BFT was having some technical problems, so all of the comms were being redirected to me. From my perspective, it seemed that we were basically splitting the tactical control of the patrol—I more or less had the west and south positions, while he had the north. I responded to the U2 on the BFT.

MEBA-CLB-B-MTPLT2: *Bones, this is Arawak 2. Roger. Can you see any traffic inbound on our position? Several pickup trucks approached on a route to our east earlier, possibly maneuvering on our position.*

9RW-5RS-ACFT1: *No more traffic inbound on your position. Cannot see any significant movement around your position.*

The U2 stayed on station for a while, observing and reporting what was going on, but could do little to influence the situation on the ground. Night was coming. We knew what was going to happen when the sun went down. I needed everyone to try to recover from the days IED attacks and get ready for the fight ahead.

"All stations, this is Buzz. An enemy attack is likely at sundown. I want everyone to eat something now, and I want all optics op-checked and new batteries put in all radios." The Marines in MTVRs had to give the batteries for their handheld PRC-152 radios to Marines in MATVs or MRAPs because the MTVRs did not have powered radio amplifiers. A couple of Marines came to get batteries for their radios from my truck. "Clean and lubricate all the crew-served weapons. Sundown is in about an hour."

Night fell. Lance Corporal Sedam set up the Driver's Vision Enhancing system in the truck. "Hey, Sir, I got the thermal camera pointed at that building over there." He watched the output on a flip-down LCD monitor mounted to the ceiling and scanned the area, panning back and forth with the DVE's joystick controller for the camera. He then pulled up some REO Speedwagon on his iPod and played it over the speakers he had mounted above the windshield.

You're under the gun, so you take it on the run . . .
We waited, watching.

Clatta-clack.
The attack began with a single burst from an AK-type weapon directly to our west. The rounds zipped just over the top of our truck.

"That's us," Corporal Sena shouted. He had been perched on the gunner's stand down inside the truck so that he could see the thermal camera picture on the DVE screen in front of the driver. He jumped up into the turret and began searching for targets.

The first burst of gunfire was a signal for the rest of the enemy to begin attacking. From multiple covered and concealed firing points to the north and west, bullets began flying at us. The L-shaped configuration of the enemy firing positions allowed the insurgents to put us in a cross-fire without risk of hitting each other. These guys knew what they were doing.

Staff Sergeant Pupillo, CLB-6's intelligence officer, was dismounted when the first shots were fired. Within seconds of the report of the guns, Captain Gallagher literally yanked him into his truck. Rounds struck the side and back hatch of the truck seconds after it was closed. It was a close call.

This wasn't a normal combat logistics patrol. This was a group of Marines on a reconnaissance patrol who happened to be combat logisticians. On this patrol, the one-to-five gun-to-truck ratio that we were normally stuck with due to limited assets didn't apply. Every one of our trucks had a machine gun on it, and a trained Marine in the turret.

Rounds impacted the front of our truck. Corporal Sena saw where they had come from, and answered with a burst from the M240. Its 7.62mm bullets were white-hot as they left the barrel and appeared as streaks of white in the hazy green NVGs. Toward the front of the convoy, the story was the same. Sergeant Williams pushed out to the east a little. He and Captain Gallagher were identifying the targets to the north, and their gunners were suppressing. "Suppressing" is a rather sterile term that does not adequately capture the stress or intensity of the fight. Repeated bursts of accurate fire were trained on any position the enemy took up.

On the radio, the call came from a truck somewhere near the middle "RPG RPG RPG!" I could hear the *kschew* of the rocket motor, but no *boom* from the warhead. Must've been a dud. The battle continued. The insurgents moved from place to place, from one compound to the next, popping up and firing. Our gunners returned fire with M2 .50 caliber and M240 7.62mm machine guns.

I saw somebody to our front popping out from behind a wall and then darting back behind cover, about 100 meters away. It looked like he was trying to set up a shot. It was a little hazy in the NVGs, but he definitely had something that looked like an RPG. Lance Corporal Sedam and I both yelled up to Corporal Sena in the turret. "Sena, watch that alley! If he pops again, shoot him."

"Got it." The insurgent popped the corner again. He squared his body to us and began to bring up the RPG. He took too long. Corporal Sena fired three bursts from the M240. The machine gun was incredibly loud inside the truck. The sound was so loud it seemed to deafen and blind me while it was firing. Metal links and empty brass cartridges clinked and clattered as they poured down out of the turret into the truck.

Streaks of white light zipped across the green display of my NVGs and disappeared in the attacker's chest. He went down and didn't get back up. Watching this man die through the green hazy NVGs and white-hot display of the DVE was impersonal—it was like a video game, but with consequences. After the man died, his body no longer produced its own heat and he cooled until he was the same temperature as the surrounding air, and was no longer visible in the DVE.

Reports of the attack with detailed grid coordinates of the enemy attackers were sent up. The attack continued. Hundreds of rounds were fired in each direction, and about seven or ten RPG rounds were fired at us, though none of them struck our trucks. We had gotten lucky that time—we'd had trucks hit by RPGs a few times before. Captain Martinez, the JTAC, had been working on getting us some close air support and ISR, to give us some eyes overhead. Finally, a pair of "fast movers," F/A-18s, checked on station, but they were coming off another mission and didn't have much fuel in their tanks.

"Hey guys, this is Chosin. The pilots can't really see anything of value and they only have a few minutes left on station. I'm going to have them do a show of force."

While one plane remained high overhead, providing overwatch, the second lined up for a low altitude show of force run. He dropped from thousands of feet down to a few hundred feet above the deck. Running from south to north, the plane flew over our position and kicked in the afterburners in a spectacular display of noise and blue flame. The message was clear. "We know what you did to us. We know who you are. And we will fuck you up." The insurgents broke contact but we were certain they remained in the area, hoping for another opportunity to attack us.

Third Battalion, Seventh Marines was operating to the west of the Western Cluster, conducting Operation Eastern Dagger. They wanted a piece of the action and began to advance into the Western Cluster, trying to get in behind the insurgents, cutting off a possible escape route. I watched the blue circular icons of their trucks come toward us. If they could get to our position, it would greatly enhance our security. I sent a BFT message to the platoon commander, describing the enemy firing positions and armament. Shortly after, I received a response.

MEBA-DIV-V37-CAAT1: *Arawak, we just hit an IED. No recovery assets. Waiting on recovery. Not going to get to you.*

So that was that. They were still three or four miles away, which may as well have been another planet, but an additional unit was also interested and pushing to get a piece of the action. First Battalion, Second Marines was sending down a Combined Arms/Anti-Armor Team (CAAT) with about six trucks. They were approaching from the north and would try to push straight down Route Red. They were moving slowly, and were also about four miles away.

We had consolidated our trucks into three separate security positions, one in the north with Captain Gallagher, one three hundred meters south, and my truck between them, a hundred meters off the road to the west. It wasn't perfect, but it wasn't bad. We had fought off one sustained attack so far; we could handle another if it came.

A pickup truck approached from the south. It stopped several hundred meters back from our rear vehicle. Then slowly, it crept forward. A few more meters forward, and it stopped again. They were trying to see what we would do. It seemed the enemy knew our rules of engagement as well as we did. If we shot them, it would be a counterinsurgency victory for them—we "infidels" would have killed innocent people in a truck. If we didn't shoot, they would keep creeping forward, stressing our Marines out. Either way, they won.

Finally, they got close enough to warrant "escalation of force," a warning to stop. The gunner in our rear vehicle fired a pen flare, a small pyrotechnic, at an angle slightly offset from the small pickup truck. The green flare streaked across the sky. The truck stopped and the driver got out. He went to sleep on the hood of his truck and stayed there for the rest of the night, taunting us with his presence.

This was a weird war.

Around 0230, Zodiac Black, the 1/2 CAAT team, arrived at our position. They reinforced our perimeter, pulling their trucks into the gaps between ours, and waited for the sun to come up. One of their trucks had a flat tire, so Sergeant Williams replaced it while we waited on Arawak 1, the recovery mission from Camp Leatherneck. They arrived around 0430 with the recovery assets we needed, along with wrecker operators who made quick work of picking up the mineroller and two damaged MATVs. I surveyed the first strike site again. The first IED looked to be a pressure-plate IED with an offset pressure plate and main charge. A small clay oven in the center of the field in front of one of houses looked to be the aiming indicator, used to help insurgents know where exactly they had buried their IEDs.

Captain Gallagher and I were to continue north in our trucks with Zodiac Black on their return trip to Musa Qal'eh. The rest of the convoy would return to Camp Leatherneck with Arawak 1. As the recovery wrapped up and we were about to go our separate ways, the enemy resumed the attack.

Clatta-clack.

Arawak 1 began to push south, and Zodiac Black began north.

The last few details were still being seen to, and there was chaos on the ground. A few of Arawak 1's Marines were still dismounted though the convoy had started to move. The trail vehicle scooped up the last few Marines, and the gunners suppressed targets as they appeared.

One of Arawak 1's gunners, Corporal Rory MacEachern, spotted an enemy team setting up an old Soviet 82mm mortar. He engaged them with several bursts from his Mk19 automatic grenade launcher. All three enemy were killed, shredded by the concussive force and hail of shrapnel from dozens of 40mm grenades.

Amazingly, no IEDs had been backlaid on us when we came north, so Arawak 1 had a smooth return to Camp Leatherneck in that regard. The trip to the Musa Qal'eh District Center was equally uneventful, even passing through the heart of Shir Ghazi, a known hostile village. Captain Gallagher had to return to Camp Leatherneck as soon as possible, so he flew back from FOB Edinburgh on a returning cargo helicopter. I embedded our two trucks on Arawak 3, Lieutenant Stacy Wood's mission from Camp Leatherneck to COP Cafferetta in Now Zad, FOB Edinburgh and Musa Qal'eh.

I told my truck team, "I don't want to even think on this return trip. I am not sitting in front of that BFT. We are just passengers on this trip back." I intended to enjoy not being the convoy commander or ACC for a mission, insomuch as that was possible. I got some practice driving, spending the first half of the trip behind the wheel, something I enjoyed doing but didn't get the opportunity to do very often. The rest of the time I was up in the turret.

Stacy ran her convoys a little differently than I did, and she drove them fast. One thing that I learned from her was how to drive momentum by allowing gaps, sometimes as big as a mile, to open up if there was a breakdown or stoppage. The idea was that while the front kept pushing, you could handle the issue at the back; the trucks at the back would simply catch up once the problem was fixed. The trucks at the front were limited to a slow rate of movement as Route Clearance cleared the route.

I adopted her gap tolerance, but since I was a little more risk-averse than she was, I would post a security truck up on a hill to watch over the gap and ensure that no IEDs were laid on our trucks by opportunistic insurgents. We'd heard reports from 1st Battalion, 2nd Marines that insurgents had actually snuck up and emplaced IEDs right next to their trucks while their gunners were facing the wrong way. We couldn't relax while we were outside the wire . . . not even for a second.

I learned a lot from her on that convoy. We hadn't been very good friends up until that point and I'll admit that I was mostly to blame. I think I had judged her unfairly and too harshly for things that weren't her fault, that were a result of circumstances that would have tripped up anyone—myself included. I'm thankful that she gave me a second chance. In the end, statistically, our platoons were about equally effective.

When we all got back to Camp Leatherneck, the whole company essentially collapsed and breathed a sigh of relief. It had been a hard week. Arawak 3 had suffered a severe IED strike to one of their embedded Afghan National Army Ford Ranger light tactical vehicles (LTV) that resulted in two Afghans killed and another wounded, as well as numerous other IED strikes. Arawak 2 had been on the Route Red Recon, and Arawak 1 had conducted the recovery mission that came under heavy attack on their exit out of the Western Cluster. The Route Red Recon was often referred to as a "clown show" or a "clusterfuck." The mission had been successful in that we had answered the question: "Can CLB-6 use Route Red to get to FOB Edinburgh?" The answer was a resounding "No." The mission had been a disaster in terms of equipment damaged and Marines injured. Was undertaking that mission a sensible risk? Why had the battalion commander approved the mission? It opened up broader questions about why we were there. What was it all for? How could we bring some kind of semblance of peace to the Helmand Province? What were we doing here?

Over the next few days I thought about the insurgent we had killed. That was the closest and best view of a confirmed kill that I'd had up until that point. I was physically sick from the thought of it. We had killed him so that he wouldn't kill us, but hadn't we started the fight by coming to Afghanistan in the first place? The second or third time we had confirmed kills, it didn't bother me as much, and over time the guilt about killing someone subsided. I was more disturbed by the fact that it no longer bothered me than I was about killing people—I wasn't a killer by nature, and didn't join the Marines to kill people. Even though it wasn't me who actually pulled the trigger, I had set up the situation and I gave the orders that ended their lives.

In all likelihood, the insurgent probably didn't want to be fighting Americans either. Most of those guys were just local guns for hire and would have just as soon been home on their farms. Only a few of the insurgents were hardened fighters. Were they fighting us because of jihad, on ideological grounds, or because we were invading their home? Would I act any differently if we switched places?

It was early May 2010. We were barely halfway through deployment, and people were starting to talk about continued pushes to the east, into one of the most dangerous areas of the Helmand Province, the Sangin District.

CHAPTER TWELVE

IED STRIKE

MAY 2010

"**F**reedom is outside the wire" became a refrain for the Marines of Alpha Company. The oftentimes overbearing chain of command gave the Marines no respite from petty requirements while they were aboard Camp Leatherneck. Invariably the "leaders," trying to maintain garrison-type standards in a war zone, were those least engaged with the actual fighting.

"Hey, Devil Dog, I know you're not walking and drinking that Gatorade at the same time."

"Chewing gum in uniform? Oh, hell no."

"When is the last time this unit practiced marching?"

Adding to the stress, the relationship between the infantry and logistics units was often strained.

"The biggest issue that logistics units have," Captain Gallagher once told me, "is that we apologize for our own existence. We've somehow come to believe that we are second-class citizens."

"But we only exist to support them," I said.

"Right. It's not about us. It's never about us. That's important to understand, but that doesn't mean we're not equals. Without them we have no reason to exist, but without us, they can't exist."

Infantry Marines refer to anyone who is not an infantry Marine as a POG, pronounced with a long "O," or Person Other than Grunt. We were POGs. Our mission set was different, and we were never sent on seek-and-destroy missions, but convoys were oftentimes no less stressful. Grunts were frequently on offensive missions—they could take the initiative and select the time and place of the battle, even setting ambushes and surprising the insurgents. My platoon was always on the defense, essentially. We were told, within a very small window, where and when we had to go. Every time we left the wire we made contact with the enemy and his weapons. Quite a few of the "grunts" recognized this, and were appreciative. Others were less appreciative, deriding the CLB-6 Marines who had risked everything to deliver vital supplies.

"Oh, gotta head back to Leatherneck, gotta get some good chow and a shower," grunts would cat-call, as if a hot shower at the end of the convoy somehow reduced the risk we faced or repaired the permanent musculoskeletal damage that every Marine in a truck platoon suffered, or erased the memories of friends loaded on MEDEVAC helicopters.

The time between missions was usually short, just a couple of days or so, and these days were filled with planning and preparations for the next operation. But we had it better than the grunts out at the FOBs. In my downtime I could watch movies on my MacBook or read a book. With internet access in the Alpha Company's tent, I could email Alison every other day or so, and was usually able to call home once or twice a week. There were long stretches without being able to call or email home, though, sometimes weeks at a time between missions and during communications shut downs. Communications were shut down whenever someone was killed in action. "River City," it was called, official jargon for "reduced communications." The idea was to prevent somebody from telling a Marine's family that their loved one had been killed before the family received the official notification. It was a somber reminder for all of us; strangely, the first way we often found out that someone in another unit had been killed was that we went into River City status.

The mail kept being delivered in River City, though. Letters, oddly, could take weeks while packages from family members might only take about eight or ten days to arrive. If you judge the war in Afghanistan by the things that we asked our families to send us, it was a strange war indeed. We asked for many of the things that Marines have always asked for—foot powder, soap, t-shirts, books and candy. But because of the "static" nature of units assigned to permanent bases, we asked for heavier comfort items too—folding camp chairs to sit in, cases of Red Bull energy drinks, sheets and blankets, and plastic Christmas trees. It was strange to come back from a mission filthy and smelling like diesel fumes, just glad to be alive, to jump in a hot shower and head back to a fairly comfortable tent to watch a movie, eating cookies sent from home. Stranger still to walk into the Camp Leatherneck barbershop to see a live Christmas tree, trimmed to satisfy even Norman Rockwell.

Truthfully, I do wish that our life on Leatherneck was a little less well-appointed. The infantrymen and Marines at the forward bases had a much rougher life. A more Spartan environment would have helped keep the Marines focused. It was hard not to get complacent among the comforts on Camp Leatherneck. We were POGs. Fortunately or unfortunately, the Marines' wish to be outside the wire and away from Camp Leatherneck was granted often.

Regular resupply runs to Now Zad, Edinburgh and Musa Qal'eh were scheduled to depart every ten days or so. Each mission took about three or four days, with time in between to rest, reset, and prepare for the next mission. Second Platoon, my platoon, was more or less on a "on-off" rotation with Third Platoon on the Now Zad/Edi run, while First Platoon focused for the most part on missions to Delaram and the forward CLSA logistics base outside of Marjeh in support of Operation Moshtarak. During our "off time" between the big missions to Now Zad, we weren't really off. In addition to prepping for the next mission, a large number of Marines from the platoon had to support the other platoon's runs (just as they did for ours). Being "off" also meant that we were the standby platoon for recovery missions.

First Lieutenant Stacy Wood's Third Platoon conducted more recoveries than any other platoon in Alpha Company, due to the way the schedule fell out when other units happened to call for recovery support, but every platoon had their fair share. The recovery missions were dangerous. They brought CLB-6 to the very front lines of the battlefield and sometimes beyond the forward line of friendly troops. A request for recovery support was called a "15 Line" because of the format of the radio report. When the 15 Lines came in, CLB-6 Alpha Company was on the road.

MAY 2010: CLB-6 COMPOUND, CAMP LEATHERNECK, HELMAND PROVINCE, AFGHANISTAN

Whenever my platoon was the designated QRF, I checked in with the battalion COC several times a day to see what the various units were doing in the battlespace. If nobody seemed to be moving around then we probably would not be tasked. On other days, one unit or another might be engaged in a major offensive; they would hit IEDs and need to have vehicles recovered, so we could be sure that we were going out.

Third Battalion, 7th Marines was in the middle of Operation Eastern Dagger I and Eastern Dagger II, largely vehicle mounted operations in the Western Cluster and Tabletop just west of the Helmand River. A lack of wreckers, organic within their own units, meant that as their vehicles struck IEDs they often had to stay wherever they were until somebody could come get them.

"Somebody" was us. At first, the missions seemed to come down to the truck platoons as a surprise, but were later organized into a more formal "Quick Reaction Force," capable of departing Camp Leatherneck within four hours of receipt of mission (and considering all the administrative red tape we had to go through before we could leave, four hours was pushing it). Third Platoon had been running recovery missions for them over the past week, so I felt pretty sure that we were going out now that we were the duty platoon. As the day progressed, 3/7 struck quite a few IEDs. They were able to drag some of the damaged trucks back to the battalion assembly area themselves, but it became clear they were going to need help with at least a few. My platoon still had not been tasked with the mission, and darkness was not far off.

The task came in around 2100. Two of 3/7's MATVs had hit IEDs and were immobilized, a mineroller had been destroyed, and the left rear axles had been blown off an MTVR. All of this equipment would need to be recovered back to Camp Leatherneck; 3/7 also needed a resupply of water, food, fuel, and ammo. By that point in the day, my Marines had been awake and standing by (waiting for the mission) for over 15 hours. While we could have gone out and pushed through the fatigue, the movement would have been much slower and more dangerous in the dark. There were also some minerollers and towbars out with another one of our company's convoys that would be useful and were due to arrive back that night. We arranged to leave at first light the next day.

As we saddled up the next morning, I hoped that nobody would remember that it was my promotion date. I wanted to get promoted over the radio while I was outside the wire—I thought it would make a good story later. Alas, the battalion XO remembered, and called me into his office to promote me to the rank of first lieutenant before I left. Staff Sergeant Caravalho pinned the new rank insignia onto the sleeve of my FROG shirt. I didn't bother to correct my rank on the manifest—it would have been just one more change and it wasn't worth it.

Just before sunrise, we departed the CLB-6 motor pool and made our way to Camp Leatherneck's entry control point. I requested permission to depart over the BFT.

MEBA-CLB-B-MTPLT2: *Red Cloud, this is Arawak 2. Request permission to depart friendly lines with 41 pax, 15 vehicles.*

MEBA-CLB-B-COC: *Arawak 2, denied. Stand by.*

MEBA-CLB-B-MTPLT2: *What is going on?*

MEBA-CLB-B-COC: *Possible follow-on mission. Stand by for more information.*

They had to be kidding. I had to *leave* on a mission before they could start giving me follow-on missions. Six hours of waiting at the front gate of Leatherneck was just beginning, but I didn't know it yet. Somewhere, there were miscommunications about a repair part that 3/7 needed to fix one of their wreckers. It took about six hours for somebody somewhere to determine which part it was, exactly, and who had one and how they were going to steal it off another truck. Three times, a mechanic in a pickup truck drove out to where our convoy was staged at the exit of Camp Leatherneck (a good six miles from the CLB-6 compound . . . Camp Leatherneck was massive). Each time, they brought us a different part that they had determined was the right one needed for the repair. Finally, around 1300, we were cleared to depart.

The terrain in the desert just to the west of the Helmand River is characterized by steep ridges or fingers and deep sands, but there is a gentle ridgeline that runs north-to-south, and is easily trafficable. Called "The Tabletop," this would become one of the most heavily IED'd terrain features in the area of operations. No route clearance support was available, so we were just "proofing" the route with a mineroller. On the trip north, though, we didn't hit a thing, and the trip to 3/7's Assembly Area southwest of Shir Ghazi was smooth.

I found their company gunnery sergeant running the assembly area and arranged to leave a few of my trucks with him. My platoon had brought a few LVSRs to put the two damaged MATVs on, but we would tow the damaged MATVs back to the AA on MK36 wreckers first—it was safer to do it that way. I also left our refueler truck with him—no sense in exposing it to any more danger than necessary. Before leaving for the recovery site, Sergeant Geising, the scout vehicle commander, and I talked briefly to one of 3/7's Marines about the area.

"Well, sir, you got two shitty routes to choose from. This one here," he said, pointing to the map on the BFT screen, "is a native road, but it's full of IEDs. The other one, over here to the east, has a hill that is steep as hell and we almost flipped a truck on it, but you're welcome to try."

"CLB-6 has some of the best drivers around. If we can get through the Lande Nawah, we can get up that wadi."

Sergeant Geising, the scout from First Platoon, was filling in because Corporal Zeitz was still sidelined after being injured on the Route Red Reconnaissance.

"Sir, whadda ya think? I figure I'm just gonna push us way east. Not risk it with the IEDs. That terrain looks nasty and a bunch of the 3/7 guys said they couldn't drive out there, but I think we can handle it."

"Ok, yeah, sounds good. I'd rather deal with rough terrain than with IEDs." We were exchanging one risk for another—rougher terrain was slow and could flip our trucks, but I felt the IEDs rumored to be on the smooth route were a more certain threat.

Darkness had fallen, but the drivers did alright getting up the hill. As our vehicles ascended, our headlights were like spotlights pointed skyward. They swiveled back to earth as each truck crested the peak, and we pulled into 3/7's forward position. I found the company commander. We probably would not be returning to the AA that night, but I wanted to load up the damaged cargo for a quick departure the next morning.

"Where in the hell did you guys come from? We were watching out for you to the southwest." he said.

"Yeah, sir, we came in from the east. Your guys at the AA said you never took that route. Too rough. Since it was rough, we figured there wouldn't be any IEDs."

"Huh. Well, ok. Right, I got three MATVs and—"

"Three?" I cut him off. "The request was only for two. I don't have assets to take all three."

"Well, yeah, there's something wrong with the wheel on one of 'em. Maybe you can just change the tire. Our guys couldn't figure it out. So I need you to take care of the MATVs, the MTVR back at the AA, and a mineroller down in the wadi to the north about another kilometer or two."

"Alright, I saw the MTVR, we can get that. We also brought the spare parts for your wrecker so you can get it up and running again."

"Oh yeah, haha" he laughed, "we ended up not needing anything. Fixed it ourselves. Thanks, though." That was six hours that we wasted sitting on Camp Leatherneck.

"Oooh-k then, sir. Umm, can you show me where this mineroller is?"

"Yeah, just drive down the trail here," he pointed to the map on my BFT screen, "and it's a ways down here in the wadi."

"Ok, who should I link up with down there? I don't see any BFT icons."

"Oh, well, the mineroller is down there by itself. They detached it from the truck when it got blown up and went on with their mission. It's down there. You can just go grab it."

"You left it?" I was incredulous.

"Well, yeah. It's pretty heavy, haha" he laughed again. "I didn't think anybody else was going to take it."

"I'm not worried that somebody may have taken it. I'm worried that somebody may have booby-trapped it." This had happened quite a few times to American units in both Iraq and Afghanistan—booby traps were placed on our damaged equipment to hit us when we came to recover it later.

"Huh. We hadn't thought of that. Well, can you still get it?"

"Well, sir, I honestly don't have a choice, do I? It's still the mission, the risk just went up is all."

I hand-picked a few trucks to go down with me into the wadi. The trail was tight and the terrain tough. When we got to the destroyed mineroller, I directed my driver to do a circle around it with our mineroller. It would be much better for our mineroller to be destroyed by a booby-trap than to damage one of our precious wreckers, which were in very short supply.

"Alright, Umoren," I said to the driver. "Next, I want you to bump the mineroller with ours. Don't crash into it, but hit it hard enough that any hair triggers or pressure-release switches will trip."

He did. Nothing happened. No explosion. At this point, I was satisfied that the enemy hadn't had the time or resources to booby-trap it. The wrecker operators loaded the damaged mineroller onto a flatbed MTVR, and we turned to the next task.

The MATV with the flat tire was just a short drive from the abandoned mineroller. It was back up the hill out of the wadi, so I dropped every truck except one of the wreckers and escorted it the mile or so to the MATV. When we got there, Staff Sergeant Taylor, our truckmaster and wrecker operator, jumped out. He took one look at the damaged tire and laughed.

"So, you guys didn't want to change this yourself or you don't fuckin' know how? I don't know what's worse." He was a sarcastic guy, to say the least. "That's the difference between a 'driver' and an 'operator.' I'd bet the lieutenant could change this tire. Aww, hell, I drove all the way out here, might as well do something. *Sure thing, I'll change your tire for ya. Do you want a cup of coffee, too?*"

One of the 3/7 Marines was about to say something in retort when Staff Sergeant Taylor snapped at him, "Listen, cupcake, you couldn't change your tire, so now you have to sit quietly in the waiting room." Maybe sarcastic wasn't quite the right word. Abrasive was more accurate. But he changed their tire, so they couldn't really complain too much.

The next morning, we returned to the assembly area along with all of the 3/7 trucks that had been forward. All of 3/7 was going to return south to Camp Leatherneck, but they were going to take several hours to get ready. We had no need to wait for them, so we set off south with our small group of 15 trucks. About halfway back down the Tabletop, our movement stopped.

WHUMP.

"IED IED IED!"

"Buzz, this is Gnome, yeah, we just hit an IED. It got the mineroller pretty good, but we're all okay."

"Roger. Ole Dirt push up with me." "Ole Dirt" was Staff Sergeant Taylor's callsign. My truck with its mineroller proofed a path for the wrecker. Staff Sergeant Taylor and Corporal Minetti used the wrecker's crane to detach the damaged mineroller and loaded it onto a flatbed MTVR.

A battle-damaged mineroller is loaded onto an MTVR flatbed truck somewhere on the Tabletop in the Helmand Province. Mineroller recoveries were difficult and dangerous.

We were acutely aware of the probability that there were more IEDs all around us. Judging from the size of the blast that destroyed Gnome's mineroller, I thought these were the biggest IEDs we had seen thus far. Both intel and EOD reports would later confirm that to be true.

As we were finishing up the recovery, the COC sent me a message.

MEBA-CLB-B-COC: *Arawak 2, how many minerollers do you have left?*
MEBA-CLB-B-MTPLT2: *Just one.*
MEBA-CLB-B-COC: *Arawak 2, which truck is it on?*
MEBA-CLB-B-MTPLT2: *Mine.*
MEBA-CLB-B-COC: *Arawak 2, what is your plan?*
MEBA-CLB-B-MTPLT2: *Pushing to the front. We are Oscar Mike.*

Generally, it didn't make sense for the platoon commander to ride up front, exposed to the most risk. The platoon commander makes sure the TMO directs the recovery, the STL ensures security, the casualties are cared for, etc. My ACC for the mission, Sergeant Belcher, argued for us to switch places.

"Sir, you shouldn't be up front. You know that."

"You're right, but I can't switch trucks with you. It might be right by the textbook but I would lose all face with these Marines. I wouldn't be able to live with myself. How could I ask you to ride up front if I'm not willing to do it myself?" Days later, quite a few people took issue with my logic during the debrief and argued it was foolish pride overriding tactical sense. However, none of the people arguing that side of the issue had ever been in combat or needed their Marines to trust them outside the wire. I stand by my decision and I think my Marines appreciated it.

I took perhaps the shortest turn at the front of a convoy in CLB-6 history. No more than a few hundred meters after we started moving again, my watch stopped, figuratively speaking.

WHUMP SLAM CRASH.

In slow motion, the air filled with brown moondust and the front of the truck was lifted off the ground. I was thrown forward into the dashboard. All the junk in the truck was thrown around, crashing about.

"FUCK." So that's what an IED felt like. "Lepinski! Lepinski!" I grabbed at the gunner's leg. Lance Corporal Lepinksi was not my regular gunner, but he had been up in the turret because Corporal Sena was out on a mission with Lieutenant Wood's First Platoon. Lepinski could have been struck with shrapnel or debris.

"Yeah, yeah, I'm okay," he shouted back, alive with adrenaline.

"Okay, good. Umoren?"

"I'm okay, I guess, sir." Corporal Umoren, the driver, was visibly in pain.

"How about you, Williams?" I turned around in my seat to check on Williams, who was sitting in the back seat.

"Fine, sir. I got the grenades." Lance Corporal Williams, the radio operator, was calm as ever. He held up a green metal ammo can with our supply of smoke grenades, one each in green, yellow, white and red.

"Okay, everyone good? Williams, have Lepinski pop the green smoke." I had tried my radios, but nothing was working and the BFT had shut down. The smoke would let everyone else in the convoy know that we were okay and they didn't need to rush to our aid. Lepinski threw the smoke grenade off to our left and green smoke began to billow. I could almost feel everyone else in the convoy beginning to breathe again, relieved that somebody in our truck was alive. I tried to get the BFT restarted. The radios were coming back on. The extreme shock of the IED had shut all the electrical systems down; it had been a big one.

"Alright, Umoren, back us up, staying in our tire tracks, and then pull forward off to the side, using the mineroller like a bulldozer if there are any secondary IEDs around. I want the wrecker to be able to stay in our original tire tracks to get this blown up mineroller off us." Our truck seemed to still be working for now; the mineroller had taken the brunt of the blast. My radios finally started working again, so I briefed the convoy on the plan and we began to execute. I wasn't so much concerned about the recovery, although it was straining the limits of the equipment. The only place we could put the mineroller was on top of an MTVR that was already carrying three damaged minerollers—it was already 7000 pounds over its max cargo capacity. What was another 9000 pounds anyway? It was also towing an MRAP behind it, but true to form, the truck did everything asked of it.

The driver said, "I'll make sure to ask nicely when I tell the truck to carry this load, sir." He handled the terrain gingerly. In the end, the truck made it back to Camp Leatherneck without an issue, but we wouldn't know that for a while yet.

What next? We had no more minerollers. While we stopped to deal with the IED strike, an adjacent unit had hit another IED nearby. The area was seeded with IEDs. I definitely didn't want to drive around here without a mineroller on my front vehicle if I didn't have to. I looked on the BFT and noticed that somebody was coming north—a Marine Route Clearance Platoon from 2d Combat Engineer Battalion, so I contacted them. Conveniently, their original mission had been canceled and they were about to turn around. Instead, they came to our position. One of the EOD technicians jumped right out of his truck and into the hole left by the IED. He started poking the dirt with his bayonet. This guy was nuts.

"Well, damn, sir, this was a big 'un, wasn't it?"

"Far as I could tell, yeah. It rocked my world."

"I'll bet." He took measurements and pictures for the post-blast analysis and searched the site for evidence that could be fingerprinted. Even a scrap of an IED that had been in an explosion could still have DNA or fingerprints of the bombmakers.

The convoy was soon headed south in trace of the RCP, following in their tire tracks, but night was falling. The shock and adrenaline of the IED strike had worn off, and everyone in the truck had a splitting headache. Tylenol and Motrin can mask some of the symptoms of life threatening head injuries, so they are prohibited after an IED strike. We would have to push through. The RCP had pushed almost due south and was no longer tracing the Tabletop ridge. The fingers and draws of the earth were becoming more distinct, and more fractured.

"Uh, Buzz, this is Gnome," on the radio, "I think the truck in front of me just rolled over."

Goddammit. "Roger, Gnome." I turned to my driver. "Umoren, flip us around." I didn't have a mineroller on the front of my truck anymore, but it was a risk we'd have to take. We turned around and I could see a pair of headlights off to the side of the path that we had been on. They appeared to be about 15° from level. Well, that wasn't too bad ... we could just tip the truck back down and it would be fine. But as we got closer, I realized that the headlights were 15° from level because the truck had rolled 195°. Goddammit. It was an LVSR with a MATV on its bed. The ground had broken underneath it, and the truck had slid about 30 feet down the ridge on the right side, rolling over in the process. The Marines inside the truck were okay, but with a total weight of over 100,000 pounds, we had nothing that could recover this truck. Staff Sergeant Taylor tried, using his MK36 wrecker, but it was no use.

Captain Gallagher laughed. "Well, Jeff, this is a good experience for you. You'll get to call for an M88 recovery." He had come along on the mission, I suspect, to get away from Camp Leatherneck and the nonsense that was going on back at CLB-6 headquarters. The RCP had received another mission and departed. I sent a 15-line recovery request to the CLB-6 COC, asking them to send an M88 Hercules Tank Retriever. It would take a while to get to us. We set up security for the night.

Throughout the night we could see people watching us off in the distance. A car full of men pulled up onto a hilltop off to our northeast, a few hundred meters away. There was movement all around. We were being maneuvered against. I still had a headache. I finally gave in to one of Staff Sergeant Caravalho's earlier predictions. "Hey, staff sergeant, you were right. I am going to smoke before the end of the deployment. Can I have a cigarette?"

"Hahaha, sir, it would be now that you ask. I'm seriously out. This mission is taking way too long. We were supposed to be back yesterday, so I only brought one pack. I'm out."

I laughed.

Staff Sergeant Caravalho laughed again. "You know, sir, I did this on purpose, just to make sure that in your moment of weakness I wouldn't have any cigarettes, so that in the end you can be right."

We prepared for an attack.

We weren't the only ones aware that we were being watched. Enemy radio communications were being monitored, and some of the info was being passed to us through our COC.

MEBA-CLB-B-COC: *Arawak 2, this is Red Cloud. Enemy radio traffic reports approximately a platoon-size enemy force watching "American trucks" near the river across from Sangin. You are the only unit in the area, be alert. They plan to attack after sunrise.*

MEBA-CLB-B-MTPLT2: *Roger, we have been watching some spotters on a hill off to our northeast.*

A few hours later, just before sunrise, another message from our COC came in with the first good news in a while.

MEBA-CLB-B-COC: *Arawak 2, enemy radio reports they are breaking contact. They were shouting "They brought a tank. We see the tank!"*

It had to be the M88. The enemy didn't know that the only thing the Hercules could do was lift some weight, and that it had no weaponry. The recovery mission was getting close to our position.

"Well, damn sir, that's another lieutenant I've had to come rescue," Gunnery Sergeant Locklear said when he pulled up. He was the convoy commander for the recovery mission that had come to recover *my recovery mission.* "You're the third lieutenant I've had to come get," he said in his North Carolina drawl. He was our company operations chief; he was also indispensable and our all-around pinch hitter and fill-in.

"Yeah, yeah, yeah. Did you bring the stuff I asked for? We need coolant pretty bad." The IED had damaged my truck's radiator—and since all the coolant had leaked out we were refilling it with water, but the truck was still overheating pretty badly. The driver shut off the engine whenever we stopped, and we ran the heater whenever the truck was on. The heater worked as a kind of "secondary radiator" to keep the engine cool, except it dumped the heat inside the cab, which made it miserable for us in the May heat.

"Sure, I brought some coolant." He held up a five-gallon jerry can of coolant. "So your truck got hit too? You guys *tryin'* to find all the IEDs? You know you can just drive around 'em?"

"I would have if I could have. Just bad luck, I guess."

The M88 operators set to work. Based on the M60 Patton tank, the M88 is a tow truck and crane built on a tank chassis. In service since 1961, it is among the heaviest recovery assets in the US military even at the advanced age of 49, as of 2010.

An M88 Hercules Tank Retriever sets up to recover an LVSR that rolled over, crushing the MATV that it was carrying.

The recovery didn't take long. The LVSR was rolled back onto the trail, started up, and driven off to be rigged for flat-tow behind another LVSR. The MATV was dragged up the hill and loaded on to another LVSR to be hauled back to Camp Leatherneck. Gunnery Sergeant Locklear and I reorganized all the trucks into one convoy for the trip back, which actually went quite smoothly. No more IEDs or attacks.

We arrived back at the CLB-6 motor pool in mid-afternoon. I finished getting all of our equipment accounted for and secured the Marines, and just wanted to get to sleep. I still had a headache from the IED. I hadn't eaten anything in over 24 hours.

"I just want a shower and some food. I'll be fine."

"Bullshit, sir, you're coming with me." The company first sergeant, First Sergeant Pat Gillespie, carted me off to medical despite my protests.

For Marines, the things we carry grow to take on a life of their own. We love and hate the way they wear against us. We hate the weight of a flak jacket with SAPI plates, but there is a comfort in the way it fits us. It sucks sharing your sleeping bag with an M4 rifle, but it is strangely comforting at the same time. For a truck platoon, it is not only the things we carry that have significance—it's the things that carried us.

CLB-6 was very fortunate to have the gear we had, even though we always felt that we were just scraping by. Compared to what soldiers and Marines had to make do with in WWII or Korea, we really had it okay. Even compared with early in the OIF in Iraq, we didn't have it too bad—I never had to survive on one MRE a day or risk running out of water. For a logistics unit, success or failure will be defined, at least in part, by how proficient the unit is with its equipment and if it has the right equipment to begin with. The equipment defined our lives, we lived and breathed it, literally living in and on our trucks for weeks at a time. I could sleep on the hood of a MATV or against the tire of an MTVR any day of the week.

My MATV, serial number 650644. Heavily armored and surprisingly quick, this truck saved my life.

My MATV literally saved my life. The best truck that the Marine Corps ever purchased was MATV serial number 650644, which I used on almost every mission during OEF 10-1. I claim that it was my truck, but Lance Corporal Ed Sedam, my driver, has much more right to it than I do. He was the one who really took care of her. Like ships, we always thought of our trucks as feminine. We lived in that truck. That truck kept us alive. Ever loyal, even when severely damaged by an IED, she limped back to Camp Leatherneck before giving out right as we got back to the motor pool. She got us back home, and it was like she knew that she had done her job and that only then would it be okay to sleep.

Several months later, right before the end of the deployment, we got her back, fixed and as good as new. The mechanics at the third echelon maintenance shop that repaired her had painted a "battle star" between the two panes of glass that made up the front windshield. This was a mark of honor, of respect, for the vehicle.

When I returned to Afghanistan in 2011, one of my first tasks was to find my truck. Sure enough, she was still being used, still alive. I told her driver to take good care of her, but I don't think he understood how serious I was.

CHAPTER THIRTEEN

BACK IN THE SADDLE

After an initial assessment by one of the battalion's corpsmen, all of us who were in the IED strike were diagnosed with Grade II concussions. After one concussion, Marines were restricted from going outside the wire for ten days; the idea was to give the brain time to heal a little before potentially being exposed to a second IED. Because of the IED strike that we had been exposed to, we were locked down on Leatherneck and wouldn't be allowed to go on the next Sar Taiz mission to Now Zad and Edinburgh.

Guilt consumed me—the platoon would be going out and I wouldn't be with them. But secretly, I felt I wasn't ready and was glad to not have to go out yet. Searing headaches that flared up with any physical exertion (even walking) and insomnia had rendered me practically ineffective. I hid as much of this as I could from the Marines and from my company commander, but after talking to the doc I realized the only thing I could do was wait. I was given some Midol for the headaches—all joking aside, it was supposed to relieve swelling and fluid retention in the brain. The only good thing that came out of being grounded was that Staff Sergeant Caravalho was to lead the next Sar Taiz mission on his own. I had every confidence in his ability, and helped him with the mission planning process.

It hurt like hell to watch my platoon depart friendly lines without me. I wouldn't have been able to forgive myself if someone had gotten hurt while I wasn't there. First Lieutenant Stacy Wood rode with Staff Sergeant Caravalho to provide a little topcover for him and to answer questions. I was in the COC every few hours to check on the mission status, to see how they were making out. The Marines performed to standard. Five months into the deployment, they were practiced and confident in their trade. When they rolled back through the gate I was there to greet them, and was able to breathe a little easier; I would not let them go out again without me.

I needed to get back on the horse. The fear of IEDs was building in my mind. I think it was a pretty justified fear, but nevertheless, I had to somehow overcome this fear so that I could continue to lead Second Platoon. On the tenth day after the IED strike, I put myself on First Platoon's milk run as a passenger to MOB Price, a friendly base run by the British and Danish forces in the outskirts of Gereshk. I knew the route well from the Route Red Recon and some of the recovery missions, and was there to advise the sergeant from First Platoon who was running the convoy—First Platoon's lieutenant had been relieved of command, so there was a leadership gap.

I rode along on two more convoys with First Platoon to force myself not to let the nerves get to me. Nevertheless, every time an IED went off it rattled my mindset and focus much more than it had before I had struck one. I hoped the Marines wouldn't notice. The Marines needed to stick together, and I needed them to have confidence in me. Rifts were forming in the battalion, and in the company.

JUNE 2010: ALPHA COMPANY TENT, CAMP LEATHERNECK, HELMAND PROVINCE, AFGHANISTAN

First Lieutenant Jamie Maynard, First Platoon's commander, was relieved of her duties. The damage she did as a leader was only marginally worse than the drama and chaos that resulted from her relief.

"I thrive on the misery of others," Second Lieutenant Bobby Fowler, our company XO, said with a smirk. We both laughed. "Misery and failure sustain me."

"You have to tell me the story." Gossip was one of the few things available to keep us entertained.

"She left here crying. The Gallagher yelled at her to get out of the company tent and to not come back. She's been fired as a platoon commander and is being sent to FOB Delaram II to be the camp commandant. She'll spend the rest of her days in CLB-6 making sure that the trash gets picked up."

"Okay, but what happened?" I asked.

"Alright, so you know how most of her platoon was attached to 3/7 out in Delaram, right? She was tasked with bringing them back from Delaram to Leatherneck. So she put in an ASR for a flight and flew to D2. But she got there and decided she didn't want to be the convoy commander, and put Sergeant Plumhoff in charge."

"But she's the lieutenant! She can't remove herself from responsibility. It was her platoon and her mission." I was taken aback. You might as well say that you didn't want to be a Marine officer anymore.

"Right," Fowler continued. "She puts herself in the last vehicle of the convoy. An MK31/870."

"A 31/870? It doesn't have a turret. Who was doing rear security?"

"Nobody. No rear security. And you know what else a 31 doesn't have?"

"A radio or BFT. So she really put herself in a 31/870 with no comm and no gun as the last vehicle in her own convoy."

"Well, she kept saying it wasn't her convoy. That it was Plumhoff's convoy. So anyway, there she is. The 31 breaks down, and slows to a crawl. But the rest of the trucks keep rolling. The vehicle in front of her sees her and slows down with her, the MK36 wrecker."

"But a 36 doesn't have comm or a gun either."

"Nope. Sure doesn't. So there they are, two trucks on the side of the road with nothing. Sergeant Underwood, the wrecker driver, says they need to post security."

"So they, like, set up a 360 with rifles?" Every Marine was ordered to carry an M4 or M16A4 rifle outside the wire; no longer do officers carry only pistols.

"Well, that's the funny part. She didn't bring her rifle with her to Delaram. She left it here at Camp Leatherneck."

"And the rest of the convoy kept going?"

"Kept trucking. Forty-five miles an hour because they were on the hardball paved road. Out of sight. They were all alone. Luckily, another Marine unit drives by a little while later."

"And they stop? Who was it? GS Motor T?"

"Wrong. It was a PSD." Fowler laughed again. A Personal Security Detachment is the small group of Marines assigned to protect and provide mobility for a VIP. This PSD was for some General.

"She explains what happens and asks to use their Iridium phone." Iridium Satellite phones look like early 1990s cell phones and can make phone calls from almost anywhere in the world utilizing satellites. While not technically a "secure" means of communication (as they are not encrypted to the same standard as our radios), most units carried an Iridium phone as a backup means of communication.

"So she calls the COC?" I asked.

"Wrong again. She didn't have a CEOI." The CEOI was like a phone book and contained all the communications information including frequencies, callsigns, BFT role names and Iridium contact numbers. Without it, you may as well be dialing random numbers. "So she asks the PSD if they know who she can call. The closest number to CLB-6 they had was for RCT COC." The RCT-2 COC was the headquarters for the regimental combat team that we supported. They were an adjacent unit, and definitely not "in house." Calling them was tantamount to airing all of our dirty laundry.

Fowler went on, "So she calls the RCT, who calls our COC. And of course, poor Graff is in there like, 'You're who? What is going on? Is this for real?'" First Lieutenant Graff was the CLB-6 battalion watch officer.

I was incredulous. "So, she put herself in the last vehicle, without comm, without a gun in the turret, she didn't bring her rifle, and she tried to put her sergeant in charge of the platoon."

"Right. And when they finally got the whole convoy back here, she tried to blame the whole thing on anybody else she could think of. It wasn't her fault!"

She had become known as "our girl" (or "your girl" when referred to by the Staff NCOs in the unit), a sarcastic term meant to emphasize the failure of our peer, a fellow lieutenant. I wish it had been the only mistake that "our girl" made. It wasn't. It was one of a veritable litany of failures that eventually spanned years. She missed deadlines that cost the unit millions of dollars when equipment had to be transported by truck instead of by train. Critical ammunition that she was responsible for ordering was not available for fundamental predeployment training exercises. She compromised highly classified mission plans by plugging a classified external hard drive into her Macbook (a serious violation) so that she could do mission planning in the comfort of her air-conditioned tent instead of in the Company Office where her Marines had to work. She utilized a unit vehicle for personal reasons while junior Marines, without the vehicle they should have had, walked miles in the hot sun to pick up the battalion's mail.

Not once, but *twice,* she was "soft-relieved," moved to another job with less responsibility where she could do less damage. The problem with a soft-relief is that, at least in this case as in many others, it was done without any real consequences. Without negative official fitness reports or counsellings, she was retained on active duty when better-qualified officers were let go, and she was promoted to the rank of captain. Marines like this are truly the rarity in the officer corps, but the few who do slip by tear through the Marine Corps like a wrecking ball, damaging everything they touch.

I think it's just human nature that failure and frustration stick out in our minds more than things that go smoothly. I don't intend to dwell on the failures of leadership for too long, but to pretend they didn't happen would be naïve. Part of being a learning organization is to learn from mistakes and try to avoid them in the future. I learned a lot from seeing the mistakes that other people made. I learned when it makes sense to acknowledge the failure and move on, and what happens when leaders fail to hold a Marine accountable for his or her mistakes. When a Marine in a leadership position isn't held accountable for their mistake, it can poison the command and paralyze the organization. What's worse, the offender will think nothing of the indiscretion, and continue to make the same mistakes over and over again. In the end, their Marines pay equally, whether the mistake was made out of ignorance or willful indifference.

The chaos of the battalion seemed to be carrying over to our missions. While Second Platoon was running Operation Sar Taiz IX, delivering supplies to Now Zad and FOB Edinburgh, the chaos reached a high point. The trip north had become a routine operation with Alpha Company making the trip every two weeks; Second Platoon had the lead on every other mission, trading on and off with Third Platoon. During the "off periods," Second Platoon took shorter runs to Delaram and Marjeh or recovery missions. Marines from First Platoon filled out the roster on every trip.

The outbound leg of Operation Sar Taiz IX had gone well enough. There were a few IED strikes, but by this point in the deployment the Marines were well practiced at vehicle recoveries and the only injuries were concussions. Cargo offload had been accomplished, and our trucks were loaded with disabled and damaged equipment for backhaul to Camp Leatherneck where it could be repaired.

The convoy had departed Now Zad fourteen hours earlier, just as the sun rose. We were headed back south to Camp Leatherneck on the final leg of what would be a four-day mission, but an early IED strike just south of the Acolyte Wadi had delayed the convoy.

The farmers of the Helmand Province, and indeed much of the Middle East are dependent on very sophisticated irrigation techniques for survival. Most villages relied on a system of kariz tunnels, an ancient innovation that predates Islam. A long tunnel, usually three to five feet in diameter, was dug entirely by hand into the side of a gently sloping plain or land mass. To assist in the construction and maintenance of this horizontal tunnel, vertical tunnels

The author aboard FOB Edinburgh near Musa Qal'eh just prior to departing to return to Camp Leatherneck. In the background, heavily armored cargo trucks and a 5000 gallon M970 fuel tanker are staged for departure. Carefully lining up the convoy in order ensured accountability and security.

were built down to it every 10 to 20 meters. The earth from the construction of the tunnels is piled up around the holes, into a long series of gigantic "molehills." The horizontal tunnel is dug into the hillside for several miles until it is below the level of groundwater, several hundred feet down. The result was a series of kariz shafts several miles long—a major obstacle for which there was usually no way around.

Driving over the kariz shafts was not an option. More than one vehicle had gone nose-first into a kariz and not come out (fortunately not any of CLB-6's vehicles). Convoys were forced to drive between two of the shafts. This greatly simplified the math for the insurgents; by putting an IED in the gap between every kariz, they could virtually ensure that we would encounter it. Such had been the case that morning. As the first vehicle slowly approached the gap between the mounds of earth, a mushroom-shaped dust cloud erupted under it.

Whump.

"IED IED IED!"

Several hundred meters back, the mushroom cloud was visible about four seconds before the shockwave and sound reached me. Inside my truck, the pressure wave and muffled *whump* were something like a solid door slam. For years afterward, the sound and change in air pressure of a door slamming or an air conditioner coming on were startling and unnerving.

While we stopped to recover the damaged vehicle, some children ran up to the convoy and started stealing things like chains and cargo straps. I jumped out of my truck and ran after them. Chains were in short supply and we couldn't afford to lose even one. As soon as the kids realized they were being chased, they dropped the chains.

With Noori, my platoon's interpreter for the mission, I took a case of bottled water and went up to the nearby Afghan adults.

"As-Salaam alaikum," I said, giving the standard greeting for the Muslim world.

"Wa alaikum as-salaam," the Afghan farmers responded. They looked nervous. I had just chased after their children.

"I want you to know that I am not mad at your children," I said in English, looking at the men.

Noori translated this into Pashto.

"We are here to keep you and your children safe, to provide security. Our trucks are very dangerous and can hurt your children. They cannot run up to them or climb on them," I continued. Noori translated for the Afghans as we went along. It was true. Quite a few Afghan children were hurt or killed every year as they jumped on our trucks trying to steal things.

"I have brought some water for the children, so they know that I'm not mad at them." It was a bribe, plain and simple. *I'll give you something, maybe you'll give me something in return*, I thought. "Do you know anything about the IED that we just hit?" I asked, pointing to where our truck was being recovered. The men all shook their heads and spoke so quickly they seemed to trip over their words as they enthusiastically denied all knowledge of the IED.

"They say they don't know anything about the IED, that they have never seen any Taliban. If the insurgents come, they come at night, and the Afghans are afraid to go out at night," Noori said. I smiled and thanked the Afghans anyway. It was amazing how nobody *ever* seemed to know anything about the IEDs that were planted right near their houses.

The convoy had to keep on. The movement was slow, but steady. We crossed through the Southern Terrain Belt and below the 60th Northing. The IED threat was diminished, but darkness was falling and visibility had been poor all day. Summer in Afghanistan is characterized by searing temperatures and lightning-fast winds, racing across the sands at over 100mph. The winds whip up the moon dust, limiting visibility. Particularly strong winds or storms would kick up walls of dust that rolled across the landscape like a tidal wave.

Such were the conditions during Operation Sar Taiz IX. With the convoy still about ten miles from Camp Leatherneck and midnight approaching, I was paying close attention to the visibility. I could see the truck in front of me and one more in front of that, but no more. The powerful spotlights on my MATV only penetrated 30 or 40 feet into the dust clouds. Suddenly, a wave of sand engulfed the convoy, the night got ever darker, and visibility dropped to zero.

"All stations, this is Buzz. Halt the convoy." I could no longer see the truck in front of me, even though it was no more than five feet away. We were running with tight dispersion because of the poor visibility. "We're going to wait a few minutes to see if this sandstorm lets up at all." Oftentimes, only a few minutes was needed to let the worst of the storm pass. After four or five minutes passed I could once again see the truck in front me. The sky opened, the moon shone through, and the haze lightened. Where I should have been able to see one long line of trucks with my truck sitting somewhere in the middle, I saw a scattered collection of vehicles. Hundreds of yards away, I saw the twinkling of headlights. Small sticks, groups of two or three trucks, were all over, pointing in every direction.

The sandstorm had scattered the convoy. Fear instantly gripped my throat. What if somebody was lost? Not all of my vehicles even had radios—they relied on hand and arm signals and shouting to the vehicle in front or behind them to communicate, and were entirely dependent on "following the leader" for navigation. I called Staff Sergeant Caravalho on the radio, "Smokecheck, this is Buzz. Let's assemble everyone at a central point and get accountability." We needed to account for every truck and every Marine.

"Roger, Buzz, they're all over . . . that's the only way to know if we have everyone. I'll set up a 'gate' here with Godfather if you want to collect everyone."

Staff Sergeant Caravalho set up a gate with his truck and Sergeant "Godfather" Galante's truck. It looked like most of the convoy's trucks were relatively nearby, but a few had gotten far off track. I drove a large, circular search pattern out to a radius of a few miles from the center of the convoy to look for stragglers. If there were any IEDs out there, I was going to hit them. Driving big circles like that was something we called the "IED Zamboni," named for the machines used to resurface ice hockey rinks. I didn't see any lost trucks and fortunately didn't find any IEDs. And by "find" I mean "hit."

The convoy slowly advanced forward, one truck at a time. As they passed through the gate, Staff Sergeant Caravalho checked them off on the roster and confirmed that all occupants were accounted for. We normally tried to maintain a set convoy order, but the trucks had been shuffled around in the sandstorm. I held my breath as the last truck passed through the gate. Staff Sergeant Caravalho looked up and smiled.

"We got 'em. Every one." He held out a closed fist.

I laughed and we fist-bumped. "Alright, let's get moving." The fear that I felt while waiting on the confirmation that all our Marines were accounted for was never surpassed by any other incident before or after, even while being shot at. I could think of no worse fate than for two of my Marines to be stranded and lost in the desert alone, without a radio or a Blue Force Tracker to navigate with. If one of the trucks had continued driving in the sandstorm they could have ended up miles from the convoy. Who knew if we would find them first . . . or if the enemy would. I couldn't imagine sentencing any of my Marines to that fate. I was overwhelmed with relief as I messaged the COC over the BFT.

MEBA-CLB-B-MTPLT2: *Red Cloud, all vehicles and personnel positively accounted for. We are pushing on.*

The rest of the trip back to Camp Leatherneck was anything but smooth. While we were back at FOB Edinburgh, the S3 had tasked us to dump our emergency fuel reserve into FOB Edinburgh's fuel tanks, part of a ridiculous campaign to demonstrate how quickly the battalion could move fuel. I should have said that I had dumped everything, instead of acknowledging that I had the required emergency fuel reserve—once the S3 found out we had it, they tasked us to dump it. I was furious as those 500 gallons of fuel poured in FOB Edinburgh's tanks—the fuel was the margin of error for my platoon. Not having that fuel meant that my trucks had left FOB Edinburgh without full tanks. Despite protesting the dumping of my fuel reserve, I was overruled, and it was coming back to bite us now. The delays from the IEDs and sandstorms earlier in the day meant that my trucks were running out of fuel. One by one, they stopped. I racked my brain for a solution to get us the last few miles back to base.

"Hey, Smokecheck, we got any rubber hoses?" I asked Staff Sergeant Caravalho over the radio.

"Buzz, we should have some airlines," he said, referring to the air hoses used to pressurize a towed vehicle's brakes.

"If we cut up some airlines, we could siphon fuel out of the blown up trucks that we're backhauling. Most of them probably still have fuel in the tanks."

It was slow and unconventional, but it worked. A few of my Marines knew how to suck the air out of a hose to siphon fuel out of a car—a few did it a little *too well*, prompting some raised eyebrows from their peers. I sent a furious BFT message to the OPSO in the COC.

MEBA-CLB-B-MTPLT2: *Red Cloud, because we were required to give up our emergency fuel reserve at FOB Edinburgh, my trucks are running out of fuel less than five miles from Camp Leatherneck. I have implemented a plan to siphon fuel from damaged backhaul vehicles. If this fails, be prepared for us to request an emergency fuel resupply.*

MEBA-CLB-B-COC: *Arawak 2, how long is this process going to take?*

MEBA-CLB-B-MTPLT2: *Red Cloud, I do not know. I have never had to do this before.*

I could have screamed, "We normally carry an emergency fuel reserve in case there are delays like the one we had today . . . an emergency fuel reserve that you tasked us to give away."

MEBA-CLBB-COC: *Arawak 2, can you do anything to speed up the process?*

MEBA-CLBB-MTPLT2: *Red Cloud, negative. We do not have proper siphons or pumps. Gravity siphons go as fast as they go.*

Again, I could have screamed. *It's science.*

Upon arriving back at Camp Leatherneck, I went to the COC to check back in. The OPSO raised his voice at me, "You took a huge risk by putting fuel from damaged vehicles in your trucks. It could have been contaminated."

I was furious and he could see it. I yelled in my head: *You think I don't know that, motherfucker? You know where I had a few hundred gallons of fuel that I knew was clean? In my emergency reserve. You put me in that position by ordering me to give away my reserve fuel. We keep that reserve for a reason, and you denied it to me so that you could look good for the RCT by saying you pushed another few hundred gallons of fuel.* The taste of the disdain I had for the man was the same bitter taste of the mouthful of JP-8 fuel I got when starting up one of the siphons.

I gave him a terse "sir," and walked out.

The Marines of Alpha Company often felt isolated from the rest of the battalion. *Alpha Company versus the world.* CLB-6 was my first unit, so there was nothing to compare it to, but the interpersonal drama between the staff sections and the companies was noticeable, and it affected our ability to do our job.

"You just have to know, Jeff," Captain Gallagher told me one day, "that this is not normal. The Marine Corps is not like this. We just have to run the company, take care of the Marines, screen them from the battalion's bullshit."

Alpha Company, CLB-6's main effort, could not get required support from staff sections. Combat action ribbon nominations for Marines with confirmed kills in multiple engagements were denied without explanation. Unfounded accusations of Alpha Company Marines engaging in drug trafficking were levied by Marines in H&S Company (an NCIS investigation cleared the Marines; the agent said the allegations were "ridiculous"). We were tasked by the Operations Shop to haul trucks that we didn't have licenses for; when I protested, I was ordered "you have been given your orders to haul the loads, but you are not to have any Marines drive trucks they aren't licensed for." The officer knew the order was contradictory, but he would not accept the responsibility for delaying the load, or for authorizing unlicensed Marines to drive—I learned a lot about who he was as a leader that day, and it wasn't good.

Freedom was outside the wire—I longed to get away from the nonsense found on Camp Leatherneck. When I was outside the wire, I was the ground forces commander. There was nobody who could tell me what to do for miles.

The tension in the unit did not go unnoticed. Twice, command climate surveys were administered to the Marines, providing them an opportunity to anonymously provide feedback about the chain of command and operating environment. The surveys got results; Marines had written some damning words. The battalion commander and sergeant major were relieved of command and sent back to the United States. It was an extreme move and while it may have given the Marines some small satisfaction, the environment did not change. It would take many months for the command climate to improve.

It was by no means everyone. Most of the members of H&S Company were great and often came along on convoys to provide extra gunners for us. The maintenance section worked around the clock, fixing our trucks. But there were more than a few leaders who shirked their responsibilities and whose decisions were self-serving; these individuals were not "servant leaders" to the junior Marines of the battalion. As a leader, your Marines come before you. Nevertheless, the Marines of CLB-6 accomplished the mission. Freedom was outside the wire. I just had to stay focused and keep the Marines focused. Unlike most rear echelon-types, our lives depended on it.

Alpha Company came together and did what we needed to do. The Marines were proud to be a part of the company, even if we were a dysfunctional family of sorts. Our company logo popped up everywhere; on trucks, on t-shirts, on PowerPoint slides—it was a skull wearing a Native American headdress (in homage to our battalion callsign Red Cloud, for Medal of Honor winner Mitchell Red Cloud). One Marine even got it tattooed on his leg when we got home. It was one of the few good signs that we were sticking together as a company.

Alpha Company's logo was designed in January 2010 by Marines from CLR-2's maintenance tool room.

We had to stay focused. The deployment wasn't over, and in addition to our regular resupply runs that were dangerous enough, Alpha Company was tasked with two more missions with rather elevated risk profiles.

The Marines were going to take Sangin.

Being no different from my Marines, the pace and stress of the deployment was starting to wear me down. When I was alone, I just tried to shut my brain off. At night, trying to sleep, I would see IED strikes and mortar attacks. Panic attacks would set in, making it hard to breath sometimes, but no matter how hard I squeezed my eyes shut, I couldn't make the images go away.

I couldn't let the Marines see me like that.

CHAPTER FOURTEEN

SANGIN

"Sangin, son! Sangin!" Gunny Locklear would exclaim with false enthusiasm. It seemed only a matter of time before the offensive in the Helmand Province pushed into the city of Sangin. Every offensive campaign needed combat logistics support, and CLB-6 would have to provide it.

I didn't want to go to Sangin. The fighting would be hard.

Limited American operations were conducted in Sangin as early as 2005, but the area was not a priority until 2006, with the construction of the small FOB Wolf, later renamed FOB Robinson, and the transfer of the area of operations to the British 3d Parachute Regiment. In 2008, 2d Battalion, 7th Marines helped expand the British influence, but it was returned to British control. Due to the relatively limited number of British troops available, they restricted their operations to the areas very close to a string of patrol bases along Route 611, conducting foot patrols and trying to provide the 14,000 inhabitants of Sangin with security. Securing the Helmand Province relied on securing Sangin, which had become a major drug trafficking hub.

By the end of June, the first infantry unit planned to push into Sangin, taking along a small augment of CLB-6 trucks to carry additional cargo. Gunnery Sergeant Locklear went as the stick commander for CLB-6's embedded trucks, to learn about the route and to help bring back information to help us plan our own convoys to Sangin. The mission was a disaster.

The unit leading the convoy had misjudged the enemy threat, and tried a tactic we called "hey diddle diddle, run right up the middle"—up Route 611, one of the most heavily IED'd routes in the country, with predictable results. The Route Clearance Platoon struck a few IEDs within the first few kilometers and was no longer mission capable. There was no chance they would make it to Sangin, so it fell to Gunnery Sergeant Locklear to get the convoy back to Leatherneck. We had a saying in Alpha Company, "If you find yourself in front of Route Clearance, you just became Route Clearance." Once again, the Marines of CLB-6, the POGs or "Persons Other than Grunts" were in the vanguard, driving momentum in the most dangerous battlefield in the Helmand. Gunnery Sergeant Locklear never got the recognition he deserved for the mission, but he and the Marines of CLB-6 got the job done, and brought everyone through the danger zone back to the safety of friendly lines.

CLB-6's first mission to FOB Nolay, the largest base in Sangin, was just a repeat of our experience on every Operation Lava and Sar Taiz, lasting days. The convoy struck several IEDs and took enemy mortar fire. IEDs and indirect fire present a similar psychological terror in Marines, as there are relatively few things that can be done to prevent them. They are initiated without warning. One lucky strike can stop the convoy, and makes the unit vulnerable to further attacks. It's hard to be "offensive" against indirect fire and IEDs—you just have to hunker down and take it.

Where two platoons of combat arms Marines failed a few weeks prior, the logistics Marines of CLB-6 succeeded and were among the very first American ground troops to push to the British-occupied FOB Nolay in June 2010, before most infantry units. We had seen the writing on the wall. In addition to the pushes to Now Zad and Musa Qal'eh, we would also be pushing to FOB Nolay every ten days or so. The last six weeks of the deployment would be busier than ever.

We were tasked with a second ground reconnaissance mission.

"Goddammit, doesn't anyone remember how the last one went? It was a fiasco," I complained to Bobby Fowler.

"Whatever, man," he said. "I think some of the battalion leadership just want to put it on their FITREP as an accomplishment."

"On their FITREP? It's my Marines who will have to run the mission."

Alpha Company was a victim of our own success. The long convoys to FOB Nolay immediately beckoned the question "is there a better way?" Just west of the Helmand River was a wide expanse of open desert that might prove more trafficable and present less opportunity for the enemy than Route 611 and the Eastern Desert on the other side. On the other hand, that was where I had hit the IED on the recovery mission, so I had my doubts about that route.

Still, if there was a way to travel that route up the west side of the river and cross over into Sangin, it might save considerable time. We had experience fording the Musa Qal'eh River with cargo trucks, and during the dry season most of the Helmand River delta didn't look any more risky. The main channel of the river, though, was too deep to ford. Some type of expeditionary bridging equipment would need to be used to span it.

I don't know why Alpha Company was tasked with conducting the Helmand River Bridge Recon mission. This was a mission in support of the Infantry Regiment who would pick a location for the Engineer Support Battalion to build a bridge. The Infantry Regiment's recon should have been supported by the reconnaissance battalion, and the Engineer Support Battalion had their own security and motor transport platoons—so I never figured out where CLB-6 came in, except for being tasked with most of the support for the mission. Captain Gallagher was going and would be taking most of my platoon with him. Though I wanted to, I was ordered not to go because I was running the next Nolay mission with First Platoon (who was still without a platoon commander after First Lieutenant Jamie Maynard was relieved). The turnaround between missions was too tight, and if the River Recon was delayed I wouldn't be back in time to take the Nolay mission out.

CLB-6 trucks pick their way down into the Helmand River basin searching for a shallow fording point.

In a complete reversal of the Route Red Recon, the River Recon was completed in mere hours. Though the area would later be a hotbed of enemy activity, no coalition forces had been there before so there was no enemy presence and no IEDs. I could have gone. At least I was able to plan parts of the mission.

It looked like a bridge was a possibility, and about a year later the bridge was constructed. It didn't do me any good, though. We had to fight our way up to Sangin on the east side of the river, paralleling the dangerous Route 611.

The FOB Nolay mission a few days later was more of the same old, same old. We were out in the open desert, paralleling a heavily IED'd route. Dickers on motorcycles followed us and crossed our path. I tried desperately to keep the Marines focused on what they knew was their second-to-last convoy. The convoy took a few IED strikes, and though they were all as terrifying as ever, one in particular stopped time—I can't even begin to describe the panic that gripped me.

A British unit was coming north as we were going south. They had coordinated to use my planned southbound route for their northbound trip. I was in touch with an American embed in their convoy over the BFT, and we coordinated the "route trade" near the midpoint at a wadi. North of the wadi, the threat was significant; south of it, the threat dropped. The British were stopped, and agreed not to move until we got to them. It was risky to have more than one unit moving at a time in the same area—we'd had a few Marines seriously injured when a truck drove by them, detonating an IED. When we had dismounts on the ground, no trucks moved.

The route clearance engineers in our convoy were clearing the final few meters of the wadi by hand.

THOOMP!

My scout Corporal Zeitz on the radio, "Buzz, this is Peewee, IED IED IED!" We had dismounted engineers from the Route Clearance Platoon on the ground. An IED that size would have killed them. Vaporized them, actually.

Holy shit. Those guys are dead. That was not a survivable blast for dismounted troops. A morbid joke we threw around went something like "How big was that IED? Would they need a trash bag to pick up the pieces or could they fit them in small little baggies?" Feeling completely numb, I keyed the radio.

"Thor, this is Buzz. What is the status of your guys?" I was ready for the worst.

"Buzz, Thor. We're a little shaken, but that IED must have been the Brits, because it wasn't us." From my perspective, I couldn't see exactly where the explosion had been. "It was about 50 meters from us, but we're okay. The sweepers up front were knocked over by the blast but I think that was more instinct than anything else. They're okay."

"Goddammit! Why didn't the British wait?" I asked nobody in particular.

"Hey, sir, weren't we taking all the risk on that one, since we were doing the clear?" my gunner for the mission, Corporal Ben Olson, asked. "I mean, if somebody else offered to clear a wadi that I needed to cross, I would let them, right?"

"Yeah, man. I don't get it. They nearly killed our guys, though."

Once we pushed past the strike site, I could see what had happened. A British Mk31 towing a 5000 gallon Close Support Tanker full of diesel had run over a pressure plate IED. It was a threat that all trailers faced—as a tractor towing a trailer hit a corner, the driver had a choice. If the tractor stayed in the cleared tracks, the trailer would end up cutting the corner short, exposing a trailer of flammable diesel to IEDs. To keep the trailer in the cleared tracks, the driver would have to swing the tractor wide on the outside of the turn, exposing the tractor and its operators to IEDs. Little details like this were my life. Thankfully the diesel tanker hadn't caught fire. They had agreed not to go until we gave them a green light. Why had they moved?

The rest of the mission went smoothly for us. We were able to drive south at a relatively high speed in the tire tracks that the British convoy had taken north, and avoided any IEDs. As we drove south we watched the British tire tracks that we were driving in, carefully, to make sure they had not been disturbed. That could mean an IED. But I felt okay about this because we had never done it before, and I could do anything once without the enemy catching on.

One more mission down, and only one mission to go. When we got back to Camp Leatherneck we found that the first few Marines from CLB-2 had begun to arrive. We were ecstatic to see them. They would replace us. They would send us home.

CHAPTER FIFTEEN

THE LAST MISSION

AUGUST 2010: THE EASTERN DESERT SOUTH OF SANGIN, HELMAND PROVINCE, AFGHANISTAN

I always taught my Marines that the mission was not over until we were back to Camp Leatherneck, with all of our personnel and equipment accounted for. No matter how close we were to getting there, "it ain't over, 'til it's over." The primary purpose of this mantra, repeated ad nauseum, was to help prevent complacency. We could be attacked at any time, even in areas that we evaluated as "low threat." Secondly though, we never knew when we were going to be tasked with a follow-on or secondary mission. Follow-on missions usually involved recovery of another unit that had become disabled for one reason or another—perhaps they had run out of fuel, had mechanical difficulties or had struck more IEDs than they had re-

Army First Lieutenant Andrew Carlstrom (from the Route Clearance Platoon), Captain John Gallagher (Alpha Company Commander), First Lieutenant Stacy Wood (Third Platoon Commander) and me before our last mission.

covery assets for. Our platoon would be tasked to provide assistance to them, allowing them to continue with their mission or to bring them back with us to Camp Leatherneck.

During the very last CLB-6 mission, karma, being the bitch that she is, ensured that we received a follow-on tasker. The mission had run smoothly up until that point. First Lieutenant Stacy Wood was the mission commander. Since it was the company's last mission, I went along so that I could bring one of CLB-2's platoon commanders in my truck, talking him through the mission and explaining how we did things to give him some pointers before CLB-2 had to do it solo. It was a standard run from Camp Leatherneck to FOB Nolay in Sangin.

Since we didn't have any future missions taking resources (because we were headed home), we threw everything we had at this last run. I was the security team commander, and took five trucks as a lead security element working closely with the Route Clearance Platoon and the Main Body. Our job was to minimize the slinky effect and keep the whole convoy moving. If the convoy got into trouble, we would respond. All of our experience was evident, and we made it to FOB Nolay in about 20 hours, close to record time. After performing our offload, we reset and prepared to leave the next day.

The return trip went fairly smoothly; one of the commanding general's personal security detachment trucks left the cleared tracks and struck an IED, but there were no serious injuries. Somebody took some potshots at the convoy from a few hundred meters with an AK-47, but it was just as likely to be

This sign was posted on walls all around FOB Nolay in Sangin, reminding us that we were never really safe. Marines loading trucks were often standing on top of trucks to strap the loads down. When they were standing this high, they were above the protective berm around the FOB, extremely vulnerable to snipers' bullets from nearby buildings.

some farmer who was mad that we drove through his fields, as it was a die-hard insurgent.

The convoy made it back down toward the paved route, Highway 1, again in close to record time. The rise in anticipation was palpable. Everyone, from Captain Gallagher, the company commander, to the most junior lance corporal, knew that once the first truck touched the hardball road the risk to the convoy decreased exponentially. The last truck didn't even need to be out of the desert—once the first truck touched the paved road, there was at least one path that was *probably* free of IEDs. Once we hit Route 1 on the return trip of our last mission, there was *basically* no chance that we would strike an IED.

Now, remember that thing about follow-on missions? We were nearly back down to Route 1, on our last mission, when a follow-on recovery assignment came in to go retrieve a broken MTVR. This truck was nowhere near us—it was at FOB Ramrod, a US Army base near Kandahar, 70 miles away. My security team was tasked with the mission, with me as the mission commander. First Lieutenant Wood gave me a few of her trucks to beef us up and give us the tools we needed to do the mission.

You can imagine our frustration and anger. We were basically done. Home free. Finally finished with IEDs, enemy, broken trucks, the whole lot. Instead, we were being tasked with a follow-on mission, sure to take at least ten to twelve hours, adding 70 additional miles each way. The worst part (from a risk standpoint) was that I had zero intelligence about where I was going. So here I was, going to a new place, in the dark, with no intel, and the exact destination kept changing. Now, keeping in mind that I had a new lieutenant in my truck (the CLB-2 platoon commander), I had a lot to prove. I had swagger . . . I was salty . . . I was a badass. At about 2200, we accepted the mission and headed towards Kandahar with about eight trucks and 25 Marines. I was only given a gridpoint. Upon arriving at that grid, we found only empty desert.

MEBA-CLB-B-MTPLT2: *Red Cloud, we are at the designated grid point, and there is nothing here. Empty desert. Please confirm that the grid coordinate for FOB Ramrod is 41SPS 65111 35223.*

MEBA-CLB-B-COC: *Arawak 2, that is affirmative. Are you sure your equipment is working?*

MEBA-CLB-B-MTPLT2: *Red Cloud, we are at the grid we were given, and your BFT should report us at the grid you gave us. We have verified against three BFTs as well a Garmin GPS.*

MEBA-CLB-B-COC: *Arawak 2, we have an updated grid coordinate for you. The FOB is at 41SPS 72111 34635.*

Was the FOB moving? What on earth could possibly be getting updated?

SOMEWHERE OUTSIDE FOB RAMROD, KANDAHAR PROVINCE, AFGHANISTAN

We finally found the sand berm of an FOB. It had only taken us about three hours to get to FOB Ramrod because we were traveling on the hardball Ring Road, Route 1. Three hours . . . should have been less than two, but there was that nonsense about changing grid coordinates. We had found it, kind of, but we couldn't find the front gate. This is really funny in hindsight, but at 0100 in the morning, with the countdown to our flight home running, it was infuriating. There were no roads around the FOB; it was just a berm in the middle of the desert. And because of the way that entry control points were built, there were no large signs at most FOBs. The moondust limited the visibility to just a few feet in front of our trucks. We had found the berm, but we couldn't figure out how to get into the damn place.

I was talking to our COC the whole time, trying to get a point of contact or radio frequency that I could talk to someone on. Nobody was responding on any of the BFT rolenames that I was pinging, and our crypto was not matching any of the frequencies they had given me (most radio communications were encrypted to prevent monitoring by enemy forces). I had even tried broadcasting in the clear on the Sheriff or Guard channel, a "911 channel." The COC was no help and said "it should be right there." It wasn't.

Finally, a message came in on Staff Sergeant Caravalho's BFT and he forwarded it to me. It was from the FOB Ramrod Operations Center, who said they were watching us on their GBOSS (a camera with thermal/infrared optics on tall tower) and were wondering what we were doing. I asked them to steer us toward their ECP and requested permission to enter. Our ordeal was nearing its end, just as the sun was coming up.

We found the truck that we were going to haul back to Camp Leatherneck and began rigging it for a flat tow behind another MTVR. What our COC had failed to mention, however, was that we were not just bringing back the truck, but also the two Marines who had been riding in the truck and who had been stranded at FOB Ramrod for the past two weeks. That would have been good to know ahead of time. I didn't really have seats in my vehicles for them, but we rearranged some things and got ready to drive the final leg of our trip home.

I led the convoy back to the front gate of FOB Ramrod and got permission to leave from my COC, clearing us for movement. The guard, a US Army soldier (since it was an Army base), refused to let me pass.

"Sir, I'm telling you that you are not allowed to leave."

"And I'm telling you that I have been cleared by CLB-6, 2d MLG and II MEF. I am OSCAR MIKE. Get out of the way."

"The Ring Road has not been cleared by Route Clearance in over a week. My command is ordering you to wait for route clearance."

"And when will route clearance be here?"

"Two or three days, and then another two or three days to clear the route."

"I don't think you understand. This is my last mission. I get on a plane out of this shithole in three days. I will not miss that plane. I have been cleared to depart. Get out of the way."

"Sir, the route is black. High IED threat. Are you prepared to deal with that?"

"Yep. Get out of the way. I am OSCAR MIKE. NOW."

I started walking out the gate, waving to my trucks to follow me, leading them out through the wire. I certainly wouldn't have run anybody over, but the soldier at the gate didn't know that and scurried out of the way. As I jumped up into my truck, I heard him shout something to his buddy.

"I don't understand these Marines . . . they're fuckin' crazy."

Whatever. I had just driven over that route on my way to get there, and had dealt with enough IED strikes to know where they usually took place in that kind of terrain. Though I didn't think the threat was that high, my ridealong lieutenant had a bewildered look on his face as we left.

"Is that how you always deal with these kinds of situations?" he asked.

I looked over with this big dumb grin and shrugged. "Eh, I just kind of play it by ear."

We left the FOB and swung west on the Ring Road, heading back to Camp Leatherneck.

ROUTE 1, GERESHK
HELMAND PROVINCE, AFGHANISTAN

Gereshk is the largest city along the Ring Road in the Helmand Province. Imagine a two-lane highway with one narrow lane in each direction. Through Gereshk, there were donkeys, and buses, and cars, and people, and bikes, and motorcycles. Oh, and also vendors with carts selling things. All on the road. Not like along the road. ON THE ROAD. At the same time.

I always made a point to cross through Gereshk in the middle of the night when the population was asleep and there were few, if any, civilian vehicles. It was safer for us, but more importantly, it was safer for the civilians who could easily be killed by our huge trucks. Now, except for this follow-on mission, we would have been through Gereshk just before midnight, but instead I had to bring my convoy through at 0900, the height of the morning rush. I resorted to dismounting and walking in front of my vehicle, trying to clear people out of the way. I was much more afraid of running somebody over with one of my 40,000 pound MRAPs than I was about somebody shooting at us.

CLB-6 trucks drive through Gereshk near an Afghan National Army checkpoint.

I saw a vendor selling the best-looking watermelons I think I have ever seen. I didn't have an interpreter with me to negotiate a price, but I pulled three dollar bills out of my pocket and hand gestured that I would like one watermelon and would be willing to pay three dollars. I'm sure I overpaid because the man smiled and nodded eagerly, took the money, and then yelled at the people to get out of the way of my truck.

We got through Gereshk without incident, thankfully, and kept going west on Route 1. Along the way, the truck we had recovered from FOB Ramrod started smoking from its back axle. More delays. My platoon sergeant and I took a look at it, and discovered that the driver hadn't properly caged the brakes. In retrospect, I was a little unfair with the kid, but it was something he should have known. "Dammit dude, this is kiddie stuff." We were back on the road in just a few minutes, thankful that it wasn't a bigger problem.

CAMP LEATHERNECK ECP
HELMAND PROVINCE, AFGHANISTAN

One of my greatest triumphs was designing the improvised refrigerator that I had in my truck. It was unfortunate, however, that I didn't think of it until the very last mission. Afghanistan gets hot. Really hot. 120°F hot. If your air conditioner goes out, it's pretty bad. If the radiator isn't working and you need to cool the engine, you turn on the heat. If you do it in the summer, it's unbearable. Oh, and we were wearing long sleeves, pants, helmets, gloves, and body armor.

But if the air conditioner is working and you put a plastic box or ice chest with water bottles in it, and you pipe in cold air with vent tubes made out of water bottles, it makes a beautiful fridge. Every time we stopped, I would grab all the cold bottles I could and pass them out to the gunners who were up in the turrets and put in new bottles to chill.

The reason that I didn't think of this idea until the last mission (or rather, devote significant brainpower to actually implementing it) was because I had bought a case of non-alcoholic beer from the British Army PX to celebrate our last mission. I wanted to hand each truck a cold beer to toast our success as we rolled "through the wire" back into the relative safety of Camp Leatherneck, with our deployment basically done. I needed the beer to be cold. Necessity is the mother of invention.

So we had completed our mission at FOB Ramrod, gotten through Gereshk, and made it back to Camp Leatherneck. As I walked up to the Marine ground guiding each truck back through the ECP to hand them the beer, there was an initial shock that I had brought "near beer." Through their gloves they couldn't tell that it was actually cold. The cold, hoppy non-alcoholic Stella Artois was the best thing I have ever tasted.

When Staff Sergeant Caravalho hopped down, we hugged (a good, manly hug, of course).

"Buzz! We're done!" he exclaimed.

"Thank God. You're the man." I couldn't and still can't articulate how much he did for me. For his actions, he was nominated for a Navy Commendation Medal with Combat "Valor" device, the Purple Heart and Combat Action Ribbon. He was promoted to gunnery sergeant in 2011.

Each and every one of us was so relieved to be done. Each and every Marine in the platoon was going to come back alive. For that, I will be forever thankful.

Corporal Jonathon Neubauer scraped "nice try" onto his mud-caked MATV door beneath a bullet embedded in the composite armor. Time after time, insurgents did their best to kill CLB-6 Marines. They were not successful.
Photo courtesy of Corporal Jonathon Neubauer

CHAPTER SIXTEEN

RETURN HOME

When I boarded that plane back to Manas, I could not have been happier. I didn't care that it was a C130 with a cargo net seat instead of an upholstered chair, or that the flight was freezing despite the summer heat of Southwest Asia. It was my Freedom Bird. Nothing could dampen my spirits. Landing in Manas, I headed straight for the chow hall. There was something that I had gone seven months without, and I needed it. Fresh milk . . . and the milk in Kyrgyzstan was amazing, without any hormones or chemicals like the stuff we get in America. I must have had four or five pints in that one sitting, with some wafer thin Kyrgyz cookies. There wasn't much that needed doing—we were just waiting on a plane to take us back to the States.

Though there was a bar in Manas, Marines were prohibited from drinking there, after some of our counterparts from 1/9 got into a brawl. I should have been irritated that my first beer was delayed by a few more days, but the joy I got from the whispers of the soldiers and airmen were worth it.

"Did you hear that the Marines can't drink here?"

"Really? Why not?"

"Dude, those guys are nuts. They are brawlers . . . they start fights."

We finish fights, is what he surely meant to say.

The flight back to the US was uneventful. First Lieutenant Brad Palm, CLB-6's engineer platoon commander, and I were the only two officers on the flight, so we made the rules for the brief layover in Shannon, Ireland. And the rules we made were real simple: Don't come back drunk. I went straight to the airport bar.

"Oh, and what'll you have?" asked the bartender in her brogue.

"Uh, I guess fish and chips. And a Guinness in the biggest glass you've got."

"It's ten in the morning. You really want a Guinness?"

"It's been seven months since the last one. Definitely." With the exchange rate and the airport fees and VAT and everything else, the meal cost me almost $45 for mediocre airport fish and chips (and a really good Guinness at 10 am). It was totally worth it.

I was one of the first Marines in the battalion to see my family. Alison, my parents and siblings, had found a dirt road that took them to a parking lot back behind the runway at Cherry Point and were waiting for the plane to land. I saw them wave from a distance. I also saw them be asked to leave by a police officer because they were in a parking lot behind the runway that nobody was supposed to be on. Pretty funny, actually.

Once the battalion arrived back at Camp Lejeune, there were hours of tasks to complete before we were released to actually go see our families. Weapons had to be returned to the armory and accounted for. Shots were administered and blood was drawn. But finally we were done. We walked from the armory over to the barracks where the families were waiting for us. We were home. Alison nearly knocked me over when she hugged me.

I really couldn't ask for more from my family. They were incredibly supportive while I was deployed, and threw a big barbecue welcome home party a couple of weeks after I got back. All kinds of family and friends were there, traveling from all over the country. Aunts and uncles from Pennsylvania, friends from Atlanta, family friends from Missouri, Washington, and any number of places around the country. People wanted so badly to be supportive, and they were. I definitely appreciated the "non-anti-Vietnam" reception. Even people who enthusiastically detested the war itself were yellow ribbon "Support the Troops"ers. One of the things that I heard more than almost anything else was, "Thank you for your service."

"Thank you for your service" seemed to be a comfort-zone phrase for many Americans, not just my friends or family. It gave them something to fall back on, and feel good about the way they handled an interaction with a veteran. To their credit, I think most people *were* genuinely thankful. I appreciated the sentiment, but I really didn't like being on the receiving end of a "thank you for your service." There's not a good response to that. I found that "thank you for your support" is the best answer. "You're welcome" is too succinct.

The "thank you for your service" was all part of the painless war experience that most Americans had—it gave them a comfortable "out" when conversing with a veteran of wars that most Americans didn't support. For some, it let them lie to themselves and think that everything was okay, that the wars didn't really end up hurting anybody and were just something that we happened to get involved in and needed to get through . . . that somehow the War in Afghanistan was not a deliberate decision by our democratically elected leadership.

Dealing with the constant "thank you for your service" was just one of many adjustments that I had to make to get used to life in the United States again. I was fortunate in that I was never exposed to any extremely gruesome injuries, and none of my close friends or Marines were too badly injured; I did not display any serious symptoms of post-traumatic stress disorder (PTSD) or some of the worst negative side effects from traumatic brain injury.

Probably the funniest adjustment was to learn how to drive fast again. My wife and I were on the highway when she asked, "Is there a reason you're only going 45?"

"I hadn't even realized I was. Weird."

It took a while to realize why I was suddenly driving slowly. Our convoys were very slow (averaging three to five mph) and I had developed an innate hesitation of driving forward for fear that the ground would literally explode in front of me (as had happened dozens of times to my platoon in Afghanistan). I ended up driving extremely slow once I got back home. There were a lot of little things like this. Even the slight pressure change caused by a door slamming would make me jump. It was nearly identical to the sensation of the shock wave that I felt when one of my platoon's trucks hit an IED. It just took a while to realize that I was back home again.

The effects of the deployment were more than mental. The long days wearing 40 pounds of body armor and sitting in truck seats that didn't seem to be designed for humans had taken their toll, not to mention the IED strike. While hiking in Yosemite Park with Alison, the aches that I had just attributed to the pace of operations and the lack of sleep in Afghanistan didn't get better. A string of doctors, x-rays, MRIs, chiropractors and physical therapists later, I was diagnosed with a torn rhomboid muscle and some damage to a few vertebrae and discs in my back. Various physical therapies and medicines did little. Months later with little improvement or positive results, I accepted the fact that I would basically have to learn to tolerate constant back pain for the rest of my life. Speaking to my Marines, most of them were experiencing similar symptoms to one degree or another.

As I read about Afghanistan in the news, I wondered what the point of it had been. Few Americans even seemed to remember that we were still at war.

CHAPTER SEVENTEEN

RELOAD AND DO IT AGAIN

A nd then we did it all over again. CLB-6 was in a deployment rotation with CLB-2 and CLB-8; 2 replaced us, 8 would replace 2, and then we would replace 8. As the Marines had climbed the stairs on the aircraft to deploy to OEF 10-1 in January 2010, they knew they would climb the stairs on another aircraft in July 2011 to do it all over again for OEF 11-2.

After all-too-brief periods of post-deployment leave, we launched head-first into a training and reset cycle. The clock was counting down. About a third of the battalion was staying for the second deployment, and almost everyone shuffled around to a new job within the battalion. I would no longer be a platoon commander—I was assigned to the S3 Operations Section as the assistant operations officer. As it turned out, I had first met my new boss, Major Chris Charles, in 2009, about a year before while CLB-6 was at Mojave Viper.

SEPTEMBER 2010: CLB-6 OPERATIONS OFFICE, CAMP LEJEUNE, NC

The first time I met Chris Charles, he was still Captain Charles, callsign Coyote 44, and he was yelling at me. I was in the S3 Combat Operations Center, waiting to talk to the S3A (Current Operations Officer) about an upcoming training event, but nobody was around. Captain Charles wanted to know why something hadn't happened yet, and I was the only one in the area. He rightfully assumed that I worked in the S3, and gave me a dressing down that I can only assume somebody deserved. I managed to extricate myself and explain that I was not the target that he was looking for. As I hurried away, I thought to myself, "Christ, am I glad I don't work for that guy."

I never really gave him a second thought. Until . . . fast forward a year. I knew we were going to get a new operations officer (OPSO), and honestly, I couldn't have been more glad—I did not have a great relationship with the outgoing operations officer. But we were getting a new one, and I was excited to be the Current Operations Officer or "COPS." I walked into the office, which was set up as a bullpen—one large room with everyone's desk along the wall. And who was sitting behind the OPSO desk? The recently promoted Major Chris Charles. He didn't recognize me but I recognized him, and I was sure that I was in for a pretty rough year and a half. He invited me to sit down and we began to talk. Major Charles had something of a stern look to people who didn't know him, and spoke with a Caribbean accent.

"There are two things that you should know about me. First, I am from The Islands. St Croix. You know. And second, some people say that I look angry. I don't know about all that."

I can say without hesitation that I learned more from Major Charles than from anyone else during my Marine Corps career, and that an incredibly small number of people understood leadership or logistics as well as he did.

We built the core of the battalion around the third of the Marines from the first deployment who would go on the second. With the benefit of a combat deployment in the area of operations that we would redeploy to, we were able to focus on the training that was essential, and skills that would have been good for the Marines to have had on the last go-around.

The pace was unrelenting, and of the 11 months, 18 days between deployments, the battalion was "home" for less than 200 days. The rest of the time was spent in the field or at major training exercises in the Mojave Desert of California. I developed training scenarios and ran exercises as an observer/controller for CLB-8 before they deployed, and again for CLB-6. As the training officer, my job was to create and coordinate realistic training opportunities for the Marines, injecting experiences from the first deployment. The days were long, but it was rewarding—I felt I had something to offer. When people asked questions, they wanted to know how we had done things. I worked as hard as I could to support and coordinate as many training opportunities as I could during those 11 months and 18 days. On that next day, we repeated the deployment process, saying goodbye to family, driving to Cherry Point, flying to Manas Air Transit Center Kyrgyzstan, and finally arriving at Camp Leatherneck, Afghanistan. We were back.

Upon arriving at Camp Leatherneck in July 2011, I was struck by how much it had been built up since my departure just under a year ago. Most of the roads were paved, and hardened buildings had replaced most of the tents.

"How long does the United States plan to have us stay here?" was a refrain often in my mind.

As the current operations officer or COPS, anything happening within the next week or so was my responsibility. Anything further out than a week was managed by the future operations officer, or FOPS. My job was to serve as the link between the infantry units at all the various bases throughout the AO and CLB-6's logistics capabilities. I tried to smooth the bumps in both directions, adjusting the flow of supplies to supported units and helping them predict when they would receive support. Oftentimes, units would not understand what it took to get what they wanted. An infantry unit requesting a capability like a Portable Ground Surveillance System (essentially a blimp with a camera to help watch over their position) wouldn't necessarily understand that it took ten trucks to move the whole system, and doing so would impact the rest of their resupply requests. On our end, I worked to minimize the last-minute changes and 110% surge efforts demanded of our truck platoons. My job was to balance everything out.

I did not have a good relationship with the S3 Section during my first deployment, and I'll be the first to admit that it was at least 50% my fault. But I didn't feel like they ever looked at things from my perspective—none of them had ever been in combat or done a convoy before. I was determined that everything the S3 did while I was there would be in service of our supported units and the battalion's platoons on the ground. I was busy.

I was, literally, not permitted to leave Camp Leatherneck. I deployed a few weeks earlier than most of the battalion, traveling on the Advance Party to coordinate bringing in the bulk of CLB-6 in an organized fashion. Major Charles had come to see us off. He looked at my bags and asked, "You got your flak and Kevlar in there?"

Both were on the packing list, and were required to go outside the wire. "Yes, sir."

He laughed. "I know you have to bring them, but you're not going to need them. Your job is on LNK," he said, giving the abbreviation for Camp Leatherneck.

He was right, and I knew it. I often felt guilty about it. It wasn't fair. Why should I sleep on a mattress every night and get a shower and hot meals every day when so many Marines didn't?

"Jeff, you are the button that we push when we have a problem. I know you would like to get out there with some of your Marines, but you can contribute more to the mission, you can do more to *take care of the Marines* here," Major Mastria, the battalion XO, told me once.

I tried to take care of the Marines by minimizing the last-minute requests and surge efforts for our truck platoons. The best way to do this was to forecast the demands that our supported units had. If I could figure out what they were going to ask for, I could figure out what we needed to move, and then do the backplanning to give the truck companies a predictable operational schedule.

JP-8 fuel was the lifeblood of operations, essential for generators and vehicles, and was always a high-visibility issue for commanders. The first project that I undertook was to develop a historical tracker to forecast requirements for all of the locations that we supported. For some locations, I could set up contracted delivery of fuel by local national truckers, but for most places, our ground convoys would haul JP-8 in armored tanker trucks. One such location was Patrol Base Mirmandab, a small special operations base south of Sangin. The MARSOC team at PB Mirmandab were true professionals, but their support staff at SOTF-W headquarters on Camp Bastion left something to be desired. For some reason, their communications networks were not connected to ours, so they were often unavailable by secure phone or email. The one time I tried to physically visit, I was denied entry for security reasons and nobody from their S4 section would come out to see me.

They were uncommunicative, but their Marines still needed support. I had a good idea how much fuel they used on a daily basis and could forecast when they would need resupply, so I tasked CLB-6 Bravo Company to deliver fuel to them. The platoon commander who regularly did that run had a good rapport with the guys at Mirmandab and agreed.

"Yeah, it's about time they needed fuel," First Lieutenant Caelyn Furman acknowledged.

I got a phone call on the day of the convoy.

"This is Captain Williams, S4 for SOTF West." This was the guy I had been trying to get in touch with for a week.

"Yes, sir, this is Lieutenant Clement, CLB-6 S3 COPS. What can I do for you?"

"I need fuel for PB Mirmandab."

"Yes, sir, I thought you would."

"How could you know that? We haven't been sending in the fuel reports and haven't requested any." *Oh believe me, I know that you haven't been sending in your fuel status reports. I noticed.*

"I track and forecast fuel for the whole AO, sir. Helps minimize the last-minute scramble on my part."

"Okay, well, I need fuel."

"Yes, sir."

"This is, like...an emergency," he said, with a tone of uncertain authority.

"Yes, sir, I'm tracking Mirmandab as having only about two days of fuel left," I tried to stay deadpan.

"That's what they said there. Did you talk to them?"

"No, I couldn't get through to them." It was true, I often couldn't get through to special operations teams.

"Okay, well, this isn't funny. We need fuel."

"Yes, sir, and I told you that I was tracking that. I wasn't kidding."

"Okay, how soon can you get fuel to Mirmandab?"

"Are you requesting support for Mirmandab, sir?" Every time I talked to CPT Williams, I harped on him to request support before it was too late. He was the S4—and it was his job. I wasn't psychic; I usually couldn't give them something they didn't ask for. Fuel was an exception because it was consumed at a fairly steady rate.

"Yes, okay, I am. I know I should have requested it sooner." Aha! A breakthrough. "How soon can you get fuel to Mirmandab?"

"Hold on, sir, lemme check." I popped my head into the COC to check on one of our digital displays to find the location of Bearfoot 1, First Lieutenant Caelyn Furman's platoon. "Sir, it'll be about thirty minutes."

"This isn't funny. It takes three hours to get from Leatherneck to Mirmandab . . . the convoy would have had to already left."

"They did, sir, about two and a half hours ago."

"And they have fuel for us?"

"They do, sir."

"Why didn't you talk to us about this? You can't just send us fuel without our asking." Wait, what? It felt so contrived, like something out of a sitcom. They remained in much better communication with us after that, though.

Beyond just supporting our platoons and the combatant units, the one other goal that I tried to accomplish wherever possible was to remind the "fobbits," people who never left Camp Leatherneck, that there were, in fact, Marines in a shooting war just on the other side of the wire. Life on Camp Leatherneck could be cushy and serene for "rear echelonites," of whom I was begrudgingly now one. The recreation facilities were greatly expanded, and there were no fewer than five coffee shops serving lattes and cappuccinos.

What kind of war was this?

First Lieutenant Adam Arellano, the battalion S6 communications officer, and I discussed this often. "Don't you just want to stand on top of one of the buildings and scream 'what in the actual fuck is going on here?'"

"Exactly. What is this? It doesn't look like a war." Most of the Marines on Leatherneck were completely disengaged from the war right outside the gates. I often felt guilty or reluctant that my life and daily schedule were so comfortable and predictable. I often wouldn't know exactly what was going to happen, but my schedule remained fairly constant. I would wake up around 0700, which felt luxuriously late.

My roommate was the battalion S2 intelligence officer, First Lieutenant Chris Barton. We shared a 10' by 20' air-conditioned room with a concrete floor and solid walls. We had beds with mattresses, as well as furniture built or acquired by previous units—we had a table and bookshelf, complete with a few dozen books. The amount of stuff that every unit left behind in Afghanistan was astounding. It was a far cry from the tents and cots that we had on the first deployment.

After a quick shave, I would grab breakfast "to go" from the chow hall, usually some yogurt and fresh fruit. I would check my email (unclassified, US Secret, and NATO Secret accounts) and get a debrief from the COC on what had happened overnight. The day really began with the 0800 Battle Update Brief, a short staff meeting and update to the battalion commander. After the meeting, I would spend an hour or two knocking out routine business and answering requests for information and submitting requests.

Around 1000, there was a lull. It eventually dawned on me that this was because at 1000, nobody had yet realized there was something they needed to freak out about. Promptly at 1000, I would go for a run or do a CrossFit workout, shower, and grab some food. Shortly after noon, the calls would start coming in (once people realized that they needed to start freaking out), and I needed to be available all afternoon. I would have all the fires put out in time for dinner, eat at one of the ten chow halls with some of my fellow staff officers, and then return to the shop.

Around 2100 the calls would start coming in again. Somebody was always in need of something and there would be questions to answer. I felt strongly that we needed to make sure we were available to support, even late at night. Things would die down again around 2300 or 0000. I would often go running or work out again, especially in the summer when it was too hot to run during the day. After one last check-out with the COC, I would go to bed, catch a sustainable five or six hours of sleep, and repeat the cycle the next day.

The regularity of my schedule was absurd, considering we were in a war. My quality of life was so good it was embarrassing to tell my friends who were in combat how good it was. The relative predictability of life on Camp Leatherneck led to widespread complacency, a disconnect between the combatants outside the wire and the FOB dwellers who never saw combat. Daily phone calls to my wife's DSN office phone and near-constant email connectivity were a luxury that most Marines did not enjoy. I did what I could to fight the complacency in myself, to not lose the sense of urgency when people requested support. Workouts and running helped. I ran the Marine Corps Marathon, 26.2 miles of laps around Camp Leatherneck, finishing in my second-best marathon time of 3 hours, 32 minutes.

The CLB-6 convoys were doing the same things that I had done on the last deployment. I often thought about how poorly I thought the S3 section had supported me, and swore that I wouldn't be that way. I tried to be visible in the motor pool, to talk to the junior Marines about issues, and to frequently check in with the platoon commanders. I might not be able to change what they had to do (though I sometimes could), but I could at least make sure they felt like they could come talk to the S3 about it. We existed to serve, and I tried to remind the Marines of the S3, including myself, of that fact.

And we always had coffee and snacks in our shop for the Marines. By encouraging the junior Marines from the truck companies to pop in and grab a cup of coffee, I could get a good picture of how operations were going.

"Hey, how are things?" I asked Sergeant Smith, Second Platoon's new platoon sergeant.

Combat Logistics Battalion 6 OPERATIONS SECTION

OPEN

FOR EVERYTHING ALL THE TIME

OEF 11-2 Helmand Province Afghanistan

The sign I posted on the door of the S3 shop during OEF 11-2.

"Good, sir. I 'preciate the coffee. We're getting loaded up and ready for the next convoy. We're having some trouble with the chits for the Class I request though."

"What? They said they were going to have it ready by yesterday. Alright. We'll call the LNO and have them fix it right away."

It was the little things. Sometimes the most important things were random bits of information that I found out when somebody was pouring a cup of coffee.

NOVEMBER 2011: CLB-6 OPERATIONS SECTION, CAMP LEATHERNECK, AFGHANISTAN

Gunnery Sergeant Mario Locklear knows combat logistics better than, perhaps, anyone else I have ever met. He could lay out convoys in his head, splitting up long lists of cargo onto the appropriate vehicles. Most people didn't know this, at least not immediately, and they would think they could convince him to give them what they wanted, whether or not it was physically possible.

We were in the S3 Ops office on Camp Leatherneck when the phone rang. It was the liaison officer for one of our supported battalions, calling to request some kind of support. I was across the room from Gunnery Sergeant Locklear, so I could only hear half of the conversation, but in this case half was enough.

Gunnery Sergeant Locklear (On the phone): "Okay, sir, I understand that."

Liaison: . . .

Gunnery Sergeant Locklear: "Well, sir, this is about priorities. I'm looking at the levels of supply and it looks like you guys are okay for now. We're going to push you about half of what you're requesting now, and we'll send the other half next week.

Liaison: . . .

Gunnery Sergeant Locklear: "I'm sorry, sir, I only have a limited number of trucks, and we're supporting four different battalions, as well as the RCT, the MEF and the Georgian Battalion."

Liaison: . . .

Gunnery Sergeant Locklear: "Sir, the priorities have already been established. I'm not going to send you something extra that you can live without for a few days and let somebody else run out of something critical."

Liaison: . . .

Gunnery Sergeant Locklear: "Yes, sir, I DO understand that you are an officer."

Liaison: . . .

Gunnery Sergeant Locklear: "Sir, this ain't about rank. This is logistics!"

I don't think he intended it to be some kind of a catchphrase, but that's what it became. The bottom line is that a dispassionate, objective approach is one that removes rank from the equation. You can outrank someone, but even so, your order will not somehow empower them to defy the laws of nature—gravity, conservation of mass, and the space-time continuum will not bow to your will. Some officers don't get that—but any time Gunny Locklear came across one who didn't, he made sure to set them straight. His mentorship (which could be summed up nicely by the phrase "it ain't about rank . . . this is logistics) helped shape my leadership style and helped me realize something—or at least to put words to it.

The days of my second deployment dragged on much more than the first, and the events felt less significant. Major Charles taught me something every day, and I tried to train myself to think through problems the way that he did—a good starting point was always a sharpened #2 pencil. I know that on the second deployment my ability to help Marines had a broader impact, but the events were less formative for me than my first deployment.

There were some unique experiences and challenges; I briefed generals and senators on the concept of support for our AO. But my daily experiences were mundane. CLB-6 was still running and gunning; the truck platoons pushed north all the way to the Kajaki Dam, and provided a forward, task-organized unit, dubbed Combat Logistics Company 6, that provided unsurpassed levels of support to 1st Battalion, 6th Marines in their push north during Operation Eastern Dagger. Those stories are not mine to tell.

CLB-6 distinguished itself once again during OEF 11-2, and after just over seven months in Afghanistan we returned home, once again. Upon returning, the battalion immediately turned to preparing for another Afghanistan deployment, scheduled for the second half of 2013. While there were a few Marines who would make a third deployment with the battalion, I was not one of them. I had been issued PCS orders to Marine Barracks Washington, D.C. at 8th and I.

CHAPTER EIGHTEEN

THE LIEUTENANT DON'T KNOW (REDUX)

This book began by way of explanation of where I was and how I came to be a platoon commander in Alpha Company, CLB-6 for our 2010 deployment to Afghanistan. The first draft of the book opened with the platoon getting on the plane at Cherry Point en route to the war zone, but after going back through, I realized that I wanted people to know how I got there, and how much preparation and training the Marine Corps gave me before I deployed.

I actually began writing this book while I was still deployed in 2010. It began as a series of long emails between me and our company XO, Lieutenant Bobby Fowler, commiserating about the mission and the conditions. The discussion broadened to encompass the war as a whole, and I began to think that I should write some of these things as a book. I worked on it off and on after the first deployment, but it was coming out too raw. Rather than a record of the things that the Marines of Alpha Company did, it came out as a rant. I wasn't enjoying writing, because thinking about all the things that had happened just made me mad. When I went back to read it, I realized it wasn't any good, and if I wasn't enjoying reading it, why should anyone else? I started writing again while on my second deployment as a way to pass the time, but again, it came out as a rant. I wasn't accurately portraying what I thought about the situation and about what our Marines were doing, because I really didn't know. It was not until I was removed from the environment of a deployable unit that I was able to accurately capture my impressions.

I gave up on writing for the second time in early 2012 and didn't touch the manuscript again until 2013. On an unexpected three-day weekend granted by the commanding officer of Marine Barracks Washington, I rode the Amtrak train from Union Station in DC to Philadelphia to visit two family members who were in ill health.

My great-uncle Joseph Joyce was 87 at the time, and like so many of The Greatest Generation, had fought in World War II. Joe never really said much about his time in the war, but we had always known that he had been injured during his time in the Army. He walked with braces on his legs, but as children we were always cautioned to not talk or ask about it.

On that Monday I connected with Uncle Joe in a way that I had never experienced before. He wanted to know all about Afghanistan, what kind of tactics were being used, what it was like for the Marines. I had talked about all this stuff with other people in different settings, but each time it was more like a lecture or a military briefing. This was different. This was a cathartic experience, unlike any of the other discussions. Uncle Joe opened up a little, too.

He told me a little bit about the campaign in the Pacific from his perspective, of the mud and the heat and the humidity. Of going against the Japanese, face to face. The rustle of leaves in the jungle, the uncomfortable silences at night, the terror of the Japanese shelling. He didn't go into detail on the injuries for which he was twice awarded the Purple Heart, nor did he dwell on the heroics that earned him the Bronze Star. He did talk of the weight of the BAR, the .30 caliber automatic rifle that he carried. There was no mention of comrades lost, though I have no doubt there were many. His perspective was that of the private soldier, the individual. The things that stuck out in his mind were the costs of war. He wouldn't say it like that, but that is what it was. I could tell, without knowing the details, a small fraction of what World War II had cost him. But he didn't want pity. After the war, he returned home and became a successful salesman, a dealer of HVAC units and a pillar of his community as a member of the Lions Club in West Chester, PA. He did what he had to do. Freedom has a cost.

He didn't want sympathy. Nor do I. However, in the days and weeks after our visit, and especially after Uncle Joe passed away a few months later, I began working on this book in earnest. I couldn't quite articulate why, but I knew I had to tell my story. I didn't quite know to whom or why yet. I wish I knew more of my Uncle Joe's story, but even so, that story is not mine to tell. I imagine, though, that it would read something like Eugene Sledge's *With the Old Breed*.

My story is not glamorous. Combat Logistics Battalions do not have a sexy mission, and logistics units are rarely the feature of a Hollywood blockbuster. No logistician's memoir can hope to be as exciting as that of a Green

Beret or an operator from Seal Team Six. After the first draft was mostly written, I despaired on that last fact. Who would ever want to read this? My story was that of a regular guy, in a regular unit, not even a front-line combat unit.

And then I realized . . . that's the point. History will judge the wisdom or folly of our venture in Afghanistan, just as history has judged the forays of the Russians and the British in that landlocked country. A perspective that must be included is that of the individuals who fought. And we did fight. We were not a front-line combat unit; neither my Marines nor I had a "combat arms" military occupational specialty. Yet our company contended with nearly 100 IED attacks and numerous combined arms attacks against a trained enemy, who rained mortars and rocket propelled grenades on us. We returned their attacks with precision fire from heavy machine guns and coordinated close air support. Even under overly-stringent rules that denied deserving Marines of them, two-thirds of the company was awarded the Combat Action Ribbon (though that number should have been closer to 90%, but for some administrators who never left the wire).

Marines froze in the January rains of the Helmand Province, slogging through the ten-inch deep waters that flooded the deserts and left Marines soaked for days. Marines were scorched in 120-degree heat of the Afghan summers. Nearly every Marine in the company suffered from some degree of lower back injury due to the weight of the gear and the poor ergonomics of our trucks. About half of the company received a traumatic brain injury from an IED, the long-term effects of which are only starting to be understood.

I do not want sympathy. I knew what I was getting into. As the saying goes, "this is the Marines, not the Girl Scouts." My story, and the story of the Marines from Alpha Company, CLB-6, is like that of hundreds of other Marines who fought in Afghanistan. What I realized is that our story, an accounting of what the War in Afghanistan cost us personally, must be recorded, so that it might be considered in the future when our country considers waging war.

Nobody ever told me why I was going to Afghanistan. Sure, I knew our unit's mission was to go resupply other units, but nobody ever came out and briefed our unit on *why* any of those units were really there in the first place. "That unit is securing this little village" is a little more of an explanation, but why do we need to secure that village? Why do we need to secure any village in Afghanistan? When asked by my Marines, I told them honestly (and in the third person).

"The lieutenant don't know." I followed it with a little more explanation, but I distinctly recall saying that to them after the deployment, when a couple of my Marines approached and wondered what it had all been for.

I feel for the people of Afghanistan. I do. I've played soccer and red rover with Afghan kids. They are fun-loving people, and the smiles are real. They don't care about the war, they just want to grow up and be happy. But that is the situation that their country was placed in, without anybody bothering to ask their opinion. Why does it have to be like that? The lieutenant don't know.

I love being a Marine. I love the Marines around me. I have worked alongside sailors, soldiers, airmen, police officers, FBI and NCIS agents, British Royal Marines and soldiers, Afghan National Army soldiers, and civilians. They all work hard, they have a creed, they are dedicated, but none of them are Marines. Marines are strange. We know that. It's really a chicken-or-the-egg type of problem. Are certain people strange, and they all choose to become Marines so we end up with a group of weird people? Or do normal people come into the Marine Corps and then get a warped sense of reality after hanging out around Marines for too long?

The Marine attitude is to push through, overcome, get it done. This attitude is one of our most valuable assets, and is a defining difference between us and some of the US Army units that I worked with, for example. Marines will work all night if we have to. We won't balk at getting on line and searching the sand for a missing cleaning brush for a machine gun, because that little $0.49 piece could mean the difference between mission success and mission failure. Like a swarm of ants, we'll have a hundred tents set up in a flash and all the tents will be covered and aligned. Five hundred seabags and packs will be offloaded and without telling them to, Marines will line up all the bags facing the same way and sort them by type. When they are getting shot at, the Marines don't hesitate. They push through fatigue and fear.

Our sense of normal is distorted. I think this is essential to getting our job done, but sometimes Marine leaders take this distorted sense of reality for granted. Like when somebody forgets to provide food to Marines in transit. "You haven't eaten in 48 hours? Suck it up . . . you're Marines! You'll get food when we get there!" Or when somebody doesn't plan for some kind of shelter in case there is a huge storm during a parade or ceremony. "You're getting wet, oh well. You're Marines . . . you're amphibious! Suck it up!" Why do the Marines do these things we ask of them? The lieutenant don't know.

The thing is, the Marines will do whatever they are asked. Conditions that would cause a mutiny in the Army or Navy will be accepted by the Marines. Sure, we'll complain—griping is a part of who we are. It's when the Marines stop complaining that you have real problems.

I am periodically struck by how different we are. Something that we don't really think all that much about will shock a civilian or member of another branch of service, and they will make a comment or have a weird look on their face. If they ask, we kind of have to shrug and smile and explain that it is "a Marine thing." You'd have to be a Marine to understand.

DECEMBER 2012: DOVER AIR FORCE BASE, DOVER, DELAWARE

"Hand . . . Salute." Appropriate honors were rendered to a Marine, 26 years old, from Mechanicville, NY. He was assigned to 3rd Battalion, 9th Marines, deployed from Camp Lejeune, NC. While on a foot patrol in Marjeh, a site of heavy fighting southeast of Camp Leatherneck, he was struck in the neck by an enemy sniper's bullet in the 11th year of his country's War in Afghanistan. I had never met him, I didn't know him, but tears rolled down my cheeks as we carried his flag-draped coffin off the C-17 to the waiting mortuary vehicle.

I am one of the few Americans who will ever know about this Marine. Was it worth it? Was this war worth the cost of even this one Marine's life? The lieutenant don't know.

I am proud of what the Marines of Alpha Company, Combat Logistics Battalion 6 did. Against all odds, the Marines accomplished something extraordinary, at great personal sacrifice and incomprehensible risk to life and limb. Will their sacrifice, and the sacrifice of their families, be remembered? Will the human cost of the war, especially a war whose "low" death toll can't describe the true magnitude of those costs, be considered next time we find ourselves deliberating conflict? What could I have done differently that could influence those things? Where do I go from here?

The lieutenant don't know.

AFTERWORD

I never really set out to write a book, and it was something I never thought I could do. I am tremendously grateful to everyone who pushed me along the way and helped me realize this project.

First, to Gunnery Sergeant Caravalho and Gunnery Sergeant Locklear, thank you for your mentorship, and for each agreeing to write a foreword to the book. Your words give our story a legitimacy that mine alone cannot. Both of you saved my life at one point or another, and I cannot thank you enough. I use you guys as examples of what it means to be a leader all the time. Thank you.

To my friend, Adam Arellano, thank you for your help editing the book. Your counsel has always been wise, and I appreciate all of our good times together. We shared many a good "EMV" (Sailor Jerry Rum and Vanilla Coke, as I recall) from a Jetboil thermos and many grand nights in the Lieutenant Morale Tent. Here's hoping for many more, only in a more prime locale.

To my family and my in-laws, thank you for your support and love while I was deployed, and for your enthusiasm for this project. Thank you especially to my siblings Maura, Stephen and Claire. You are the best cheerleaders anyone could ask for.

My mom was my first editor all through school, and has continued to help me when things came along. She warned me to "be careful what you ask for" with regards to her edits, but they have greatly improved the quality of the book. There was no way she knew how much work she was signing on for when she agreed to be a first reader and revise the first draft. Thank you.

My dad also ran through the manuscript. I am always amazed at his ability to work with words. There are many spots in the book where from my uncertain language he was able to distill the precise meaning I wanted to achieve.

Thank you for your tremendous attention to detail. He also provided sage legal and financial counsel for the venture.

My wife Alison has put up with everything, and I'm so lucky to have her as my best friend. She was incredibly supportive while I was deployed, and she had every right to say "Enough. I'm done hearing about Afghanistan," but she didn't. She read through the manuscript more than a few times, making corrections, challenging my viewpoints, and making it something that somebody else might want to read. Thank you.

I wish I could name each Marine, Soldier, Airman and Sailor who I served alongside in combat, but the limited space I am allotted here will not allow it. In particular, there are dozens of Alpha Company Marines from First and Third Platoons who were on nearly every mission with Second Platoon, but whose accomplishments are not recognized by name. Your bravery and sacrifice is worthy of emulation and you have my gratitude.

Finally, to the Marines of Second Platoon, Alpha Company, Combat Logistics Battalion 6: Thank you. Thank you for bravery, your intelligence, your humor, your dedication, and thank you for teaching me. I regret that despite your efforts, the lieutenant *still* don't know. I wish that the limits of this narrative allowed me to better record each of your individual contributions. In lieu of that, please let me record each of you, by name, for posterity.

STAFF SERGEANT	Caravalho	Joseph
SERGEANT	Belcher	Thomas, D
SERGEANT	Crouch	Justin, R
SERGEANT	Galante	Ryan, L
SERGEANT	Williams Jr.	Calvin, D
CORPORAL	Aguilar	Gerardo, J
CORPORAL	Anderson	Eric, J
CORPORAL	Jacobs	Christopher, J
CORPORAL	Olson	Benjamin, K
CORPORAL	Prickett	James
CORPORAL	Salsberry	Jeremy, D
CORPORAL	Schueder	Jesse, A
CORPORAL	Umoren	Edet, S
CORPORAL	Uranga	Richard
CORPORAL	Zeitz	Jesse, G.W.

LANCE CORPORAL	Acevedo	Angel, D
LANCE CORPORAL	Avila	Cristofer, L
LANCE CORPORAL	Berdahl	Ian, J
LANCE CORPORAL	Burke	Jordan, B
LANCE CORPORAL	Chisholm	Anthony, J
LANCE CORPORAL	Coppenhaver	Ryan
LANCE CORPORAL	Eddy	Thomas, J
LANCE CORPORAL	Espinosa	Angel
LANCE CORPORAL	Fuller	Anthony, J
LANCE CORPORAL	Garcia	Jonathan, C
LANCE CORPORAL	Gordon	Quinn, D
LANCE CORPORAL	Gorton	Samuel, D
LANCE CORPORAL	Hale	Michael, A
LANCE CORPORAL	Hernandez	Clemente
LANCE CORPORAL	Hickle	Austin, D
LANCE CORPORAL	Hollis	Albert, W
LANCE CORPORAL	Jenkins	Darius, E
LANCE CORPORAL	Johnson	Robert, M
LANCE CORPORAL	Laday	Roy, D
LANCE CORPORAL	Leiter	Eric, L
LANCE CORPORAL	Lepinski	Nicholas, M
LANCE CORPORAL	Malarkey	Mark, A
LANCE CORPORAL	Martin	Andrew, J
LANCE CORPORAL	Moore	Joey, L
LANCE CORPORAL	Neubauer	Jonathan, C
LANCE CORPORAL	Partin	Joshua, J
LANCE CORPORAL	Paul	Michael, J
LANCE CORPORAL	Pietras	Krzysztof, J
LANCE CORPORAL	Porter	Trey, M
LANCE CORPORAL	Randolph	Nicholas, S
LANCE CORPORAL	Rea	Thomas, A
LANCE CORPORAL	Renno	Jacob, A
LANCE CORPORAL	Rial	Phillip, D
LANCE CORPORAL	Rusk	Travis, E

LANCE CORPORAL	Sedam	Edwin, L
LANCE CORPORAL	Sena	James, M
LANCE CORPORAL	Sobecki	Cale, J
LANCE CORPORAL	Staaf	Benjamin, B
LANCE CORPORAL	Stimson	Zechariah, M
LANCE CORPORAL	Wasmer	Kenneth, A
LANCE CORPORAL	Williams	Garrick, D
LANCE CORPORAL	Zelaya	Jorge, H
PRIVATE FIRST CLASS	Achig	Jack, L
PRIVATE FIRST CLASS	England	Andrew, T
PRIVATE FIRST CLASS	Joycereyes	Yoan
PRIVATE FIRST CLASS	Milliren	Adam, J
PRIVATE FIRST CLASS	Minozzi	Calvin, R
PRIVATE FIRST CLASS	Pineiro	Rosa, M
PRIVATE FIRST CLASS	Smith	Bradley, D
PRIVATE FIRST CLASS	Sypnewski	Robert, J
PRIVATE FIRST CLASS	Vankuren	Anthony, E

COMBAT LOGISTICS VEHICLES

MINE-RESISTANT AMBUSH PROTECTED ALL-TERRAIN VEHICLE (MATV)

ROLE: Security Guntruck, Command and Control
CREW: 4-5
WEIGHT: 27,500 pounds

MINE-RESISTANT AMBUSH PROTECTED VEHICLE (MRAP)

ROLE: Security Guntruck, Command and Control
CREW: 3-6 (4 Wheel Variant), 3-8 (6 Wheel Variant)
WEIGHT: 32,000 pounds

MRAP with Panama City Generation III Mineroller designed to set off IEDs in front of the truck instead of underneath it.

MEDIUM TACTICAL VEHICLE REPLACEMENT (MTVR)

ROLE: Medium Cargo Hauler, Command and Control
CREW: 2-3
WEIGHT: Varies, 27,000-34,400 pounds
VARIANTS: MK23/MK25 Short Bed (14 foot) cargo hauler/Command and Control
                 MK27/MK28 Long Bed (20 foot) cargo hauler
                 MK29/MK30 Dump Truck
                 MK31 Fifth-Wheel Tractor (for pulling M870/M970 trailers, shown)
                 MK36 Recovery Vehicle/Wrecker (shown)
TRAILERS: M870 Low-Boy Trailer (for hauling vehicles and machinery)
                 M970 5000 Gallon Fuel Trailer (shown above)

MK23 MTVR with a Panama City Generation III mineroller. This truck has its cargo bed empty as a "bump space" to recover damaged minerollers or other equipment that may be damaged during the mission.

MK36 Wrecker towing a MATV whose front end was destroyed by an IED.

MK31 MTVR Tractor towing an M970 Fuel Trailer.

LOGISTICS VEHICLE SYSTEM (LVS)

ROLE: Heavy Cargo Hauler
CREW: 2
WEIGHT: Varies, 40,000–60,000 pounds
VARIANTS: MK48/14/14 Tandem Tow (2 x 20 foot cargo beds)
               MK48/15 Recovery Vehicle/Wrecker
               MK48/16 Tractor (for hauling vehicles and machinery, shown)

MK48/16 Tractor using a M870 trailer to haul a piece of equipment.

LOGISTICS VEHICLE SYSTEM REPLACEMENT (LVSR)

ROLE: Heavy Cargo Hauler
CREW: 2-3
WEIGHT: Varies, 53,700–63,700 pounds
VARIANTS: MKR15 LVSR Recovery Vehicle/Wrecker
            MKR16 Fifth-Wheel Tractor (for pulling M870 trailers)
            MKR18 Self-Loading Cargo Vehicle (shown)

LVSR MKR18 hauling a Mobile Trauma Bay.
Photo credit to Lance Corporal Jonathon
G. Wright; photo courtesy of the
United States Marine Corps.